Baseball on the Web

Rob Edelman

A Subsidiary of
Henry Holt and Co., Inc

MIS:Press
A Division of Henry Holt and Company, Inc.
115 West 18th Street
New York, New York 10011
http://www.mispress.com

Printed in the United States of America

First Edition—1998

ISBN: 1-55828-568-7

MIS:Press and M&T Books are available at special discounts for bulk purchases for sales promotions, premiums, and fundraising.

For details contact: Special Sales Director
MIS:Press and M&T Books
Divisions of Henry Holt and Company, Inc.
115 West 18th Street
New York, New York 10011

10 9 8 7 6 5 4 3 2 1

Associate Publisher: *Paul Farrell*
Editor: *Andy Neusner*
Copy Edit Manager: *Karen Tongish*
Managing Editor: *Shari Chappell*
Production Editor: *Gay Nichols*
Copy Editor: *Geneil Breeze*

Cover photograph by Simon Metz Photography (NYC)

To Sam, who would have enjoyed this book.

ACKNOWLEDGMENTS

Writing a book about the World Wide Web is a solitary task. You sit at your computer, day in and day out, exploring search engines and logging onto Web sites by the dozens, then hundreds, and finally thousands. But if you are researching a topic you enjoy, that assignment, however occasionally frustrating, is anything but a chore. Nevertheless, several individuals deserve heartfelt thanks for assisting me when assistance was needed. They are: the Bohman-Fannings; Marialana DeRossi of C&C Computer Solutions; Greg Spira; Bill Nowlin; Mike Shatzkin; Clayton Dreslough; Jeff Suntala; Daniel Levine; Harry H. Hollingsworth; and my agent, Andy Zack. This book never could have been completed without Klink Net Communications, my ever-reliable Internet access provider, and its owners, Robin and Eric Padua. Extra-special thanks go to Andy Neusner, my editor, and David Pietrusza, whose baseball knowledge is vast and whose friendship is valued. Finally, a note of gratitude to my wife, Audrey Kupferberg, whom I love even more than baseball.

Contents

Chapter 11: Minor and Independent Leagues 149

Chapter 19: Fun and Games 249

Chapter 20: Baseball for Sale 259

Chapter 22: Chat Rooms/Mailing Lists/ Message Boards 291

Chapter 23: Newsgroups 299

Introduction

Upon receiving the go-ahead to write this book, Andy Neusner, Associate Development Editor at MIS: Press, sent me two previously published volumes in the "On the Web" series: *Judaism on the Web* and *Catholicism on the Web.* Several days later, I was pondering how peculiar the jump seemed from Judaism and Catholicism to baseball. Then in the instant it takes for a bat to smash a fastball across a cloudless sky on an idyllic summer day, it dawned on me: This association really isn't strange at all because, to the true believer, baseball *is* a religion.

In one of my earlier books, *Great Baseball Films*, I quote Annie Savoy (Susan Sarandon), the baseball groupie created by former minor leaguer turned writer/director Ron Shelton in *Bull Durham.* "I believe in the church of baseball," Annie declares. "I've tried all the major religions, and most of the minor ones...I know things. For instance, there are 108 beads in a rosary, and there are 108 stitches in a baseball. When I learned that, I gave Jesus a chance. But it just didn't work out between us. The Lord laid too much guilt on me....

[But] you see, there's no guilt in baseball. And it's never boring."

So if you are in the know about baseball, as Annie Savoy certainly is, you will understand all about bats and balls and faith. And anyone in your sphere who might judge Annie's declaration as blasphemous most likely will neither understand, care about, nor be reading this book.

Throughout my life, I have had two all-consuming passions: motion pictures and baseball. Although my favorite baseball movies are *Bull Durham* (for its authenticity) and *Field of Dreams* (for its sheer poetry), my top baseball-fan movie is *City Slickers*: a knowing ode to statistic-spewing baseball fan-atics, which comes courtesy of its star, Billy Crystal. I feel that I *am* one of the characters played by Crystal, Daniel Stern, and Bruno Kirby. They are aging Baby Boomers who debate the virtues of Henry Aaron versus Roberto Clemente as the 1950s''60s' top left fielder; spew forth baseball factoids as if they are passages from the Bible; and readily acknowledge that the best days of their childhoods were spent in the sun, in the company of their fathers, watching their favorite outfielders chasing down fly balls.

It is for these reel (as well as real) life enthusiasts—not just Baby Boomers but fans of all ages and both genders—that *Baseball on the Web* has been designed.

Lately, it has become fashionable to knock baseball. Critics complain that the game is too slow and lacks the flash of basketball. The players are selfish multimillionaires who play only to fill their pocketbooks while charging youngsters big bucks for autographs. The owners are robber barons who blackmail taxpayers into paying for new ballyards while raising ticket prices so that only the wealthy can afford to attend major league games.

Anyone who truly understands the appeal of baseball will know that neither labor disputes nor escalating player salaries nor contentious owners can tarnish the essence of the game. Additionally, and pointedly, that essence cannot be captured in a sound bite. It is something you savor, as you might a creamy rich dessert, a steaming hot cup of coffee, or Fred Astaire and Ginger Rogers dancing across a movie screen.

It transcends whatever problems exist at the major league level. In the 1990s, baseball across the land and the world is alive and well, thank you. For one thing, interest in minor league teams has skyrocketed. Rotisserie/fantasy baseball leagues and baseball card collecting have become popular hobbies among adults, and record prices are being paid for baseball memorabilia. Any sporting goods/clothing store or department store casual dress section will feature an array of baseball caps, T-shirts, and warm-up jackets.

Baseball is not a game to be played only by the young. More and more adults are pitching, hitting, and chasing down fly balls in newly minted local baseball, softball, and townball leagues. Meanwhile, the sport is increasingly being played across the globe, a fact reflected in the growing number of foreign-born players making the majors and the establishing of baseball as an official Olympic sport.

All this has translated into a saturation of baseball-related Internet Web sites. Their exact numbers change weekly (if not daily) as new pages debut and others go unmaintained and drift off into the cyberspace heavens. Moreover, transitory URLs are not limited to those that are small and individually hosted and that expire for lack of payment to Internet providers. Some—including high-profile sites that exist to cover the major league postseason—are by their very nature temporary. They are here today and gone with the last out of the World Series.

Despite their short life spans, these pages do not go unseen. Upon completion of the 1997 Fall Classic, it was reported in *Sports Business Daily* that "the World Series site, *www.totalworldseries.com*, was viewed in more than 40 countries. Viewing of the site increased from 842,241 hits and 421,759 page views on the day of Game One, to 4,361,189 hits and 2,219,022 page views on Sunday for Game Seven."

These numbers were achieved without the New York Yankees or Atlanta Braves, Ken Griffey, Jr., or Cal Ripken battling for the world championship. Shame on Don Ohlmeyer, president of NBC (the network that aired the series) West Coast, for declaring before the Cleveland Indians and Florida Marlins went into battle, "We're looking for four and out....The faster it's over with, the better it is."

Whereas some Web sites enjoy brief lives, others keep evolving. Near the beginning of my research for *Baseball on the Web*, I came upon two separate "super" URLs. The first, the *Sports Illustrated*-hosted SIonline, was a solid site: eye-popping; information-filled; and offering the latest headlines, scores, and stats; major league scouting reports; and information on *SI*'s Baseball Manager and Baseball Manager Lightning fantasy games (priced at, respectively, $94.95 and $24.95, and promising "Real Stats. Real Players. Real Ulcers."). One of the site's foremost features was a handy search engine, allowing you to look up previous *Sports Illustrated* pieces. On the day I explored the page, a search for Cal Ripken resulted in 95 documents, all of which could be downloaded. One for Derek Jeter yielded 38 documents; one for Ty Cobb brought forth 11 documents; and one for Jimmie Foxx yielded 2 documents. Also noteworthy was a section spotlighting current and recent *SI*-generated features. On my visit, there were stories on "The Other Alomar" (Sandy, not Roberto), a survey of "Black Baseball" highlights, and various pieces under the heading "Baseball Preview 1997."

Meanwhile, the home page of CNN Sports included up-to-the-minute sports headlines. To get to the baseball nitty-gritty, you had to click on the "Baseball" icon. This led you to all the bat and ball-related links, as well as a search engine that could be used to download major league team pages. Here, you could find further links to team stats, rosters, logs, schedules, ticket information, and attendance reports.

Several months later, however, SIonline and CNN Sports were no longer on the World Wide Web. They had been replaced by CNN/SI, a completely different Web site with many new features—and quite a few deletions, especially from the material available on SIonline.

As fleeting as some baseball Web sites may be, the sheer number of URLs remains permanently mind boggling. A HotBot search for the word "baseball," made while writing the book proposal for *Baseball on the Web*, yielded no less than 289,752 Internet documents. An AltaVista search produced "about 100,000 [documents] matching the query." An Excite search yielded 229,772 documents. WebCrawler and Infoseek searches may have produced only 12,100 and 14,357 documents respectively, but a Lycos search resulted in an incredible "66,557,959 unique documents."!

Try narrowing the search to specific individuals. The word "Griffey" alone yielded "1,342 relevant documents" (via Lycos); "about 3,000 (documents) matching the query" (AltaVista); 8,276 documents (HotBot); and 7,151 documents (Excite). "Babe Ruth" produced "25,836 relevant documents" (Lycos); "about 3,000 [documents] matching the query" (AltaVista); 5,810 documents (HotBot); and 3,238 documents (Excite). "Cal Ripken" yielded "7,341 relevant documents" (Lycos); "about 2,000 [documents] matching the query" (AltaVista); 5,543 documents (HotBot); and 3,174 documents (Excite).

Which of these and all the other baseball Web pages are the most informative?

Which are fascinating?

Which are funny?

Which are visually arresting?

And which are unique?

How does the individual baseball fan process all the data offered by Internet search engines? He or she can waste hours perusing baseball-related URLs and downloading sites that are repetitious or boring (not to mention semiliterate). This, in fact, was my own experience as I began exploring baseball Web pages prior to beginning work on this book.

So it is my hope that *Baseball on the Web*, by its very nature, will simplify the process of exploring baseball on the Internet.

However, one essential point must be stressed regarding the entries in this book: the inclusion of an URL is no guarantee that every bit of information contained in it is accurate.

If I am an expert in one area of baseball research, it is baseball on film. In my Internet wanderings I continuously came upon lists of, and information on, baseball movies that were incomplete and in error. While exploring Negro League Web sites, I downloaded David Marasco's Negro Leagues Page (*http://pubweb.acns.nwu.edu/~dmarasco/david.html*), a visually spiffy site that includes "original research" on the topic. While exploring the site to determine whether it should be included in this book, I came upon a link to *Soul of the Game*, the HBO movie about Jackie Robinson, Satchel Paige, and Josh Gibson. Marasco referred to it as "a short film"—yet, in fact, *Soul of the Game* is a 95-minute feature.

The point of all this: If Marasco cannot properly describe the length of a movie, how can I trust the rest of the research contained on his page?

Just because you are seeing it on the Internet—or, for that matter, just because you are reading it in a newspaper or watching it on television—does not make it the gospel truth.

While compiling *Baseball on the Web*, I have done my best to weed out faulty URLs and select only the very best Web sites. They are the most fact-filled, the most enjoyable, the most unique. And they are the ones that the boys of *City Slickers* would enjoy almost as much as they relish lazy summer afternoons spent in ballyards from Anaheim to Altoona, New York City to Sioux City, St. Louis to Salinas.

Up-to-the-Minute Baseball

You wake up in the morning, sip a cup of steaming java, log onto the Internet—and hope to be able to satisfy your craving for baseball information.

Did your hometown team win that late-night game on the coast? How did their closest rivals fare? Did your favorite ballplayer smash a dinger or toss a shutout in yesterday's game? Who was sent to the minors? What heralded rookie just made his debut in The Show? What are the latest controversies and trade rumors?

Or maybe you just feel like perusing some baseball-related features or examining a few box scores and statistics.

All the Web sites listed in this chapter should satisfy your hunger for baseball news. Some offer the meat-and-potatoes basics; those with longer descriptions generally include more links, sidelights, and other features. Quite a few, beginning with Total Baseball Online, also provide extensive coverage of baseball history. These sites are included here because of their up-to-the-minute information.

Bear in mind that many of these sites offer similar or overlapping material: box scores and stats for the same games or features about the same ballplayers, managers, or owners. The fact that Milwaukee beat Kansas City or St. Louis bested Montreal will not change from site to site—much to the disappointment of Royals and Expos fans. The key is to find the sites you like the best and make them your regular baseball super-sites. But if you are like the media junkie who must peruse all the city's papers every day, you will not want to limit yourself to any individual site.

Total Baseball Online

http://www.totalbaseball.com/

This is the online home of *Total Baseball*, the "Official Encyclopedia of Major League Baseball." Ruthian in scope, it is an impressive, intelligently written and designed site that offers a smorgasbord of information related to all aspects of baseball present and past.

Because a piece I co-authored can be found here ("Reel Baseball"), it would be easy to downplay the quality of this site to avoid accusations of hyping a professional connection, but that would be unfair to the site. The amount of information contained here is staggering. A baseball fanatic could spend endless hours perusing this site.

Total Baseball Online is loaded with links. One, "Total Baseball Daily," is the equivalent of a newspaper sports section. It is updated every day and includes extensive game reports, hot-off-the-wire major and minor league news items, opinions galore, trivia questions, events that happened "today in history," and links to the previous week's postings.

You do not even have to log onto the site to download Total Baseball Daily. Every 24 hours via e-mail, you can have the Total Baseball Online "newsboy" deliver a free edition.

This Web site is listed here because of "Total Baseball Daily," but its coverage of a rainbow of subjects would easily qualify it for any of several chapters. In particular, there are plenty of links to baseball's past. "Biographies" features photos and detailed bios of Hall of Famers and Hall of Famers-to-be; "Statistics" offers the batting, fielding, and pitching stats of every man who ever played in the majors; "Team Histories" chronicles the histories of all present major league teams; "Postseason" and "All-Star Game" offer year-by-year accounts of all major league postseason play and all-star games; "Chronicle" highlights more than two dozen links related to the history of professional baseball from "Cincinnati 1869" to "AL 1991—" and "NL 1991—."

The "Records" link includes batting, baserunning, fielding, and pitching marks. This section is a stat-freak's delight. You will find not only the standard single season or career records for hits, home runs, and RBIs, but also such new-age categories as "Clutch Hitting Index," "Isolated Power," "Adjusted Batting Runs," and "Runs Created."

"Team Roster" offers the rosters of all nineteenth and twentieth-century major league ballclubs from the Atlanta Braves to the St. Louis Cardinals, the Altoona Pride to the Wilmington Quicksteps (both of the old Union Association). Once you retrieve a roster, you can link to each ballplayer's stats for that year.

"Awards" features a list of all major league prizes and their winners, from Cy Young to Gold Glove, Rookie of the Year to MVP. One intriguing highlight is Bill Deane's list of "hypothetical" award winners—ballplayers who might have won citations in the years prior to the establishment of each prize.

"Features" includes links to a wide range of baseball-related subjects: historical ("Robinson Signing" and "Father of Baseball"); statistical ("Phantoms," "Sabermetrics," and "Pinch Hitters"); other leagues (including "Black Ball," "Women in Baseball," "Minor Leagues," "College Baseball," "Caribbean Baseball"); baseball and the arts (the broadcasting, televising, and reporting of baseball; baseball in the movies and in music). Still others focus on the game's managers and mascots, umpires and commissioners.

The Web site also offers its own newsgroup and chat group in addition to a question-and-answer column called "Ask Total Baseball" in which you can submit baseball-related queries trivial or not-so-trivial. For example, if you ask, "Who was the first player elected to the Hall of Fame posthumously?" you not only will receive an answer (Christy Mathewson) and the year of election (1936) but a smartly written brief bio of the "great pitcher" and "man of moral convictions who inspired an entire generation of fans." A query about "the date and place (in which) the Minnesota Twins played their first game as the Twins" gets you a detailed response from Dave Smith of Retrosheet (*http://www.retrosheet.org/*), including an expanded box score and complete play-by-play account of the game.

Total Baseball Online offers several SABR (Society for American Baseball Research) related links. One allows you to take a peek at the SABR-maintained list server (SABR-L), which features give-and-take baseball repartee. Here you will find data as diverse as a list of major leaguers who hit game-winning grand slams with two outs in the ninth inning and the proper pronunciation of the surname of Emil Yde, a five-year major leaguer who pitched for Pittsburgh and Detroit back in the 1920s.

Major League Baseball (MLB@BAT)

http://www.majorleaguebaseball.com/

Simply put, this is the "official site of Major League Baseball," and what you get here is the "official" party line of the sport—in other words, no controversy and no strong pro-or-con commentary regarding the game's pressing issues or the quality of a team's play.

This is not to say that the Web site is the equivalent of a grounder dribbling through a second baseman's legs. Far from it. The site is beautifully designed and crammed with photos and visuals. You even can download video, from *This Week in Baseball* clips to such classic baseball moments as Don

Larsen's perfect game in the 1956 World Series, Joe Carter's game-winning dinger to end the 1993 Series, and the play-by-play for the New York Giants' and Brooklyn Dodgers' broadcasts of Bobby Thomson's legendary 1951 pennant-winning shot-heard-'round-the-world. However, an appropriate video player and software are required to view videos.

The site provides helpful and fact-filled links galore to current major league standings, yesterday's game highlights and line scores, information on today's games (including the TV networks on which they will be broadcast), a wide variety of stats, major league franchise histories, a photo archive, minor league teams, a special *This Week in Baseball* page, a special section devoted to the Negro Leagues, and future events (such as the All-Star Game and All-Star Fanfest, if not already held, and postseason activity). You also can link to each major league team and get instant access to a club's roster, batting and pitching reports, schedule, franchise history, and minor league affiliations. A "Fan Forum" enables visitors to post comments and, on occasion, chat with ballplayers. Transcripts of conversations with past "Fan Forum" guests (who have included a wide range of names, from Alex Rodriguez to Ralph Branca) can be downloaded via the site's "Archive" link.

One of this site's 1997 highlights should remain a permanent feature: an extensive (and stunningly designed) homage to Jackie Robinson, spotlighting Major League Baseball's recognition of the Brooklyn Dodgers legend who "shattered the conscience of the nation and manifestly moved the United States to a higher level of equality."

But the other end of the professional baseball scale is in no way ignored. During the 1997 season, Montreal Expos minor league hurler Shayne Bennett wrote a chatty, entertaining weekly Web journal chronicling his life as a Harrisburg Senator/Ottawa Lynx. Readers could even e-mail their questions and comments to Bennett, who would post his responses in his columns.

Additional Web site highlights are news items and press releases issued directly from the (still embarrassingly vacant) Office of the Commissioner, special features written for kids, and lengthy articles relating to all aspects of the game. Some of the latter are informative, whereas others are puff pieces that do little more than market products. For example, one piece was directed at children and headlined "Pinnacle Inside Locks Cards In A Collectible Player Can." It includes a self-serving quote from the senior business director of Pinnacle baseball cards on how "many baseball fans will be buying the cans as a collectible."

Or so he hopes.

A less manipulative marketing link can be found at this site, one that enables the browser to e-mail away for a free catalogue offering items from the Major League Baseball "Clubhouse Shop" and purchase officially licensed MLB merchandise and home videos.

ESPN SportsZone

http://espnet.sportszone.com/

This all-purpose Web site offers up-to-the-minute information on the NBA, NHL, NFL, college football and basketball, soccer, golf, auto racing and baseball.

Links related to the latter include plenty of features: for example, a piece on Houston Astros hurler Billy Wagner, from ESPN's *Baseball Tonight*; and a lengthy and informative Curt Schilling-bylined piece titled "Curt Schilling's Big League Diary: Curt talks about injuries, workouts and the strike zone as he answers some of your questions."

The site offers book excerpts from Roger Kahn and columns from the likes of Kahn, Peter Gammons, Stan Isaacs, and Bob Klapisch. Rob Neyer's highly personalized and delightfully opinionated "Chin Muzak" is a special treat; it reads less like a column and more like a conversation with a baseball-savvy buddy. And there are scores and schedules, statistics, reports on yesterday's games, chats with ballplayers, and links to teams. One outstanding feature, well worth highlighting, is under "Player Profiles"; you can link to every current major leaguer and download his up-to-the-minute stats, professional baseball history, scouting reports, and so forth.

However, be forewarned: ESPN SportsZone is a highly commercial site. Its "Baseball Challenge" contest is presented by Pizza Hut. The online fantasy league you can log onto is ESPN SportsZone's "Fantasy Baseball '97 Late Season" and is described (not surprisingly) as "the best value on the Web at just $29.95."

Furthermore, to completely access all data on this site, you have to take a "premium subscription" and become a SportsZone subscriber.

This Web site hits you with the hard sell: "You could spend hundreds of dollars on newspapers, magazines, videos, and books and still not get all the information available to a SportsZone subscriber."

Or, you could log onto any number of totally free Web sites, each of which can keep you engrossed for hours.

Nevertheless, if you do not allow yourself to fall for its sales pitches and self-promotion, ESPN SportsZone definitively is worth perusing for its wealth of free information.

SportsChannel

http://www.sportschannel.com/

SportsChannel is a cable network that offers regional sports programming in Chicago, Florida, New England, New York, Ohio, the Pacific—specifically Oakland A's and San Francisco Giants territory—and Philadelphia.

Happily, the SportsChannel Web site is not ruled by hype and self-congratulation. After you get beyond the gigantic SportsChannel logo, which fills your computer screen upon logging onto the site, you will find information, features, and editorials relating to the professional teams (baseball and otherwise) that play in each region. Separate links are provided to each team, with further links to stats, news and features, previews, recaps, and standings.

The editorials are notably refreshing in that they are not afraid to criticize and take sides. One, written by Brian Webber and posted on the "Pacific" link less than a month into the 1997 season, noted that the "Giants or A's will have to make a serious postseason run for fans to come back" to the respective ballparks. The reason: in the post-strike era, "people won't go to the park unless the home team is in serious contention or [is playing] an attractive opponent like the Dodgers or the Braves." Another editorial, written by John Sanders and posted on the "Ohio" link, began with a flat statement (which would reverberate as the season progressed): "I am opposed to interleague play in major league baseball."

SportsChannel and ESPN are not the only sports-oriented cable television outlets to feature reportage on their Web sites. For example, NESN SportsCircuit (*http://www.sportscircuit.com/*), the Web site sponsored by the New England Sports Network, includes Boston Red Sox coverage. However, just because a network broadcasts sports does not mean its site will feature stats and game highlights.

On the Internet, MSG stands for many things: Monosodium Glutamate (of course), as well as Modeling, Simulation, and Gaming; and even Miranda Sex Garden.

For our purposes, MSG means one thing: Madison Square Garden (*http://www.msgnetwork.com/*), which has its own cable network (described as "the nation's largest regional cable sports network") and Web site. The network broadcasts New York Yankees (along with Knicks and Rangers) games. However, the Yankee information on the site is negligible at best. The most helpful feature is a season "Events Schedule."

The site exists to promote the MSG Network. While logging on one morning, the first visual to appear on my computer screen was a mini-Emmy Award and the message that "MSG Network Sets New York Emmy Record."

Several endless seconds later came a "CLICK HERE TO GET SOME HOT STUFF" icon, the Hot Stuff being MSG merchandise for sale (including *Pinstripe Destiny*, a video chronicle of the 1996 New York Yankee season).

Finally, there was a photo of MSG's on-air personalities—from seasoned (and, now, controversial) pro Marv Albert and all-around solid Al Trautwig to obnoxious Bob Page—garbed as rock musicians, along with the station's current tag line, "We're All Over It" (which might be reworked as "We're Full Of It").

CBS SportsLine

http://www.sportsline.com/

The free offerings on this Web site include major league game reports, features, player profiles, fantasy baseball information, minor league data, and the like. On a typical visit, the home page headlines told the story: "Rocket lands on 20"; "McGwire goes deep twice, takes overall lead with 41 HRS"; "Maddux, Kyle keep sizzling, share NL lead with 17 victories each"; "Saberhagen can't overcome shaky start in return to mound."

But keep in mind that the site also hypes CBS. I was not at all surprised to find a link titled "CBS Sports: The best in sports coverage," which offers information on upcoming events to be broadcast on the network.

Furthermore, it will cost you $4.95 per month, or $39.95 per year, to receive, among other extras, daily e-mails, regional sports coverage, "exclusive scoops," "Big Discounts" on sports publications, "Automatic Entry into Dozens of Contests and Giveaways," and "Free Customer Service" phone support to answer Sportsline and Internet questions.

On one of my visits, I checked out the "Baseball Online Library," which spotlights various aspects of baseball history. I enjoyed perusing this link—but also was informed that the Library "is FREE for a limited time. To ensure continued access, get your CBS SportsLine membership now."

The site features a free search engine, which allows you to look up news, schedules, statistics, and standings from the "SportsLine NewsWire." However, although you can download some of the results, you must be a SportsLine "member" to be able to peruse others.

Like ESPN SportsZone, CBS SportsLine is a site worth scanning—as long as you do not succumb to its sales pitches.

The network also maintains its own sports Web page, the content of which mostly hypes CBS Sports programming. On it, you can link to the "CBS Sports Team Schedule" or "check out the new CBS Store and find great CBS Sports merchandise." Its URL is *http://www.cbs.com/sports/*.

FoxSports

http://www.tvguide.com/sports/

This Web site's home page features sports headlines. Clicking on the "Baseball" icon will take you to specific baseball features and columns along with scores, standings, stats, team pages, today's games, and transactions.

When I visited, there were solid articles on the Giants-Dodgers rivalry, Don Baylor's youth, Fay Vincent's views on realignment, and a projection of "how would history have changed if realignment had taken place in 1969."

Other links include "Team Notebooks," "Home Run Quiz," "Past Features," and, as you might expect, the weekly baseball broadcast schedule for the Fox and FX networks.

MSNBC

http://www.msnbc.com/news/SPT_Front.asp

This Web site's baseball home page features the latest scores, standings, schedules, odds for upcoming games, features, columns (written by MSNBC correspondents and the Associated Press), and a bulletin board (in which you can post your opinions on who will win the pennant or your pro- or anti-DH feelings). "Live votes" are also solicited. When I logged on, the question (which then was pertinent to the moment) was "Who should win the AL Cy

Young?" Others soon were added: "Will (the) Giants win the NL West?" "Is Reinsdorf more meddlesome than Steinbrenner?" "Do you like the proposed realignment plan?" "Should Rose make the Hall of Fame?" Also on the page is an "MSNBC Sports Fantasy Baseball" game.

Concerning baseball, the MSNBC site is far superior to the one maintained by NBC, the site's parent company. NBC Sports (*http://www.nbc.com/sports/*) primarily serves to hype the peacock network. There may be a Major League Baseball link on its home page that takes you to further links to previews, schedules, and the like. But the first words at the top of the page on the day I visited were, "The 1997 Major League Baseball season is here, and NBC Sports takes you into the on-deck circle with analysis and predictions."

You will not find baseball coverage on the site. But you will find additional links to the "NBA on NBC," "NFL on NBC," "NBC Golf Tour," "NBC Sports Announcers," "NBC Sports TV Schedule," and "NBC Merchandise."

On one of the days I logged onto this *sports* site, there was a link headlined "Vote for your favorite Dennis Rodman Hairdo!"—which serves to reflect on the sorry state of American pop culture in the mid-1990s and the manner in which the mainstream media embraces the absurd.

Finally, a word about the sports Web page maintained by the final major non-cable network, ABC (*http://www.abcsports.com/*). This site is strictly oriented to ABC Sports programming. You will find no baseball scores, features, and such here. Instead, you'll find press releases for whatever upcoming shows the network is broadcasting along with announcements of promotions, hirings, deals between the network and sports organizations, and plugs for America Online (with whom ABC has a partnership).

CNN/SI

http://cnnsi.com/

This solid Web site is cosponsored by CNN and *Sports Illustrated*. The home page features the day's top stories in all sports. Click on the "Baseball" icon, and you will be taken to the baseball page. Here, you will find loads of links to feature pieces covering the major baseball happenings of recent days. On my visit, there was a brief overview of the previous week's baseball events, trades, and so forth, presented in a conversational format involving *Sports Illustrated* senior writer Tim Kurkjian and CNNSI's John Sullivan.

This site features a lively question-and-response message board. One typical query: "What are the best rivalries in baseball?" The variety of answers—from Yankees/RedSox to Yankees/Orioles to Yankees/Mariners to Angels/Mariners to "I don't think there are any good rivalries in MLB because nobody has any team loyalty"—exemplify the diversity of opinion among baseball fans.

If you click on the "Live Video" icon (found under the "Resources" heading), you can find out whether any celebrity chats have been scheduled. And you can watch major press conferences covered by CNN/SI as they occur. All the needed plug-ins can be downloaded directly from the site. If you click on the "Video Almanac" icon, you will learn how to "peek into (CNN's) vast archives and view a sampling of some of the more meaningful and newsworthy sports stories we've covered." Some of the baseball-related clips are "Royals prevail in bizarre 'pine tar' game" (1983); "Pete Rose becomes baseball's all-time hits leader" (1985); "Billy Martin becomes Yankees manager once again" (1987); "Wrigley Field finally gets lights" (1988); "San Francisco earthquake rocks World Series" (1989); "Nolan Ryan tosses record seventh no-hitter" (1991); and, most ignominiously, "Baseball players strike against proposed salary cap."

Total Sports

http://www.totalsports.net/
and
http://www.sportinggreen.com/

This Web site offers thorough, frequently updated coverage of all popular sports from baseball to boxing, the NFL,

NHL, and NBA. Perusing its home page and links is the equivalent of scanning a national daily sports newspaper.

On this site, you will find games reports and features, box scores and "breaking news," and photos of last night's big league action. You also can type the name of your favorite major league team onto a search engine and be led to appropriate stats, schedules, and so forth.

And you can link to one of Total Sports' other sites: Total Baseball Online, reviewed previously in this chapter.

Baseball Weekly

http://www.usatoday.com/bbwfront.htm

This Web site, maintained by *USA Today Baseball Weekly*, offers a taste of what can be found on the publication's pages.

Several links on the home page will take you to extensive feature pieces. An "Index" link will lead you to a list of additional articles, columns, and editorials. They will cover major league teams ("Rockies can handle curves on the road"); major league ballplayers ("Blauser battles back to answer his critics," "Walker is Canadian clubber"); fans ("Making room for the Orioles," a piece about a kid who has transformed his basement into a Baltimore Orioles shrine); trivia (Major leaguers' birthdays); fantasy baseball ("Fifth starters will begin to exert influence"); the minors ("Uncommon prospects in the middle infield"); and colleges ("Utah's Heidemann battles cancer").

In case you missed previous issues, you can link back to more than a year's worth of papers. This can be helpful if you are in need of schedules or want to know a ballclub's radio and TV broadcast outlets (all of which can be found in issues published just before Opening Day).

Baseball Weekly is a rock-solid publication and a must for die-hard baseball fans—a view that certainly is reflected in this first-class Web site, which you can spend endless hours exploring and enjoying.

Additionally, *USA Today*, the MacNewspaper that is the parent publication of *Baseball Weekly*, has its own Web page. The URL is *http://www.usatoday.com*. Click on the "Sports" icon on the home page, and you will find links to all sports. Click on the link marked "Baseball," and you will find scores, schedules, features, columns, and the paper's AL and NL game round-ups, news, and notes.

Baseball America Online

http://www.fanlink.com/ba

Baseball America is published every other week and describes itself as "the nation's most complete all-baseball newspaper." On this outstanding Web site, you can get a taste of the publication via selected articles from current and back issues. On the day I explored the site, there were entertaining features with major league slants (a piece on the Florida Marlins' Kevin Brown), minor league slants (a profile of Baltimore Orioles' top prospect Sidney Ponson), and historical angles (one headlined "Money helped break color line" and another, about Jackie Robinson's lone season on the UCLA baseball team, headlined "Robinson hibernated as a Bruin"). Also available are the newspaper's Top 25 college and high school rankings and Top 100 Prospects. You should enjoy perusing the latter, which comes complete with snappy one-liners on each player.

On this Web site, you also will find "Fan Link" (for more information, see Chapter 12, Minor and Independent Leagues.

The Sporting News

http://www.sportingnews.com/

The Sporting News, which began publication on March 17, 1886, is among the elder statesmen of American sports periodicals. Its Web site is, in a word, exceptional.

On the home page, you will find links leading to hot-off-the-wire sports stories, baseball and otherwise. Click on the "Baseball" icon, and you will be led to feature pieces and columns along with additional links to scores, standings, transactions, and contests. A search engine allows you to search current articles.

But what makes the site special is its living history of *The Sporting News.* By linking to the "Archives" section, you will learn all about the Spink family, which owned the paper from its inception through 1977. You can read pieces published in the inaugural edition and find other historical goodies.

Pure Baseball

http://www.purebaseball.com/

Here is a thorough, intelligently written Web site that offers plenty of knowledgeable analysis (especially of major league team play and individual players) along with roster activity and injury reports.

When I logged onto the site, there were links to Part 1 and 2 of an ongoing feature, "Designing a Fantasy Team." On another occasion, the headlines were especially pointed: "Dodgers Concede Rookie Of The Year Award...Ship Wilton Guerrero to Albuquerque"; "Braves Activate Lockhart As They Disable Lemke...The 'Lemmer' must be the best second sacker on the planet because his offense is decrepit."

I also loved the idealism (which might be questioned by many contemporary owners of all professional sports teams) in a declaration found at the top of the site's home page. It was made in November, 1979, by Edward Bennett Williams, "new owner of the Orioles, on why he was inactive in the free agent market": "I believe there are certain things that cannot be bought: loyalty, friendship, health, love, and an American League pennant."

Fastball

http://www/fastball.com/

The focus of this nicely designed, fact and feature loaded Web site is the major leagues. Its links will lead you to the latest big league scores, news, stats, and dugout chatter; team coverage; features; a bookstore (in association with the Amazon.com book emporium); a chat line; and so on.

This site is crammed with surprises. The content of some of the features—for example, ones on baseball lingo and the Atlanta Braves ground crew—are out of the ordinary. However, the highlight on the day I logged on was the complete testimony of Casey Stengel's 1958 testimony before the Senate Anti-Trust and Monopoly Subcommittee.

The Sports Network

http://www.sportsnetwork.com/home.asp

This basic, information-packed Web site includes data pertaining to all sports, from arena football to tennis. If you scroll down the home page, you will find the latest baseball-related news headlines.

The heart of the site's baseball coverage can be found by clicking on the "MLB Live Scores" link. Upon doing so, you will be taken to a list of further links, which only begins with "Scoreboards," "News," "Schedule/Standings," "Statistics," "Probable Pitchers," "Teams," "NL Injuries," "AL Injuries," "NL Previews," "AL Previews," "Weather," "Odds," "Minor League Scores," "Sportsbook," "Bookstore," and so on.

Nando X Baseball Server

http://152.52.2.152/SportServer/baseball/

Nando Net offers "continuously updated worldwide news and sports coverage." Its Baseball Server offers daily features, major league box scores and game recaps, stats and standings, team-by-team disabled lists, and the day's pitching lines. A "Down on the Farm" section is devoted to the minor leagues.

This Web site is crammed with endless information. Especially illuminating is the "Ghosts of Baseball Server Past" section, featuring several historical links (including a simulation of the rest of the 1994 season, had there been no baseball strike).

SportsFan Online

http://www.sfan.com/mlb/home/

On this Web site, you will find coverage of all sports. The baseball section includes feature articles, player profiles, interviews, injury reports, stats, standings, even Jackie Robinson in RealAudio. Much of the material comes courtesy of Street & Smith sports publications.

Click on the "MGM" icon, and you will be whisked to the "MGM Grand Sports Book," which during the baseball season offers betting lines and data on upcoming major league games.

Oscar Madison would love this link!

The Extreme Fans: Baseball Daily

http://www.baseballdaily.com/
or
http://www.extremefans.com/

Here is yet another Web site featuring coverage of yesterday's games, trades, news and notes, and so forth. A search engine allows you to download current data on each major league team. The "Leaderboards" icon will take you to comprehensive lists of major league batting and pitching leaders.

On one of my visits to this site, the teasers on its home page were especially clever. The reportage—which, by the way, was all-around solid—of Anaheim Angel Tony Phillips's drug bust came under the headline "He's No Angel."

The Extreme Fans: Baseball Daily includes some welcome humor. David Letterman might want to claim the

"Top Ten Reasons to Retire the Dodgers' Nelson Liriano's Number," "Top Ten Signs You're at the Little League World Series," and "Top Ten Unknown Loopholes in Baseball's Drug Policy." All are contributed by the "extreme fans" who peruse the site.

SportsExtra!

http://web.sportsextra.com/www/

This solid, fact-filled Web site features news, notes, scores, interviews, contests, Interactive Radio, an "On-Line Magazine," and the like, covering all sports.

Click on the "Baseball Scoreboard" link, and you will be taken to oodles of further links: "National League Home Page"; "American League Home Page"; "Minor League Home Page"; "Schedule/Scoreboard"; "Standings"; "Highlights for today's games"; "Weather Report"; "News Wire," (which includes archived baseball news); "Team Power Ratings"; "Fantasy Pitching Stats"; "Fantasy Batting Stats"; "Rolaids Relief Man Standings"; and more.

Plus, there are plenty of features involving individual ballplayers and current baseball issues.

2 Local Color

Increasingly, daily newspapers are offering editorial content on their Web sites. This allows any baseball fan with Internet access to scrutinize the manner in which local sportswriters use local angles to cover the major league teams.

Regional newspaper sports reporting is particularly fun to read. In the livelier papers, you will often find the kind of personal, incisive (and highly opinionated) off-the-field coverage that baseball diehards savor. The latest team gossip, clubhouse chatter, and mini-controversies both real and imagined receive the kind of extensive reportage that would be briefly alluded to (if not completely ignored) in the national media.

Many of the Web sites mentioned in this chapter offer five-star coverage. Others are merely rock-solid. But the ones with the most colorful writing, those that are the most amusing to read day-in-and-day-out, exude an ingratiating wear-your-emotions-on-your-sleeve quality. The reportage is gloriously, vividly upfront. If a team loses two straight at the season's outset, well, it's high time that the manager and general manager bow their heads and hand in their resignations. If the hot-shot free agent whom the team signed for $10 million strikes out twice in a row, well, his contract really should have been for ten cents. If a rookie is called to The Show and belts a game-winning homer, he must be the newest second coming of Willie Mays—even though, by the following week, after several days' worth of "oh-fers," he will be heading back to Tidewater or Tucson. If last season's rookie of the year dares to take an oh-fer or allow a hot grounder to roll past his outstretched glove, he surely must be heading into a sophomore slump of major proportion. And if the season is winding down and the team is mired in the depths of its division's basement, the caustic asides and obituaries are printed with predictable regularity.

In general, newspaper baseball Web pages include current standings, statistics, rosters, schedules, and other basic coverage. But their most irreplaceable features are their inning-by-inning game reports, player profiles, and columns. All these are sure to be savored if you are a New York Yankees fan living in California or Florida, or a long-suffering Chicago Cubs rooter residing in Maine or New Mexico, and you cannot get your favorite team's local newspapers at your corner newsstand.

Unfortunately, some Web site sports pages maintained by papers in major league cities are too flawed to earn their own individual listings in this book, which is after all about elite Web sites. In certain cases, they are cited within the write-ups of their much-superior competitors in this chapter. But on occasion, they are their city's sole major dailies. I'll give them a quick nod here and leave it to you to decide whether you are desperate enough for local flavor to access their sites.

The sports home page of the *Atlanta Journal-Constitution* (*http://www.accessatlanta.com/sports/*) is colorful and well-designed. The logos representing the various sports are a nice touch. Beyond that, this site is a disappointment. From it, you can link to the paper's basic

Atlanta Braves coverage. Clicking on the "Braves" icon, however, takes you to the team's Web page maintained by the Fastball Web site. Additional baseball coverage is culled from the Associated Press.

The site does feature a search engine. Using it, you supposedly can download between 5 and 100 articles on any given subject. However, I set the number selector at 100, typed in Chipper Jones—and only came up with 16 documents. I did the same for Bobby Cox, and the search engine yielded 20 documents. Andruw Jones brought up just 10.

The time period covered by this search engine was not listed. The publication dates of the pieces were not clear. Although they made enjoyable reading, I felt as if I was in a vacuum while scrutinizing them. (Additional Braves coverage can be found at the Web site maintained by the *Athens Daily News/Athens Banner-Herald* [*http://www.athensnewspapers.com/sportscape.html*].)

On three occasions, I logged onto the Web site of the *Montreal Gazette* (*http://www.montrealgazette.com/PAGES/stories.html*). During each occasion, I could have copped a snooze in the time it took for the "story index" page to download. The online Montreal Expos coverage consisted of one piece by *Gazette* reporter Jeff Blair. However insightful—the thrust of the story was the team's recent dismal road trip and how "the Pittsburgh Pirates have supplanted the Expos as everyone's favourite small-market flavour of the week"—that was it for baseball coverage of any kind on this site.

The Web site maintained by the *San Diego Union-Tribune* (*http://www.uniontrib.com/sports/index.html*) features the day's top San Diego Padres story; when I logged on, it was a piece on Ken Caminiti's being tossed out of a game. You also could link to a piece describing how Padres owner John Moores and Hall of Famer-to-be Tony Gwynn were dead-set against the DH.

But for "complete sports coverage," you will have to register and receive a User ID and Password. At the time of my visit, the service was free. But I also was informed that,

"Later this year we expect to restrict access to paying subscribers."

One only can hope that charging money to download newspaper Web sites, or making them available only to subscribers, will not be the wave of the future.

Finally, a word about the Web site maintained by the *Tampa Tribune* (*http://www.tboweb.com/sports/baseball/devlhome.htm*). While researching this book during 1997, there was little Tampa Bay Devil Rays coverage to be found on this site beyond information on the team's minor league affiliates (which already were in operation) and pieces with such upbeat headlines as "Before long, dome will turn into new home"; "Rays built on solid foundation"; and "Long wait will prove worthwhile." That was because the team did not yet exist as a full-fledged major league ballclub, with active rosters and in-season games under its belt.

All that hopefully will change when the Devil Rays become daily newsmakers.

ANAHEIM ANGELS/LOS ANGELES DODGERS

Los Angeles Times

http://www.latimes.com/HOME/SPORTS/BASEBALL/

This solid Web page offers impressive and extensive coverage of both Los Angeles-area teams, the Dodgers and the Angels. On my visit to the site, I found lively reportage of the previous day's games; an insider piece relating to problems between Tommy Lasorda and Bill Russell, the former and current Dodger managers; a report on the rehabilitation of Angels' hurler Mark Langston, who was pitching in the minors after recovering from elbow surgery; an analysis of the manner in which newly acquired Rickey Henderson might impact on the team's lineup; plus reports on other major league teams, games, and players. You can search the paper's archives for any related stories; however, a fee is required to retrieve them.

Unfortunately, the links to the paper's generic home pages devoted to the Dodgers and Angels (*http://*

www.latimes.com/HOME/NEWS/SPORTS/TEAM/DODGERS/ and *http://www.latimes.com/HOME/NEWS/SPORTS/TEAMS/ANGELS/*) are in serious need of updating. Both pages do offer helpful links to team records, ticket information, schedules, and rosters. However, the introduction at the top of the Angels page begins, "A new name, new uniforms, new manager...It's clear the Angels are determined to make some changes. Jim Leyritz, Eddie Murray, and Terry Collins teamed with Tim Salmon certainly could make a bigger difference than any wardrobe changes..."

The only trouble is, by the time I perused this page, Leyritz had been traded to Texas, and Murray had been released.

The Dodgers page offers more of the same: predictions for a baseball season that already was well underway.

In fact, quite a few newspaper Web sites include this kind of information, even when it is way outdated.

Orange County Register

http://www.ocregister.com/news/index.shtm#sports

Scroll down to the "Sports" heading, near the bottom of the home page, and you will find links to Dodgers and Angels game reportage, team-related features, news and notes, and columns, as well as additional sports coverage. You even will find pieces on the Mission Viejo Vigilantes of the Western Baseball League, Southern California Little League, and Connie Mack baseball.

On the day I perused the site, I was amused by one headline in particular: "Nixon is not a crook, but he robs Expos."

ARIZONA DIAMONDBACKS

Arizona Republic

http://www.azcentral.com/depts/dbacks/dbacks.html

I visited this Web site during the summer of 1997, and the Arizona Diamondbacks were not set to begin play until spring, 1998. Yet there already was plenty of Diamondbacks coverage.

Dozens of pieces are available on a range of topics, especially the accomplishments of the team's already-in-operation minor league affiliates and the exploits of a number of hot prospects. However, although serving to pump up interest in the Diamondbacks, this site is anything but a public relations arm of the front office. On the day I perused the site, a pair of columnists, E.J. Montini and Joe Gilmartin, offered differing views in their pieces on "the Diamondbacks' food-ban controversy."

After the Diamondbacks begin play, this promises to be an A-one Web site for the team's fans.

BALTIMORE ORIOLES

Baltimore Sun

http://www.sunspot.net/sports/orioles/

The main feature on this Web site's home page (titled "SunSpot Orioles Extra") is a link to "CyberSkipper," a free forecasting game spotlighting major league baseball in Baltimore. However, be forewarned: you must register to play, and while doing so, you will be asked to submit information on your occupation, family income, and other personal data.

On to the good news. The "Sun Articles" link will take you to Orioles-related pieces published in the paper during the previous few days, plus links to articles from recent months. You will find game coverage, player and team-related features, minor league reports, and various other organizational pieces. One of the more illuminating pieces was a well-written (by Brant James) feature on ex-Baltimore flychaser Al Bumbry and his work as outfield and base-running coach of the Colorado Silver Bullets.

Additionally, there is a "sports bulletin board discussion area," where you can peruse readers' postings or post comments of your own.

Washington Post

http://www.washingtonpost.com/wp-srv/sports/orioles.htm

Because the Washington Senators have long been consigned to the baseball heavens, there is no Washington D.C.-area team for the *Post* to cover. Instead, you will find detailed reportage on the Baltimore Orioles, the major league team closest to the nation's capital. Included are game scores and highlights, links to other Orioles-related sites, statistics, player biographies, and ticket information. There are also features and mini-features by *Washington Post* sportswriters and columnists—notably Thomas Boswell, one of the most eloquent baseball writers in the country. Boswell began his column on the death of ex-major league hurler and long-time Orioles public address announcer Rex Barney by observing, "For several years, Rex Barney has been dying, an amputated leg and a heart attack at a time...." He continued, "Barney was knocked out of the baseball box for good when he was still just a kid. He had a no-hitter against the Giants and a couple of losses in the World Series, plus a perfect opportunity to chew on a mouth of sour grapes all his life. Instead, he turned it all around. He laughed with the world at the humor of a man being given a 100 mile-per-hour fastball and the worst control on earth...." Boswell closed the piece by noting, "For the past 23 years, I've bugged Rex Barney. Thousands of times he's turned from his mike. Every time with a smile. I don't really miss him yet. But I will."

At *http://www.washingtonpost.com/wp-srv/sports/baseball.htm*, you will find the more generic up-to-the-minute scores and summaries of major league games; plenty of current and recent baseball-related news, features, and opinion pieces written by *Washington Post* and Associated Press sportswriters; and even "Baseball News By Team" links, which allow you to download data on your favorite major league ballclub.

Finally, on my first visit to the Web site of the *Washington Times* (*http://www.washtimes.com/sports/sports.html*), the "other" daily paper in our nation's capitol, the entire sports section consisted of two pieces. The first was a feature on the Washington Redskins breaking training camp. The second was an opinion piece damning sports agents ("Sports agents are masters at the art of the ridiculous").

There was nothing on the Orioles. And this was mid-August!

BOSTON RED SOX

Boston Globe

http://www.boston.com/globe/

This fact-filled, lively looking Web site offers coverage of yesterday's Red Sox game and related reportage, pieces on the previous week's contests, an AL and NL Roundup, and similar features. Plus, there are columns galore—by Peter Gammons, Will McDonough, Bob Ryan, and Dan Shaughnessy. A week's worth of each columnist's pieces is readily available, and you can search the paper's archives for additional ones.

If you want to link to Peter Gammons' pieces on ESPN SportsZone, you will have to become a subscriber to the site—and shell out money. But Gammons' jottings are available for free on the *Boston Globe* Web site—as they very well should be.

The other major Boston paper is the *Boston Herald*. Be forewarned that there is subtle advertising on the *Boston Herald* Web site (*http://www.bostonherald.com/*). At the top of the paper's home page is a colorful illustration of the Boston skyline. Right in the middle is a sign for a certain brand of gasoline—as if that is the lone type sold in the state of Massachusetts!

And you won't find baseball information (or, for that matter, Boston-area news or entertainment) on this site—at least, perhaps, for the time being. When I visited, it consisted of little more than job search-related information and business/stock market stories, and even that took what seemed like weeks to download. But the site promised that it is "new & improving," so in the future you actually might find Red Sox coverage.

Additional reportage may be found on the Web site sponsored by the *Providence Journal* (*http://www.projo.com/report/sports/offthewall/*), which features coverage of both the Sox and Pawsox (Pawtucket Red Sox), the team's AAA affiliate.

CHICAGO CUBS/CHICAGO WHITE SOX

Chicago Sun-Times

http://www.suntimes.com/sports/index.html

The *Sun-Times* Web site's sports section home page features links to, among other subjects, "Top Sports Stories," "Sports from the Past Seven Days," "Area Prep Sports," and "Prep Sports from the Past Seven Days." During my perusal of the site, the "Top Sports Stories" headlines reflected the paper's coverage of the beleaguered Cubs and White Sox: "Another day, another Cub giveaway"; "Cubs wilt again, this time vs. Padres"; "White Sox pitching collapse continues"; "Buckner booted in power struggle with Bevington."

Here is the first line of the "Cub giveaway" piece, penned by staff reporter Mike Kiley: "Ed Lynch has started making trades for players to be identified later only if you own a fingerprinting kit. In the case of Class A relief pitcher Frisco Parotte, the odds are huge that no one will ever be parroting his name."

Gotta love it—that is, unless you are a Cubbies' diehard. A "Calendar" search engine will lead you to Sox and Cubs team schedules. And a "Columnists" search engine will do the same for the paper's sports section opinion writers. Included are about a month's worth of columns for each scribe. I particularly liked Rick Telander's piece, headlined "Reinsdorf knows what's bad for us," which began: "I get it now: The White Sox signed Albert Belle for a hundred gazillion dollars to be... the Official Greeter. There he'll be at the door to the dungeon known formerly as Comiskey Park, but soon to be renamed the Baseball Hall of Torment, Whining and Fan Manipulation."

Gotta love it—that is, unless you are a Pale Hose diehard.

Chicago Tribune

http://www.chicago.tribune.com/sports/cubs.htm
and
http://www.chicago.tribune.com/sports/sox.htm.

The Web site address for all *Chicago Tribune* sports coverage is *http://www.chicago.tribune.com/sports/current/sports.htm.* Baseball fans, however, will want to go directly to the colorfully designed pages devoted to the White Sox and Cubs. On the day I explored them, the headline and content of the main coverage on the hapless Cubs illustrated the joy of local newspaper baseball reporting. The headline was "Road Wimps: Cubs losses piling up in record fashion." The accompanying piece began, "The only certainties in life anymore are death, taxes and Cubs road losses..." The staff writer went on to dub the Cubbies "Team Road Kill" and "The Boys of Bummer," and offer some theories as to why the team could not win outside Wrigley Field in 1997. The last and most logical: the "Cubs Just Stink Theory."

I happened to log onto the White Sox page a couple of weeks after team owner Jerry Reinsdorf tossed away any chance for catching Cleveland in the AL Central by trading away Wilson Alvarez, Roberto Hernandez, Danny Darwin, and Harold Baines. Although condemnation of these moves could be found on countless Web sites, the *Tribune*'s coverage was particularly pithy. In a piece on shortstop Ozzie Guillen's future with the team, a staff writer reported, "On the night of July 29, Guillen hit the clubhouse so angry he could not control himself. A few hours after learning that longtime friend Harold Baines had been traded, Guillen had dropped an infield pop that Ozzie Jr. could have caught. Instead of taking it out on Mr. Rawlings, he made Mr. Zenith pay. Guillen took his bat and smashed a television set in the clubhouse. It was described as the best hit of the night..."

White Sox and Cubs history is not ignored on these Web pages. Also featured on the White Sox page during my visit was a fascinating piece headlined "Chicago's 55-year-old secret," charting the events surrounding an "obscure tryout" Jackie Robinson had with the team in 1942.

CINCINNATI REDS

Cincinnati Enquirer

http://enquirer.com/today/sports.html

On the day I logged on, the sports section home page featured a number of baseball-related pieces, including Reds game coverage and a nice feature on Cincinnati native Ken Griffey, Jr. The latter offered a lengthy and thoughtful analysis of the pressures on Junior as he attempts to lead the Seattle Mariners to a championship.

Clicking on the "Reds Page" icon brought me to a dynamite page crammed with Cincinnati Reds features. There were player stories; a piece on the Reds' fate in the wake of major leagues realignment; a story on the team's financial status during the 1990s; an article on recently dismissed manager Ray Knight; the first of three daily excerpts of a book on the Big Red Machine; a solid piece on a Reds minor leaguer named Pete Rose, Jr., who earlier in the season had made it to Triple A for the first time; and a fine Tim Sullivan column on Rose Senior, which began, "Despite the brief buzz about it Friday, Pete Rose will not be managing the Cincinnati Reds next season. No way. No how. Know why? Because he cannot manage himself...."

Cincinnati Reds fans, whether they revere Rose or think his punishment suits his crime, surely will savor this site.

Cincinnati Post

http://www.cincypost.com/sports/

This Web site's sports section home page also spotlights up-to-the-minute Reds pieces. When I visited, there were three: the previous day's game coverage, an article on Deion Sanders' thoughts on the then-impending football season, and a "Reds Notebook."

After scrolling down to and clicking on the "Reds Page" icon, I found many additional Reds-related stories dating from the previous month, a recollection of Warren Spahn and his record against the Reds, player profiles, game stories and box scores from throughout the season, and a large collection of columnist Bill Koch's pieces in which he offers "his perspective on the team."

There even are links to other Web sites spotlighting the team—a thoughtful and welcome gesture that mostly was missing from other newspaper sites.

CLEVELAND INDIANS

Akron Beacon Journal

http://www.beaconjournal.com/

Here you will find Indians game and team coverage and "Tribe Notes," along with columns and opinion pieces. During my visit to the site, there was an illuminating detailed analysis of the managerial status of Mike Hargrove. In addition, you can download previous team coverage using the "Indians Archives" link.

Even though Kenny Lofton had been traded to Atlanta months earlier, the Web site still included no less than nine pieces, plus assorted photographs, on what the paper referred to as the "DEAL OF THE DECADE." The rationale for this was made clear via the comment that the trade "means the core of (the) Tribe's 1995 World Series team now (is) just a memory": a sentiment with major implications for Indians fans.

Cleveland Plain Dealer

http://www.cleveland.com/sports/

Even though this Web page took a while to download, it was worth the wait. At its top is a snazzy "Cleveland Sports" logo. From this page, you can link to game recaps, interviews and features, "Tribe News," and so forth.

"Tribe News" is the place to go for Indians fans. It is link-loaded, and you will find additional interviews, game stories, player profiles, and information on Jacobs Field. Of special note: the pieces on Indians history not only celebrate the likes of Bob Feller, Larry Doby, and pennant-winning seasons but recall, in the "Hall of Shame," "the tragi-comic history that is our team's legacy."

This is a truly interactive site. Viewers are encouraged to vote on the team's performance in individual categories and offer their opinions on the team's then-recent release of Julio Franco and whether Jack McDowell "will pitch next season for another team."

COLORADO ROCKIES

Denver Post

http://www.denverpost.com/sports/sports.htm

This Web site's sports home page features nice Rockies coverage plus additional baseball-related links. "AP Sports" includes further baseball and non-baseball reporting. "Baseball" (which, during my visit, took forever to download) brought me to the same page as "AP Sports."

"Rockies," however, whisked me to where I wanted to be: a link-loaded page featuring additional Rockies game pieces and columns, game archives, team information, selected features, minor league reports, "AL and NL Notes," and even a chapter of "High-Country Heat," a serial authored by *Post* staff writer Kevin Simpson.

In addition, previously posted sports stories that are still on the server can be retrieved via a search engine.

On this site, in a Woody Paige column, I first saw the team referred to as "The Rox."

Rocky Mountain News

http://www.denver-rmn.com/sports/sports.htm

The sports section home page includes the latest on the Colorado Rockies and other area sports. The "Rockies" icon brought me to the previous weeks' team coverage. On my visit, a survey of the headlines reflected the local focus of the coverage.

DETROIT TIGERS

Detroit Free Press

http://www.freep.com/sports/index.htm

Click on the "Tigers" link, and you will find game coverage and features written by *Free Press* staffers. There also are links to Associated Press box scores and statistics, a Tigers Forum discussion group, and a search engine.

The latter is especially handy. A request for Kaline (as in Al) yielded 20 recently published pieces. Requests for Tony Clark and Buddy Bell did the same. To download older items—dating all the way back to 1982—click on the "News Library" icon (found on the search engine page). Searching is free; a $1 fee is charged for downloading each article. Other rules also apply.

You can select the year you want to search. Articles can be sorted from newest to oldest, oldest to newest, or by relevance or term frequency.

One cannot begin to imagine the total number of articles one can retrieve by entering the word *Kaline* here.

Detroit News

http://www.detnews.com/1997/sports/

Even though I scrutinized this Web site in mid-August, Detroit Tigers baseball was not a high priority on this paper's sports section home page. The Pistons' signing of free-agent center Brian Williams and the departure of Red Wings goalie Mike Vernon to the San Jose Sharks received bigger play than baseball. That the Tigers were not pennant-bound was no excuse.

To glean the full extent of its Tigers reportage, click on the "Sports: Tigers" icon. Here you will find all the game coverage, features, and opinion pieces. On my visit, I liked Joe Falls' analysis of the team's competitive status, headlined "Uncertainty is certain as Tigers continue down the long road toward title contention."A search engine allows you to download pieces published during the past three years. Also available are up-to-the-minute sports updates from *USA Today* and additional coverage from the Associated Press.

While researching this book, this site could be located at the URL shown earlier. However, it is safe to assume that, in the new year, the "1997" will be replaced by "1998."

FLORIDA MARLINS

Fort Lauderdale Sun-Sentinel

http://www.sun-sentinel.com/sports/

In addition to chronicling the goings-on of the Miami Heat, Miami Dolphins, and Tampa Bay Buccaneers, this South Florida newspaper offers extensive coverage of the Florida Marlins. In addition to the usual scores and game reportage, you can tour Pro Player Stadium, the home of the Marlins, and "get a Marlin's-eye view of the field and the dugout." (However, to take full advantage of this feature, you will need to download Apple's QuickTime viewer.)

You also will find some scintillating commentary from columnist Dave Hyde. Here is what he had to say on the chances of the Marlins catching the Atlanta Braves in the 1997 pennant chase: "...Suddenly, you see, the Marlins are dangerous enough to be hated. And not just by Atlanta fans. Braves third baseman Chipper Jones' first thought upon waking up Saturday morning—'Right when I opened my eyes,' he said—'was about beating the Marlins...'"

Miami Herald

http://www.herald.com/sports/

After logging onto this Web site's sports section home page, I was greeted by the headline "Moises Alou rocks as Marlins roll to rout." The piece that followed, authored by *Herald* sportswriter Clark Spencer, was solid reportage. There also was a short, sweet piece written by Spencer on career minor leaguer Kirt Ojala's call-up to the Marlins.

The "Marlins" link took me to nine additional team pieces, plus further links to day-by-day season accounts as reported in the paper; a link to the team's official Web site; and one to the "Florida Marlins Interactive Magazine," a colorful page with illustrated palm trees at its bottom.

Back on the home page are links to the paper's columnists that included the previous two weeks' pieces. The lead paragraph of one was a textbook example of solid, localized analysis: "Gary Sheffield was speaking in the clubhouse two hours before the baseball game was to start Thursday night, and as he did, thick rain pounded the former Joe Robbie Stadium. This kind of rain on a rice paddy in Cambodia is called a monsoon. This kind of rain on a Marlins game in Miami is called a metaphor for Gary Sheffield's 1997."

HOUSTON ASTROS

Houston Chronicle

http://www.chron.com/content/sports/index.html

Click on the "Baseball" icon on this Web site's sports section home page, and you will be taken to the *Chronicle*'s Astros game coverage and other major league action compiled by the "*Houston Chronicle* News Services." Additional baseball reportage from the Associated Press also is available.

On the home page are links to the paper's columnists; included are pieces published since the beginning of the year. During my visit, I enjoyed a nice reminiscence (by Mickey Herskowitz) of ex-Astros hurler Vern Ruhle's 1980 season; a solid piece on ex-Astro and current Met Pete Harnisch as he faced his old team; and a colorful example of localized team coverage ("For the Astros, it was 11 runs on 12 hits with no errors or heroes, only survivors. Any spectator who stayed to the end should be sentenced to a free trip to Philadelphia.").

Also on the home page are links to other URLs, including the Astros' official Web site. These are welcome, as is a link to "Breaking the Barriers: Blacks in Sports," a feature-filled *Chronicle* special section. And a baseball-related "Sports Forum" is available that requires a username and password to download.

Inexplicably, however, there also is a sorely outdated link offering team predictions for the *previous year*!!!

KANSAS CITY ROYALS

Kansas City Star

http://www.kcstar.com/sports/royals/royalspg.htm

In addition to Kansas City Royals reportage and other baseball news, this site offers a nice feature that stat freaks will savor and that other papers would do well to include. During the baseball season, the home page features links to each and every Royals game already played. Clicking on that link will lead you to that game's complete box score.

Additional Royals reporting can be found on the Web site maintained by the *Topeka Capital-Journal* (*http://www.cjonline.com/sports/index/html*).

MILWAUKEE BREWERS

Milwaukee Journal Sentinel

http://www.onwis.com/sports/brew/

On the day I visited this Web site, the lead sentence in the lead story on the home page, headlined "Ground Chuck:

Finley beats Brewers for No. 10," perfectly illustrated the take-no-prisoners viewpoints found in a team's juiciest local media coverage. The sentence began as a "Memo to the Milwaukee Brewers," and continued, "Even in the American League Central Division, you have to win a game every now and then to stay in the pennant race."

This site includes, among other items, Brewers game stories for the previous week; Brewers' news and notes; a team photo gallery; a "Brewers Fan Forum,"; ongoing coverage of the building of Miller Park, the team's new stadium; plus a general major league baseball round-up. You even will find descriptions of Brewers schedule highlights and promotions and a list of players' salaries.

MINNESOTA TWINS

Minneapolis Star-Tribune

http://www.startribune.com/twins/

The home page of this paper's baseball section is among the more cleverly designed: a mini-section of a playing field, on which are the various links to "Players," "Twins stories," "Twins photos," "Twins talk," "AP baseball news," "Game schedule," "Trivia," and "Baseball ticker." Another nice touch is an additional link, to the previous game's coverage and that game's score.

Under "Twins stories," you will find further links to individual articles. Jim Souhan's piece, headlined "Twins skid hits eight games," began "Forget about the Twins being shifted to the National League Central. They deserve to be realigned into the Northern League. They have become that inept. Problem is, even ball-carrying pigs and massaging nuns wouldn't distract from what might be currently the worst on-field product in baseball."

And the baseball sufferers in Chicago think they've got gripes!

If you click on the "Players" icon, the upper left side of your screen will be filled with baseball card-like visuals of

Twins team members. A search engine allows you to effortlessly find your favorite player. The "Twins photos" icon leads you to further links to a number of Twins game stills—and it is nice to see the picture taker receiving prominent credit. "Twins talk" is the site's discussion line; participants are urged to "keep it 'above the belt.'" "Twins trivia" is a mini-trivia game. When I played, the first question was, "Which Twins player holds the major league record for most indoor home runs?" After scouring my brain and not finding a logical answer, I typed in Rod Carew and clicked on "submit." In an instant, I was informed, "Whoops! You typed Rod Carew but you probably meant Kent Hrbek."

Who would have guessed!

You do not have to be a Twins fan to have fun with this Web site.

NEW YORK METS/NEW YORK YANKEES

Daily News

http://www.nydailynews.com/most/SPORTS/sports.htm

After Pete Hamill became the *Daily News'* editor at the beginning of 1997—unfortunately, he was to depart nine months into his stewardship—an ad began appearing on New York-area TV stations. It featured Hamill (who is one of the city's outstanding tell-it-from-the-heart-with-intelligence journalists) counting...and counting...and counting the paper's sports pages.

Although sheer numbers do not necessarily translate into quality, they certainly do in the case of the *Daily News* and the paper's Web site.

For openers, its sports section home page is among the more colorfully designed. On it are the day's major headlines, along with icons that enable you to link to coverage of all sports. The baseball link is loaded with pieces—each and every one colorfully written, as one would expect from a big-city tabloid—along with Mets and Yankees schedules, a fantasy baseball contest, a Sports Fan Ticker (for which you will need a Java-enabled browser), and a special tribute to Jackie Robinson. The latter is exceedingly comprehensive and deserves to remain a permanent feature on the site. The logo on the Robinson section's main page even features within its artwork an image of Jackie swinging a bat!

Of all the New York newspaper sites, this easily is the most enjoyable to browse.

The two other New York City dailies also have sports Web pages. They are the *New York Post* (*http://www.nypostonline.com/*) and *New York Times* (*http://www.nytimes.com*). The highlight of the *Post*'s Web site home page is a reproduction of the paper's front and back pages, which makes for a nice newspapery feel. It is worth viewing during the baseball season for the back page, which introduces the sports coverage and usually features an imaginative headline. On one visit, it was "OH NO, O'NEILL," referring to a ninth-inning error by Yankees flychaser Paul O'Neill that cost the Bronx Bombers a game against the lowly A's.

Beyond this, the *Post*'s sports coverage is surprisingly skimpy. It can be downloaded by clicking on the "Sports" icon, which will whisk you to a selection of the paper's baseball and non-baseball reportage.

At the bottom of the home page, it is noted that the paper is "constantly developing this website and would appreciate any comments you might have." Here is one, regarding its baseball (as well as other sports) content: More of the same! Much, much more! For starters, how about links/indexes to previously published pieces on the Mets and Yankees and spiffier graphics to match those on the home page.

On another occasion, while exploring additional media Web sites, I came upon another *New York Post* sports URL: *http://www.nypostonline.com/thursday/sports/sports.htm*. This seemed odd because the day was Monday and the link was not on the paper's home or sports page. Yet here, I was able to download additional pieces and also learned that I could "join *New York Post*'s Sports Columnist Phil

Mushnick in a live chat session every Monday night from 9:00-10:00 ET at *www.tvguide.com.*"

I usually enjoy reading the *Post*'s juicy, opinionated sports coverage. However, its Web site at this relatively late stage of Internet development seems to be a work in progress.

The *Times* prides itself on being the most influential paper in the country. A positive or negative movie, book, or theater review, for example, can solidify or destroy actors' or directors' careers, close down shows or certify them as hits, establish literary reputations or consign books to the bottom shelves of stores. But its Web site is a bureaucratic maze, and its Web site sports coverage is embarrassingly thin.

To "join *The New York Times* on the Web community," you must register (at no cost) and secure an ID and Password. To the paper's credit, its request for your "total household income, yearly, in US $$" is optional. But you might have to hire a lawyer to decipher the Subscriber Agreement.

After you have done so, you can click on the "Sports" icon. However, the first images to appear on the screen are ads. (I logged on several times, with the same result.) The section's home page offers links to articles on all sports, including Mets and Yankees Web Forums.

As hard as I tried, I was unable to find pieces by any of the paper's columnists. So I typed in the name "Berkow" (as in *Times* writer Ira) on a search engine. I had 13 responses: a letter to the editor; several links relating to Berkow's book, *To the Hoop: The Seasons of a Basketball Life* (including its first chapter, the presence of which seemed to be a teaser to get me to go out and purchase the entire tome); and—finally, at the very bottom—a trio of Berkow's columns.

Newark Star-Ledger

http://www.nj.com/mets/
and
http://www.nj.com/yankees/

These Web pages (which are linked to a Web site named New Jersey Online) are chock-full of Yankees and Mets coverage from the pages of the *Newark Star-Ledger*. You will find solid general reportage along with a "Story Archive," consisting of pieces dating from the beginning of the season.

You can link to the sites' "Fan Zone," described as "your place to gloat about your team's latest win or to complain about somebody's stupid play-calling. Propose blockbuster deals. Gripe about overpaid crybabies. Or just sit back and learn something. Let the spittle fly!" And you can download several months' worth of columns—baseball-related or otherwise—penned by the paper's fine columnist, Jerry Izenberg.

An extra attraction: Send in your e-mail address and receive, free of charge, "Mets Inside Pitch" and "Yanks Inside Pitch," the "daily e-mail scoop" on the each team. They include all-too-brief news items, current records/standings, and information on the teams' upcoming games.

Newsday

http://www.newsday.com/mets.htm
and
http://www.newsday.com/yankees.htm

These Web pages are loaded with information. In addition to team-related pieces from the Long Island paper's pages, you will find oodles of links devoted to the teams' histories.

The Mets page includes "A Gallery of Mets Greats," featuring lists of the team's Cy Young winners, Rookies of the Year, World Series MVPs, Gold Glove winners, Relief Men of the Year, batting and pitching leaders, and players selected to the All-Star game and Hall of Fame. You can download lists of the team's season-by-season records, information and trivia tidbits on the history of Shea Stadium, and recollections of the team's postseason successes. At the bottom of the home page are the Mets' retired numbers: 14 (Gil Hodges); 37 (Casey Stengel); and 41 (Tom Seaver). Each is a link in itself, which will take you to a mini-biography of the honoree.

Among the goodies on the Yankees page are a "Time Line," which offers the team's history by era; a game-by-game recap of the 1996 World Series; four features on Mickey Mantle, plus Bob Costas's eulogy at Number 7's funeral; features on Babe Ruth and Lou Gehrig; bios of those Yankees whose numbers have been retired; a Yankee Stadium history; and recaps of the myriad Yankees World Series appearances.

Both pages work as nifty quick pocket references to Yankees and Mets lore. The sites also have some slick graphics. I especially liked the mini-animated pitcher winding up and letting go with a fast one, found on the left side of "the Bullpen" logo at the bottom of the Mets page.

One minor disappointment: I was expecting to be dazzled by some clever imagery in the links to the Mets "Virtual Baseball Cards." But all I found was the kind of data one might see on a real baseball card, plus an unimpressive mini-image of the player.

Finally, near the bottom of the sports section home page (*http://www.newsday.com/sports/sports.htm*), you will find a "Sports Column" link. This will take you to an index of recently published baseball and non-baseball-related pieces.

Another helpful feature, the kind that other newspapers might emulate is the "Batting Ranges" link; you will find a handy list of Long Island batting ranges.

OAKLAND ATHLETICS/SAN FRANCISCO GIANTS

San Francisco Chronicle

http://www.sfgate.com/sports/

When logging onto this Web site from a search engine, I first was informed that I must register to enter. Although registration is free, it also is cumbersome. I was asked to submit a "Username," and an optional identifying code. I also could "check here (to) grant... permission to share or sell (my) profile information." Translated, this means check here if you like receiving junk mail and telephone solicitations.

Within an hour, I received an e-mail informing me that I now could download "fishWrap, E-mail alert and Gate TV." These pages (or whatever they are) might be of interest to those in the San Francisco area. But all I wanted was to download the *Chronicle*'s sports pages.

Happily, by using the URL listed above, I was able to do exactly that without a request for my "Username."

In addition to the day's A's and Giants coverage, there are three handy search engines: "Live Results, Stats" (with one of the selections "Baseball, AL/NL"); "Sports/Teams" (including the selections "Baseball," "Giants," and "Athletics"); and "Sportswriters." "Baseball, AL/NL" features what one might expect the previous day's game coverage. "Baseball," "Giants," and "Athletics" all lead to the same page, a stunningly designed one devoted to both teams and featuring plenty of major league stats and standings links.

Not all newspaper or magazine Web sites include the journalistic offerings of all their sports scribes and columnists. This site's "Sportswriters" search engine contains them all; the star columnists are neither omitted nor highlighted. You can read a week's worth of pieces from each and also search for several years' worth of additional articles.

On my visit to the Web site of the other San Francisco daily, the *San Francisco Examiner* (*http://www.examiner.com*), I found headlines both clever ("Giants' loss puts wraps on Rapp") and generic ("A's squander four-run lead in gift to Brewers").

But beyond these basics, there was no emphasis on baseball coverage here—not even A's and Giants stats!

San Jose Mercury

http://www.sjmercury.com/sports/athletics/
and
http://www.sjmercury.com/sports/giants/

At the top of these Web pages, you will find the upcoming week's Oakland A's and San Francisco Giants schedules.

For the games already played, you can link directly to the paper's reportage.

Plus, there are enough features and columns, along with A's and Giants-oriented chat lines, to keep the teams' fans well occupied.

PHILADELPHIA PHILLIES

Philadelphia Inquirer/Philadelphia Daily News

http://sports.phillynews.com/phillies/

This Web page offers extensive Phillies coverage, from the pages of the *Philadelphia Inquirer* and *Philadelphia Daily News.* When I explored the site, one day's worth of headlines mirrored the scope of the coverage: "Baseball's laughingstocks suddenly look bullish"; "Expansion draft has Phils thinking"; "Rolen is a rare rookie indeed"; and "Here's a to-do list for Phils president." Each piece, whether news item or column, was insightful and a pleasure to read.

In addition, you can download the previous weeks' worth of Phillies coverage. And there is a search engine, which will enable you to easily download the various pieces on a specific subject or individual that were published during the current season.

PITTSBURGH PIRATES

Pittsburgh Tribune-Review

http://tribune-review.com/pirates/

Included here is Pittsburgh Pirates game coverage, both current and recent, plus opinions galore from the paper's columnists. The headlines alone, from the "*Trib* Columnists" link, mirror the depth included here: "Pirates, Indians would make for fine rivalry"; "Baseball's realignment only a matter of time"; "Bonifay must work hard for Pirates to stay in contention"; and "Womack deserves to be an All-Star." You can link even further into the site to a "Pirates Column Archive."

Especially illuminating is "Joe Rutter's Baseball Notebook," which appears every Sunday during the season in the *Tribune-Review*. The online notebooks include plenty of gossip, facts, opinions, and other Pirates-related tidbits.

Team history also is served on this site. You can download a wealth of data on everything from Pirates awards and yearly records to managerial history and trivia.

SEATTLE MARINERS

Seattle Times

http://www.seattletimes.com/todaysnews/#Spor

As I logged onto this Web site, I half-expected a gigantic full-color photo of a smiling Ken Griffey, Jr. to fill my computer screen. If not running for president, Junior would be hawking any one of a number of products he is paid zillions to endorse.

What I found instead was a blandly designed page offering a link to coverage of the Mariners' most recent game. An additional link, to the *Seattle Times* Mariners Web page, is a real curiosity. It is an almost completely white (translate: empty) page, with links on the left-hand side to Mariner profiles, "Mariner history," "Kingdome seating," "Game calendar," "Fun facts," and "Ask the M's."

The good news is that these links lead to oodles of Mariners data: closer looks at the players, a Kingdome map (a helpful extra for those wanting to order seats), three online games, baseball factoids, and players' answers to readers' questions. The "Mariner history" link is especially interesting; it took me to further features relating to the team's past—especially its expansion 1977 season—along with readers' remembrances of the team's debut. A search archive allowed me to download pieces printed in that day's edition, during the previous week, or during the past year-and-a-half.

Just so you do not think that the *Seattle Times* ignores the Mariners' franchise player, a search for "Griffey" yielded 200 documents.

One more point: Clicking on the "Hot Diggety Dog!" logo will take you to further links to the various dining establishments found in the Kingdome. At the top of the page is a clever comic illustration—described by my wife as "cute"—of a hungry boy being chased by a moving hot dog.

Visually speaking, this is a real Dr. Jekyll-Mr. Hyde Web site. But in most ways, it is vastly superior to the site maintained by the city's other daily, the *Seattle Post-Intelligencer* (*http://www.seattle-pi/mariners/*). When I explored this site, it appeared to be a work in progress. There was no daily Mariners coverage, just generalized player profiles, season predictions, and Opening Day game stories and columns—even though it already was late summer!

Nonetheless, the generic pieces (on A-Rod and Junior, among others) were worth a look.

Tacoma Tribune

http://www.tribnet.com/news/sports.htp

The sports section home page offers links to the day's top stories. Baseball-wise, they cover both the Mariners and Tacoma Rainers, the team's AAA Pacific Coast League affiliate.

The home page's baseball link will take you to further Mariners and Rainers coverage. Of special note are columnist Larry LaRue's pieces, which are vividly written and to the point. On the day I visited the site, his portrait of Tony Phillips, written days after the ballplayer's drug bust, was poignant and revealing. And the "search news" search engine is a database of more than 16,000 online stories.

ST. LOUIS CARDINALS

St. Louis Post-Dispatch

http://www.stlnet.com/postnet/sports/CardsExtra.nsf

This meat-and-potatoes Web page includes links to loads of Cards-related features and game coverage, box scores, and commentary. On my visit, there were solid pieces on manager

Tony La Russa's future with the team; the "McGwiremania" in St. Louis since the team acquired slugger Mark McGwire, which included the observation that "Cardinal Nation, so hungry for a power hitter for so many years, has worked up a ravenous appetite for this Big Mac"; and *three* separate pieces on what the Cards will have to do to re-sign the slugger.

There were several wonderful nostalgia-oriented pieces by legendary St. Louis sports scribe Bob Broeg (who now is the paper's contributing editor). They ranged from a reminiscence of Joe Medwick to a discussion of no-hitters to a pair of Hall of Fame-related stories.

Also here were several minor league reports; links to additional baseball related URLs (starting with the Cards' official Web site); and a "Cards Talk" forum, which allows you to sound off about the team.

TEXAS RANGERS

Forth Worth Star-Telegram

http://www.arlington.net/today/news/sports/baseball/rangers/index.htm

This paper's Rangers Web page really gets in the baseball spirit. Typing in its long URL is worth the finger exercise, if only for its dazzling design: a red, white, and blue motif, with a subtle pattern of miniature baseballs.

You will find team schedules, rosters, box scores, and the like, and you can link to a complete list of the paper's daily team coverage. There also are additional links, to the Oklahoma City 89ERS, the Ranger's Triple-A franchise, and the Single-A Charleston Riverdogs, among others.

The *Star-Telegram* site wins out over the one maintained by the *Dallas Morning News* (*http://www.dallas-news.com/index/sposrch-nf.htm*). On its sports section home page, you will find links to "Top Stories," the "Texas Rangers," and "Baseball" as well as other professional leagues and area teams. The "Top Stories" link is self-explanatory. The "Texas Rangers" link takes you to game-related pieces and a "Rangers Forum," in which you can read and post comments. The "Baseball" link hooks into the paper's major league coverage.

A "Columnists" link leads you to several days' worth of offerings by *Morning News* opinion-makers. However, on the day I visited the site, there were, in order of appearance, pieces on pro athlete endorsements, the PGA championship, golfer Tiger Woods, dove hunting, hockey player Mike Modano, the Dallas Cowboys, golfer John Daly, a plan to dome the Cotton Bowl, golfer Tom Kite, the Dallas Cowboys (again), Texas big game hunting, pro athlete contracts, the NFL preseason, and the Dallas Cowboys (again).

The time was mid-August, yet not one of these columns focused on any aspect of the Texas Rangers. The lone baseball-oriented piece, placed in the middle of the pack, involved Pete Rose.

Did I log onto this Web site on an off-day? Or are *Dallas Morning News* readers more interested in football, golf, and hunting than major league baseball?

TORONTO BLUE JAYS

Toronto Sun

http://www.canoe.ca/BaseballALTOR/home.html

Here, you will find the usual: a Jays scoreboard, game recaps, feature pieces, scouting reports, and links to individual player profiles (the pages of which resemble those in team yearbooks). The game-related pieces cover the previous week.

Several welcome extras: links to the two top Blue Jays minor league teams, the Syracuse Sky Chiefs and Knoxville Smokies; and a link to the "Jr. Jays CyberMag," a children-oriented page that includes comic strips, jokes, and riddles and is described as "new," "cool," and "fun."

The latter feature is a rarity for newspaper sports sections. More Web sites should include such features; they not only add to viewership but also help spur youngsters' interest in baseball.

The other Toronto city papers are the *Toronto Star* (*http://www.tsnl.com/thestar/editorial/sports/index/html*) and the *Globe & Mail* (*http://www.theglobeandmail.com/docs/news/summary/Sport.html*).

The sports home page of the *Star* is crammed with coverage of the Blue Jays and other Canadian and American athletics. In addition to game reports, clicking on the "Blue Jays" icon will take you to several days' worth of pieces plus an archive linking you to the previous six months' worth of team coverage. For each date, you will find two or three Blue Jays pieces.

The baseball coverage on the *Globe & Mail* site was lackluster. I visited it twice; each time, the reporting was devoted as much to other major league teams and players as to the Blue Jays.

Baseball History: Research

Countless Web sites spotlight baseball history, from the game as it existed in the nineteenth century to the Negro Leagues, the Black Sox scandal, and the way the sport is represented in museums and Halls of Fame. Some pages are devoted to individual players of yesteryear, both famed and long-forgotten. Other sites focus on teams that abandoned municipalities decades ago and endure only in the collective memories of their aging fans.

Some sites highlight serious baseball research. Others feature fascinating memorabilia and artifacts. Still more explore the most incendiary and intriguing baseball controversies. Combined, they bring to life the yellowed pages of baseball's past and are reminders that there is much more to the sport than who won last night's game and who will be on the mound in tonight's contest.

Many sites that feature baseball history are described elsewhere in this book. For openers, check the Total Baseball listing in Chapter 1, "Up-to-the-Minute Baseball." Selected exemplary Web pages from sites listed elsewhere in

Baseball on the Web are also included in these history chapters because they deserve further emphasis.

SABR (Society for American Baseball Research)

http://www.sabr.org/

SABR describes itself as "the world's largest sports research organization," which "fosters research into all aspects of Baseball."

This Web site is primarily informational. It includes excerpts from SABR-published books and links to SABR regional groups and publications as well as research committees and their current projects. SABR committees cover a range of baseball-related subjects, from ballparks to Negro Leagues and oral history to pictorial history. Several of these groups have separate entries in this and other history chapters.

This Web site features information on SABR's Internet Committee and the SABR Research Library Index (which includes a variety of baseball material, from features published in *Baseball Digest* to SABR-sponsored research articles/presentations to recorded interviews conducted by SABR member John E. DiMeglio). Unfortunately, the articles and interviews themselves are not online.

The site also offers tips on how to obtain answers to baseball-related questions along with information on SABR-L, a-SABR-members-only moderated chat line whose commentary (under the name SABR-L Digest) is e-mailed daily. SABR-L participants are articulate and baseball-savvy and share a knowledge of and passion for the sport. Postings are often lengthy. For example, a belief on the part of one participant that Sandy Koufax would have been something less than a Hall of Famer had he pitched in the 1990s resulted in several days' worth of heated debate.

Access to SABR-L alone is worth a SABR membership.

RBI—Research in Baseball Index

http://student-www.uchicago.edu/users/tmc5/dataserv.htm

This "catalog/database to baseball literature" (formerly known as Baseball Online) is a project of SABR's bibliography committee. It includes more than 65,000 baseball-related books, magazines, newspaper feature articles, pamphlets, dissertations, music scores, recordings, and film and television programs—with thousands more being added each year.

RBI is available to SABR and non-SABR members. Requests for information are free. However, nominal fees are charged to view the results.

Retrosheet

http://www.retrosheet.org

Stat-freaks will relish this Web site. Retrosheet is a volunteer organization founded in 1989 that collects, computerizes, and distributes play-by-play accounts of pre-1984 Major League games, most of which come directly from ballclubs. Games played since 1984 are available on the Project Scoresheet-Baseball Workshop Database.

On this Web site, you will find "how to" links, Retrosheet newsletters past and present, and the utilities programs you will need to download to be able to access information.

To date, Retrosheet has compiled more than 100,000 game accounts. When I explored the site, an "Index of Game Accounts" link was under construction.

Original Baseball Research

http://pw2.netcom.com/~proboy/orb.htm

This Web site features several serious, original historical essays. Most are authored by the maintainer, Clifford Blau.

The title tells all in "The History of Major League Tie Games," which is based on Blau's "recorded data on 794 of the approximately 1128 tie games in major league history."

"How Hitting and Pitching Contribute to the Success of Division Winners, 1969-1989," written by Cyril Morong, is a study that "looks at the run scoring ability and run preventing ability of division winning teams" during the specified years.

In "Nonplaying Rules—A Work In Progress," Blau is "attempting to collect the complete history of such things as roster limits, waiver rules, disabled lists, and minor league drafts."

Blau is the author of "Offensive Replacement Levels," which is his term for what Bill James calls "sustenance level." Blau describes this as "the rate of return for regulars at different levels of offensive production." He offers his study, the results of which he claims will allow one to "determine the amount of hitting needed for players to keep their jobs."

Sean Lahman's Baseball Archive

http://www.baseball1.com/

So much material is available on this Web site that it was a tough call deciding where to place it. Lahman describes the site as "constantly evolving. Our intent is to... provide the largest amount of free baseball data available on the web."

Most of Lahman's links are self-explanatory: "Records/Feats"; "History/Almanac"; "Current Data"; "Statistics"; "Awards"; "Minor Leagues"; "Essays"; and "Economics/Law." For starters, "Records/Feats" includes data on current, active, and yearly batting and pitching leaders and single season records and feats (such as no-hit hurlers, Triple Crown winners, and four-homers-in-a-game sluggers). "History/Almanac" is divided into "History of Baseball," "Team Histories," "Post-Season," "All-Star Game," and "League Histories."

One highlight of the "Statistics" link provides team batting and pitching stats from 1871 to the present!

Describing this site as a mini-baseball encyclopedia would not be an overstatement.

The SABR Home (Run) Page

http://www.sabr.org/homerun.htm

Ever wondered how many inside-the-park grand slams have been hit in the history of Major League Baseball? Or who are the ballplayers with the longest names who hit back-to-back homers in The Show? Or what professionals other than Babe Ruth and Roger Maris have hit 60-plus dingers?

The answers to these and many more questions can be found on this SABR-sponsored site. Its data is compiled from the Tattersall/McConnell Home Run Log, described as "the world's largest collection of data regarding home runs (homers, four-baggers, round-trippers, Ballantine Blasts, and so on)."

(For the record, countless ballplayers have hit inside-the-park grand slams. Tony Gwynn, Chico Walker, Mike Greenwell, Ron Karkovice, and Luis Polonia have done it in the 1990s. Honus Wagner smacked five of them; Tommy Leach did it four times; Joe Jackson has three to his credit. The longest-name back-to-back-homer combo is Andy Stankiewicz/Mark Grudzielanek [23 letters], followed by Dom Dallessandro/Bill Nicholson; Carl Yastrzemski/Tony Conigliaro; and Rico Petrocelli/Yastrzemski [all at 21 letters]. And ten minor leaguers have hit 60 or more homers, with Joe Bauman heading the list. In 1954, he belted 72 while playing for Roswell in the Longhorn League.)

Home Run Hitters

http://www.pacificnet.net/~sroney/HRdata/index.html

This Web page, maintained by Steve Roney, is a work-in-progress offering his research on major league home run patterns.

Roney is interested in ballplayers who had big-dinger seasons at young ages and how this impacted on their career outputs and those who preceded Mark McGwire by hitting 20 or more long shots in a season in which they played in both leagues.

Has the baseball been juiced in the 1990s? Has the quality of pitching been depleted by expansion? Or is the present-day increase in power among major league sluggers cyclical? Those who are curious about these questions can come to their own conclusions after checking out Roney's chart, covering the years 1919 through 1996, which shows the numbers of players who belted 20 homers for the first time during each season.

The Wisdom of Bill James

http://www.cfmc.com/adamb/sabr/bjames.htm

This Web page, a link on a site maintained by Adam D. Barnhart, is an homage to Bill James. James, of course, is synonymous with *sabermetrics*, a term he coined and defined as "the mathematical and statistical analysis of baseball records" and "the search for objective knowledge about baseball."

"It has come to my attention," Barnhart notes, "that there are a great number of intelligent, literate people, some of whom even like baseball, who aren't aware of who Bill James is. To me, this is somewhat criminal, since I think of him as the greatest sportswriter (if that is, indeed, what he is) who's taken pen to paper... or finger to keyboard."

Barnhart offers a taste of James's work via links to three articles: "Inside Out Perspective," from James's *1984 Baseball Abstract*, which Barnhart describes as "perhaps the one thing (James has) written that's referred to most by other people in the field"; "Oakland A's," also in the *1984 Baseball Abstract*, which "should be required reading for anyone who's using a computer for research purposes"; and "You Don't Say," from the *1986 Baseball Abstract*, in which James "debunks a basic myth about sport that one hears endlessly."

Jim Albert's Home Page

http://www-math.bgsu.edu/~albert/

James H. Albert is a professor of mathematics and statistics at Bowling Green State University. He also is a sometime baseball fan. "I follow the Phillies when they are playing well," he observes, quickly adding, "I don't have to follow them that often!"

Albert has written a number of articles on how to interpret baseball data. One of them, an introduction to sabermetrics, can be found on his Web site. Skip "the game of baseball" section at the top unless you are completely new to the sport and want to understand its basic rules. Albert begins massaging your mind when he commences his discussion and analysis of statistics and how they are derived.

I came away from Albert's site wishing that, way back when I was in school, I had been taught math using batting averages, pitching stats, and other baseball-related calculations.

4 Baseball History: Teams

Brooklyn Dodgers

http://www.bayou.com/~brooklyn/
and
http://www.brooklyn-dodgers.com/

Fans of Dem Bums will savor this colorful, information-packed Web site. For starters, you will find decade-by-decade Brooklyn Dodgers histories, lists of Brooklyn Dodgers Hall of Fame (as opposed to National Baseball Hall of Fame) inductees, several discussion areas, links to other Dodgers-related sites, a tribute to the 1955 World Champions, even home addresses of living ex-Bums, for those who want to drop a line to the likes of Gino Cimoli, Shotgun Shuba, Randy Jackson, or Rocky Nelson. (Plus, there are the dates of death for those Dodgers already residing in that great ballpark in the sky).

This site is at its best when offering brief nostalgia pieces on the Duke of Flatbush; The Sym-phony, Knot-Hole Gang, and Hilda; and A Field in Flatbush (if you are a Brooklyn Dodgers fan-atic, you know who or what these are).

St. Louis Browns

http://www3.primary.net/~tdalton/stlbrown.htm

Once upon a time, the Baltimore Orioles were the St. Louis Browns, a perennial second division team. This Web site, maintained by Tim Dalton, features a decade-by-decade Browns history. You will find data on everything from yearly statistics to the history of the team's emblem to the "St. Louis Browns March." And there are stills (and, in some cases, mini-biographies) of "notable Browns players." You won't find Mantle, Aaron, or Musial here. But you will find George Sisler ("the best player ever to don a Browns uniform"), Ken Williams (who led the league in homers in 1922, with 39), Johnny Tobin, Baby Doll Jacobson, Urban Shocker, George McQuinn, Pete Gray, Ned Garver, Satchel Paige, and even little Eddie Gaedel.

A related site is Baseball in St. Louis (*http://spot.colorado.edu/~winterp/BBstl.html*), which features information on the Browns as well as other St. Louis professional teams (beginning with the Red Stockings and Brown Stockings of 1875).

The Buffalo Head Society: A Red Sox Journal

http://www.ultranet.com/~kuras/bufflohd.htm

Among this Web site's features are Red Sox-related data and essays. Especially enjoyable are David Nevard's descriptive portrait of "Tony C." (as in Conigliaro); Nevard and Larry McCray's essay, "The Evocative Power of Mere Cloth Numerals," a history of major league uniform numbers (with a special emphasis on the Sox); and McCray's list of "Who Wore That Number the Longest?" on the team.

If you are numeral-obsessed, you will want to know that the Bosox's Johnny Pesky wore number six for 14 years, with Rico Petrocelli in second place at 11 years. Rich Gedman and Billy Goodman both wore number ten for a decade; Bob Montgomery and Lefty Grove are next in line at nine and eight (which proves that a back-up catcher from the 1970s can have something in common with a Hall of Fame hurler of the 1920s and '30s). Additionally, long-forgotten Lou Lucier and Johnny Lazor respectively own the records for wearing numbers 81 and 82: one year (1943).

Love that 1965 Topps Frank Malzone baseball card!

A link is provided to Red Sox Nation (*http://www.geocities.com/Colosseum/Field/1289/*), which is accurately described as an "unofficial Red Sox site for Diehards."

Boston Red Sox Stats, and FAQ

http://www.best.com/~kwoolner/redsox/

Keith Woolner hosts this no-frills Web site, which offers much to cheer about for Bosox fans. For example, he posts an essay in which he builds a statistical case for the ranking of Roger Clemens among the all-time-great pitchers. (No matter that the Rocket, unlike Yaz and Teddy Ballgame, will not be finishing his career in Fenway.)

Woolner includes a reminiscence of the "single defining moment" of his Red Sox fandom: the "first major league game I ever attended—naturally it was at Fenway...."

Nevertheless, we are talking Boston Red Sox, so Woolner has much to lament. Remember Roxy Walters, Phil Todt, Ski Melillo, Ossie Vitt, Rabbit Warstler, Shano Collins, Tom Oliver, and Denny Williams? They comprise Woolner's proposed list of all-time-worst Bosox players.

Particularly unnerving is "The Ones Who Got Away," a list of players who had the most success after leaving Boston. As one might expect, Babe Ruth is on it. He is joined by Tris Speaker, Lefty O'Doul, Cecil Cooper, Reggie Smith, Gavvy Cravath, Red Ruffing, Waite Hoyt, and Eddie Cicotte. And they are joined by Wilbur Wood,

Sam Jones, Carl Mays, Bobo Newsome, Frank Tanana, John Tudor, Sparky Lyle, Dennis Eckersley, and, lest we forget, Jeff Bagwell.

The Curse Lives On!

http://acs5.bu.edu:8001/~jfarb/babe.html

This Web site, maintained by Joshua Farb, just may be more painful for Red Sox devotees to download than Keith Woolner's "The Ones Who Got Away."

Suffice to say that Farb charts the "horrible, heart-breaking" fashion in which the Sox have faltered ever since team owner Harry Frazee sold Babe Ruth to the New York Yankees in 1920.

Glenn's Pirates Page

http://www.primenet.com/~gearhard/pirates.html

The names that dominate this entertaining, fact-filled Web site are Kiner and Clemente rather than Womack and Kendall.

Plenty of history-related links are provided, beginning with "Pirate Firsts," "Pirate Notable Achievements," "Tales of the Tape" (data on Pirate sluggers and long balls), "Retired Pirate Uniform Numbers," "Pirate Championships," and the "Best Pirate Moments of All-Time."

Players are featured on the links to "Pirate Hall of Fame Members" (here is where Kiner and Clemente come in); "Other Pirate Greats" (which spotlights such Cooperstown not-quites as Babe Adams, Matty Alou, Ginger Beaumont, Steve Blass, and John Candelaria through Kent Tekulve, Andy Van Slyke, and Bob Veale); and "The Near Great Pirate Players" (such "players you remember from your childhood" as Gene Alley, Carson Bigbee, Smokey Burgess, Donn Clendenon, and Frank Gustine).

Glenn tops it all off with an impressive list of Pirates-related links.

World Champion New York Yankees

http://www.geocities.com/Colosseum/Field/4776/

Admittedly, this fan site, hosted by Lee Sinins, spotlights a month-by-month recap of the Bronx Bombers' 1996 and 1997 seasons. However, it is listed here because of two of its history links: "Greatest Yankee World Series Moments" (which date from Babe Ruth's performance in the 1928 Fall Classic in which he hit .625 and belted three dingers in Game Four and—as one would expect—his 1932 Called Shot and its subsequent controversy) and "All Time Yankee Leader Lists" (featuring the top 30 Yanks in 36 statistical categories).

Although there is nothing innovative on this site, Yankee fans should savor it.

Sinins also maintains Baseball City (*http://www.geocities.com/Colosseum/Field/6849*), where he offers generic historical data and other information on all major league ballclubs.

Total Yankees

http://www.totalyankees.com/

The focus of this impressive and exhaustive Web site (which is maintained by the folks who bring you Total Baseball) is not how many runs the Bronx Bombers scored in last night's game. Rather, it is the team's storied past, from its legendary players to its almost two dozen world championships.

The "Biographies" link takes you to extensive bios of Yankees-of-the-past—not just Mickey Mantle and Babe Ruth but also Hank Bauer, Chris Chambliss, Ryne Duren, Gil McDougald, Bobby Richardson, Everett Scott, and Tom Tresh. The "Chronicle" link spotlights memorable events—mostly the arrivals of Hall of Fame ballplayers—which helped shape Yankee dynasties. The "Timeline" link dates from 1903 when American League president Ban Johnson shifted the struggling Baltimore Orioles to New York. From the "Roster" and "Postseason" links, you can download year-by-year lists of players and their records and descriptions of Yankee postseason successes and failures.

You also will find lists of Yankee records. Bet you didn't know that second in the number of games caught for the team (after Bill Dickey's 954 and before Yogi Berra's 797) are the 835 of Jeff Sweeney, who played in New York between 1908 and 1915! Links are provided to Yankee-related chat lines and newsgroups, and if your browser is Java-capable, you even can create your own Yankee Dream Team.

Total White Sox

http://www.totalwhitesox.com/

The structure here is the same as for Total Yankees, only the biographies are of Nick Altrock, Zeke Bonura, Chico Carrasquel, Eddie Fisher—not the 1950s crooner—Kid Gleason, Fielder Jones, Sherm Lollar, and Jim Rivera; and the history section focuses less on Pale Hose postseason highlights and more on the Black Sox.

If you have never heard the term "Hitless Wonders" or are unfamiliar with a madly inspired genius named Bill Veeck, you will know them after scanning this site.

Total Giants

http://www.totalgiants.com/

New York/San Francisco Giants fans will enjoy this Web site with its features on Johnny Antonelli, Roger Bresnahan, Roger Connor, Art Nehf, Dusty Rhodes, and Hal Schumacher along with all the "Ms" in the team's past: Maglie; Marichal; Marquard; Mathewson; Mays; McCovey; McGinnity; McGraw; Merkle; and Mize.

The history section spotlights everything from Merkle's Boner to Mays's Catch, and the fact that "the Giants are consistent: they never have an easy time of it."

Total Dodgers

http://www.totaldodgers.com/

This Web site serves as a nice complement to the Dodgers page listed earlier in this chapter. The site offers bios of ancient Bums and Daffiness Boys (including Jake Daubert, Babe Herman, Willie Keeler, Mickey Owen, Wilbert Robinson, Nap Rucker, Whit Wyatt, and, yes, Casey Stengel); Boys of Summer (from Campanella to Snider); and more modern Los Angelinos (from Cey to Sutton, Mondesi to Piazza).

Similarly, the history of the Dodgers is not just the history of the Boys of Summer. There is the building of Ebbets Field and the futility of the 1920s/30s all the way through the Fernandomania of the early 1980s.

Total Braves

http://www.totalbraves.com/

Here, you will be reminded that this franchise did not originate with Ted Turner and Maddux-Smoltz-Glavine (or even Aaron-Mathews-Spahn-Burdette).

The Boston-Milwaukee roots of the now-Atlanta Braves are highlighted via bios of Joe Adcock, Wally Berger, Tommy Bond, John Clarkson, Jimmy Collins, Del Crandall, Hugh Duffy, Bob Elliot, and many others—and by the opening sentences of the introduction to the "History" section: "When they beat the Cleveland Indians in the 1995 World Series, the Braves became the first team to win a World Championship in three different cities. They had won previously as the Boston Braves in 1914 and the Milwaukee Braves in 1957. That's not many titles for a team that traces its origins to 1871, but the Braves have filled their many lean years with players whose individual accomplishments superseded those of the club."

Total Indians

http://www.totalindians/com/

In the 1990s, the resurgence of the Cleveland Indians as a perennial powerhouse has garnered much media coverage. Not too long ago, the team and the city in which it plays could be mercilessly lampooned for its decades-long ineptitude in the movie *Major League*.

This Web site serves notice that the history of the Cleveland franchise does not extend only as far back as the previous glory years of Boudreau-Feller-Garcia-Gordon-Lemon-Lopez. Such stars and semi-stars as Johnny Allen, Earl Averill, George Burns, Stan Coveleski, Elmer Flick, Jeff Heath, Addie Joss, Joe Sewell, Hal Trosky, and Cy Young played in Cleveland. There even were some memorable Indians who played for the team between the late 1940s and the 1990s, including Rocky Colavito, Sam McDowell, Luis Tiant, and Buddy Bell.

Indians third baseman Ken Keltner's sparkling defense on the night of July 17, 1941 helped end Joe DiMaggio's 56-game hitting streak.

On the downside, way back in 1920, Indians shortstop Ray Chapman died 12 hours after being struck on the left temple by a pitch thrown by the Yankees' Carl Mays.

Seattle Pilots

http://www.brandx.net/pilots/

Before the Seattle Mariners, there were the Seattle Pilots—and you will not find a Web site called Total Pilots.

That team existed for just one season, playing in the American League in 1969. The following year, the franchise was moved to Milwaukee and renamed the Brewers.

The Pilots had no Juniors, A-Rods, or Big Units on its roster. Among the more familiar names were Steve Barber, Gene Brabender (who led the team with 14 victories), Tommy Davis, Greg Goossen, Tommy Harper, Mike Hegan, Skip Lockwood, Mike Marshall, Jerry McNertney,

Don Mincher, Marty Pattin, Ray Oyler, Rich Rollins, Diego Segui, and Dooley Womack.

This Pilots homage includes team batting and pitching records; box scores; a franchise history (which is, appropriately, short); brief clips from *The First Voyage*, a documentary on the team; a reproduction of a 45 rpm single and picture sleeve of "Go, Go, You Pilots," the team's official song; even a list of Puget Sound-area outlets for purchasing Pilots tickets.

At the latter, you will learn that tickets were available at Art's Driftwood Inn, Brandy's Furniture & Appliances, Bud's Cafe, Kim's Broiler, King Oscar's, Sullivan Florist, and Vito's Restaurant. Mike Fuller, who maintains the site, notes, "Please don't... visit these businesses to buy Pilots tickets (especially since many of them have joined the Pilots in oblivion)."

Fuller is looking for audio tapes of Pilots radio broadcasts, which featured announcers Jimmy Dudley and Bill Schonely.

The Best & Worst Baseball Teams of All Time

http://members.aol.com/tomho13/top30.html

Although this Web page exists to hype the book *The Best & Worst Baseball Teams of All Time*, by sports statistician Harry Hollingsworth, enough information is found here to make it worth a visit. The highlight is a list of the top 30 best and worst teams as determined by computer analysis.

Not surprisingly, the 1927 Yankees are ranked Number One as all-time best. However, only three Yankees teams rate in the top ten; Chicago National League fans who lack a knowledge of ancient baseball history will be pleased to learn that the 1906 Cubs come in at Number Five.

Break out the champagne, all you Choo Choo Coleman fans! Among the poorest teams, the 1962 Mets rank fifth (rather than first). Ahead of them are the 1916 Philadelphia Athletics (at Number One), the 1919

Athletics, the 1904 Washington Nationals (later Senators), and the 1935 Boston Braves.

A History of the Spokane Indians Baseball Team

http://www.iea.com/~sallyep/

This Web site easily might be placed in Chapter 11, "Minor and Independent Leagues." However, it is here because it focuses entirely on its subject's history. The page is maintained by S. K. Prenger, a graduate student at Eastern Washington University who started the page as a history class assignment.

A History of the Spokane Indians Baseball Team features, as one might expect, a general history of baseball in Spokane. Some features are especially interesting, including citations of nineteenth-century newspaper articles, a picture of the 1910 Indians ballclub, a 1940 team program cover, a 1946 team picture, and a list of leagues in which the Indians played and fields on which the team played.

5 Baseball History: Players

Major League Baseball Players Alumni Association

http://mlbpaa.org/

At the top of its home page, this beautifully designed Web site features repeated silhouette images of a ballplayer swinging a bat. This site is maintained by the MLBPAA, which was "formed in 1982 in order to promote baseball, raise money for charity and protect the dignity of the game through its former players."

The site is loaded with tidbits on ex-major leaguers. You can find out how some of them are spending their post-baseball careers. Dan Quisenberry, for one, is living in Kansas City and studying poetry. Al Hrabosky resides in St. Louis and has become a radio talk show host/Cardinals broadcaster. Bert Campaneris lives in Arizona and has a golf handicap of 20. Herb Washington owns six fast-food restaurants in upstate New York.

The site offers interviews with and advice from former big leaguers on the art of hitting, fielding, pitching, and stealing bases. Those offering the tidbits include Boog Powell, Tommy Davis, George Brett, Billy Williams, Brooks Robinson, Bob Feller, and Campaneris. And you will find a motivational poem titled "The Game of Life" authored by Jim "Mudcat" Grant.

If you want to be in touch with a former major leaguer, contact the association. If the player is a member, your message will be forwarded to him.

The POP Award

http://www.popaward.com/

You've heard of the Most Valuable Player Award, Cy Young Award, Rookie-of-the-Year, and Gold Glove. This Web site is the Internet home of the POP Award, given to players who, "while having enough plate appearances to qualify for the batting title, reach the peak of offensive production for a season by qualifying in all three of these categories: Batting Average (.300 or better); On Base Percentage (.400 or better); Slugging Average (.500 or better). The combination of the baseball player who can hit for average, get on base, and hit for power is the Perfect Offensive Player, or POP...."

The links on the home page will take you to previous POP winners. Most interesting is the "POP 1500 Cub," which lists ballplayers who have achieved the all-time-best POP seasons. One will not be surprised to see Babe Ruth appearing most often (nine times); others listed include the expected (Jimmy Foxx, Lou Gehrig, Rogers Hornsby, Stan Musial, Ted Williams), the unexpected (most notably Norm Cash), and a quartet of active players (Jeff Bagwell, Albert Belle, Mark McGwire, and Frank Thomas). Among the missing are Hank Aaron, Willie Mays, and Frank Robinson! The list of "POP Career Leaders" begins with Ruth, Williams, Gehrig, Hornsby, Foxx, Hank Greenberg, Ty Cobb, Stan Musial, Joe Jackson, Lefty O'Doul, Dan Brouthers, Tris Speaker, Harry Heilmann, Ed Delehanty, and Mel Ott.

Part of the fun of the POP Awards is pondering whether the criteria present a more complete picture of a player's value or are seriously flawed in that they diminish the worth of a non-home run hitter like Pete Rose or Tony Gwynn.

The site is sponsored by Perfect Player Partners Ltd., developers of the Perfect Offensive Player Awards.

St. Louis Walk of Fame

http://www.st-louis.mo.us/st-louis/walkofame/

There are Walks of Fame in America other than the one located on Hollywood Boulevard. One is in St. Louis and honors fabled city sons and daughters—quite a few of whom are baseball personalities.

Click on the home page's "Tour the Stars" link, and you will be taken to a list of inductees. Among them are Cool Papa Bell, Yogi Berra, Lou Brock, Jack Buck, Harry Caray, Bob Costas, Joe Garagiola, Bob Gibson, and Stan Musial (not to mention Phyllis Diller, William Burroughs, Buddy Ebsen, and Masters & Johnson). Click on each name, and you will be taken to a photo of the individual along with a mini-biography.

This Walk of Fame and Web site are splendid ways for a city to honor its most accomplished citizens.

Baseball Greats

http://www.iexp.com/~gcascar/baseball/

This Web site, which also is available as a CD-ROM, consists of an impressive list of ballplayer links. Some links are for contemporary major leaguers, but the majority feature legends from Hank Aaron, Roy Campanella, and Ty Cobb to Honus Wagner, Ted Williams, and Maury Wills.

Click on a name, and you will be taken to a dramatic photo of that ballplayer. You can see a very young Stan Musial posing in front of a vintage scoreboard, Shoeless Joe Jackson intently awaiting a pitch, Joe DiMaggio finishing a swing, Warren Spahn in a dramatic wind-up, Bob

Feller serving up a pitch, Rogers Hornsby with bat in hand, Josh Gibson eluding a catcher's tag, Willie Mays sliding head first into home plate, and Mickey Mantle scoring a run in a Yankees-Dodgers World Series.

Oh, yes, you also see Frank Thomas in the batting cage, Greg Maddux firing a fastball, and Ken Griffey, Jr., staring off into space as he watches one of his titanic blasts head for the bleachers.

Historical Profiles

http://www.cnnsi.com/baseball/mlb/historical_profiles/

Here is yet another case where a link on a super-site—in this case, CNN/SI—is so outstanding that it merits its own separate entry.

You will find a complete baseball player index, covering the years 1871-1996, plus all-time rosters for teams in the various nineteenth- and twentieth-century leagues and associations.

By following a couple of links, you can download complete career stats on thousands of players from Hank Aaron, Tommie Aaron, and Don Aase through Paul Zuvella, George Zuverink, and Dutch Zwilling. And you can find out who played for the Federal League Brooklyn Tip-Tops in 1914—Mordecai "Three Finger" Brown was on the pitching staff—or the Union Association Altoona Mountain Citys in 1884, or the Players' League Cleveland Infants in 1890.

Legends of the Game

http://www2.cybernex.net/~jfox/legends/legends.htm

The legends of the game found on this site are not Ted Williams and Willie Mays, Mickey Mantle and Stan Musial. They are the heroes of baseball's "silver age": the Dead Ball Era (1903-1919). Jeff Fox, who maintains the site, observes, "The mission of this fan is to acknowledge and pay tribute to the ball players of this era who played and loved the game."

There are links to scores of players, beginning with Ed Abbatichio, Fred Abbott, and Bill Abstein. Click on a name, and you will be taken to an image of the player (where available), his statistics, and a mini-biography.

ML Players' Uniform Numbers

http://www.wp.com/elondon/numbers.htm

If you are curious about how many ballplayers have worn the numbers 7, 11, and 13, or 75, 77, and 88, this Web site is for you.

First, a bit of history: "Numbers on uniforms did not come into existence until 1929. On April 18, 1929, the Yankees introduced numbers on the back side of their player's (sic) uniforms—the numbers corresponded with the players' (sic) position in the batting order. It was an idea whose time had come: on June 22, 1932, the National League's policy required numbers to be worn on all uniforms."

The site consists of an ever-expanding master list of major leaguers' uniform numbers, which can be downloaded via handy links.

So, in addition to Mickey Mantle, the likes of Mark Belanger, Rocky Colavito, Ed Kranepool, Fred Lindstrom, Joe Medwick, and Al Simmons have worn number 7. Number 11 belonged to Luis Aparicio, Lefty Gomez, Carl Hubbell, Manny Mota, and Paul Waner. Ralph Branca, Dave Concepcion, and Lee Mazzilli sported number 13. Alan Mills, Jack Armstrong, and Rene Gonzales have respectively worn Numbers 75, 77, and 88.

And little Eddie Gaedel, in his one major league appearance, wore number 1/8!

The Official George Burns Site

http://home.earthlink.net/~myeates

On this Web site, you will not find a photo of the *other* George Burns, the chap who appeared in vaudeville, on television, and in the movies and was married to Gracie

Allen. This George Burns was one of two ballplayers sharing the name who enjoyed lengthy major league careers.

The Burns featured here lasted in The Show for 15 seasons, beginning in 1911, and mostly played outfield for the New York Giants. He compiled a .287 lifetime batting average with 2,077 hits and 383 stolen bases. Burns's namesake, nicknamed "Tioga George," was active during the same period. He came to the majors in 1914 and hung around for the next 16 seasons.

The site is maintained by Michael Yeates. At the top of its home page is a vintage photo of his George Burns sliding into a base. "It is rare that a player so great as he is ignored for so many years," writes Yeates. "So why is it that today you never hear of the great George Burns? Many players have done far less than him, but they are still talked about at every stadium and sports bar. Maybe it is the fact that no person is old enough to have seen him play, or maybe it was the fact that he was always 'silent George,' never wanting fame or glory, but always putting the team in front of himself....He is what baseball is all about, or once was."

The Jackie Robinson Society

http://www.utexas.edu/students/jackie/

The Society, an official student organization of the University of Texas at Austin, is "devoted to preserving the memory and spreading the legacy of Jackie Robinson...." Among the highlights of this well-done and informative site are an article, by Eric Enders, titled "Athlete of the Century"; interviews with Carl Erskine and Branch Rickey III; quotes by and about Robinson; a look at blacks who were barrier breakers in other sports; biographies of the players who integrated each major league team; Jesse Jackson's eulogy, delivered at Robinson's funeral; another piece by Enders on Robinson's brief stint as a basketball coach; a piece by Marc Fisher on the Brooklyn neighborhood that once was the home of Ebbets Field; information on the Jackie Robinson Foundation; and an "image gallery."

In addition, the Society is sponsoring a "Larry Doby for the Hall of Fame" campaign.

Nike Commercial: "Thank You, Jackie Robinson."

http://www.utexas.edu/students/jackie/robinson/nike.html

This short, sweet Web page can be found on The Jackie Robinson Society site and merits its own entry. Its content: the text of the 60-second version of a Nike commercial, "Thank You, Jackie Robinson," which aired in April, 1997, and featured snippets of an array of major leaguers, from Tony Gwynn through Buck O'Neil, tipping their caps to Robinson. The sum total of their words makes for a poignant homage and a valuable mini-history lesson.

The page opens with these words: "We are bombarded daily with television advertising that insults our intelligence and, all too often, disturbs our conscience. There are exceptions, however, and (this) is certainly one of those. Nike is not perfect—indeed, their (sic) use of cheap labor in Asia is disgusting—but in this commercial, if only for an instant, corporate America finally got it right."

Jackie Robinson

http://www.afroam.org/history/Robinson/intro.html

This thorough and perceptively written Web site explores the personality of Jackie Robinson and the social implications (which, of course, extend way beyond the confines of baseball) of Branch Rickey's "great experiment" to integrate the National Pastime.

The site is loaded with links, facts, opinions, anecdotes, and photos relating to Robinson's life and times. "Robinson is heroic, in part, because of the excellence of his athletic achievement; and equally important, for his political commitment to racial equality," writes Avonie Brown, the site's author. "He reaffirms for blacks in America that ours is a history of struggle, survival and accomplishment."

Cobb

http://wso.williams.edu/~jkossuth/cobb/

James Kossuth, who maintains this Web site, describes its subject as "the most fascinating baseball player ever, and one of the most intriguing people in the history of mankind...." On the site, he attempts to "highlight those points (about Cobb's life) that I find most important, fascinating, and disturbing."

The page is divided into three sections with appropriate links: "His Family, His Youth and the Road to the Majors"; "Life in the Big Leagues"; and "The Aftermath." Cobb has been written about in countless baseball histories and biographies and was depicted on screen by Ron Shelton in *Cobb.* If you haven't read the book or seen the movie or simply are interested in this endlessly complex man, Kossuth's site offers much food for thought.

Ty Cobb Letters

http://www.sportingnews.com/archives/ty/index.html

This page is connected to the previously described *Sporting News* Web site, but it is so intriguing and revealing that it deserves its own separate entry.

Taylor Spink, the paper's longtime publisher, kept up a correspondence with the Georgia Peach over the course of several decades. Here, you will find reproductions of Cobb's actual letters to Spink, including his payment for a lifetime subscription to the paper (dated June 16, 1941); his defending the spiking of an opposing player (February 15, 1955); and his comments on what he considered "unjust criticism" and how "it hurts but I try and toss it off..." (July 12, 1957).

On this page, history literally comes alive.

Shoeless Joe Jackson's Virtual Hall of Fame

http://www.blackbetsy.com/

This Web site is aptly described as being loaded with "interesting facts, pictures, statistics, tidbits, merchandise and much more about one of the greatest baseball players of all time." Its purpose, however, is not just to honor Shoeless Joe Jackson's memory but to "help get Joe reinstated into baseball so that he may take his rightful place in the National Baseball Hall of Fame."

This page is certain to be controversial, given its pro-Jackson stance and the diversity of opinion regarding Shoeless Joe's involvement in the Black Sox scandal and worthiness of a place in the Hall.

One of the site's highlights, found under the link labeled "The Truth," is a copy of "the only interview Joe Jackson ever gave concerning the infamous World Series between the Chicago White Sox and the Cincinnati Reds." It appeared in the October, 1949, issue of *Sport* magazine and was told to sportswriter Furman Bisher.

Another Shoeless Joe site is the Shoeless Joe Jackson Times (*http://userwww.service.emory.edu/~tkram01/*), which features an online petition that you can sign if you "are strongly opposed to the lifetime ban on Joseph Jefferson Jackson, and regardless of guilt or innocence believe he should be eligible for induction into the National Baseball Hall of Fame."

A related site is Pete Rose—Hall of Fame (*http://www.bright.net/~naphtali/peterose.html*), which argues for Rose's—and Jackson's—inclusion in the Hall of Fame. On the other side of the issue is How Good Was Pete Rose? (*http://www.nashville.com/~Don.Sibrel/Rose.htm*), which argues that he should be excluded because of his off-the-field conduct and his acceptance of a lifetime suspension from baseball.

Then there is the Official Pete Rose 4256 Hit King Fan Club (*http://www.peterose.com/*), which lists celebrities who are "Pete Rose Supporters" and features an article by former President Jimmy Carter headlined "It's time to forgive Pete Rose" that was published in *USA Today*.

Oh, yes, and for a mere $28, your "name will be registered as an official supporter of Pete Rose's Reinstatement...," and you will receive several "fabulous Bonus Items."

Willie Mays

http://www.orst.edu/~protherj/bbl/mays.html

This Web site is special because of its lengthy compilation of Mays-related memories contributed by fans.

As one would expect, many involve nostalgic recollections of dramatic home runs, circus catches, and childhood encounters with the Say Hey Kid.

Another, submitted by "Dave G," is worth repeating: "I was a Willie Mays fan for years. Some time ago I found a beautiful color photo of Willie at a collectors store and purchased it with the thought of getting Willie to sign it for me. I packed it up with a personal letter and sent it to him and received the following 'price list' in response. Willie would sign my photo for $40, plus $10 s&h. If I wanted it personalized it would cost me another $50. That's $100 for an autographed photo that I was supplying! I am disgusted with the commercialism of today's athlete, and believed that yesterday's ballplayer was a different type of person. Receiving this message back from Willie's 'foundation' literally broke my heart. Mickey Mantle signed several items for me for free. Stan Musial and others have done likewise. I understand that former players must make ends meet as well, but this was excessive. My bubble has been popped!"

Mickey Mantle (1931-1995)

http://members.aol.com/alvertc/Mantle.htm

This reverential Web site, which features a background pattern of the New York Yankees' insignia and pinstripes, is an homage to Mickey Charles Mantle. Its highlights is a nice assignment of photos and quotes from baseball personalities who span the generations: Gene Woodling, Hank Aaron, Ron Darling, Casey Stengel, Whitey Ford, and George Steinbrenner.

At *http://members.aol.com/mindycpa/Eulogy.htm*, you will find Bob Costas's moving eulogy to Mantle. It begins, "It occurs to me as we're all sitting here thinking of

Mickey, he's probably somewhere getting an earful from Casey Stengel, and no doubt quite confused by now." And it ends, "So long, Mick. Thanks."

755

http://cwws.com/~schubert/aaron.htm

This Web site is, simply, "Dedicated to the Greatest, Hank Aaron." For openers, there is the following quote from Hammerin' Hank, upon his being asked by Bob Costas to compare himself and Willie Mays: "Just look at *my statistics*, they do the talking for me."

The site contains everything from visuals of Aaron memorabilia to quotes attesting to his greatness to notable dates in his playing career. If by chance you want to see whether Aaron smacked a homer on your birthday—assuming that you were born between April and October—you even can find this out. With the proper software, you can see a video clip of Aaron's 715th homer, which he belted on April 8, 1974, off Al Downing; hear Atlanta Braves announcer Milo Hamilton call the shot; and listen to Aaron's complete Hall of Fame induction speech.

Most intriguing is a scouting report on Aaron written by Billy Southworth to Braves General Manager John Quinn in 1952. At the time, Aaron was 18 years old and playing shortstop for Eau Claire in the Class C Northern League.

Hank Aaron: Chasing the Dream

http://TBSsuperstation.com/hankaaron/Aaron9.html

This Web site essentially serves as a press kit for the Academy Award-nominated documentary *Hank Aaron: Chasing the Dream*. As such, it is not necessarily hype-free. (When you read such sentences as "[Director Mike] Tollin skillfully combines this melange of interviews and testimonials," remember that it was written by a publicist and not a reviewer.)

Nonetheless, from this site you can glean some telling insights into Aaron's life, his on and off-the-field careers, and the challenges he has faced; lots of visuals along with audio and video clips; and data on how Tollin (who is a faithful Phillies fan) came to direct, write, and executive-produce the film.

Babe Ruth's "Called Shot" Legend

http://members,iglou.com/kirk

Did the Bambino actually "call" the home run he belted off Chicago Cubs hurler Charlie Root in the third game of the 1932 World Series? To this day, this did-he-or-didn't-he question remains one of baseball's legendary controversies.

On this Web page, you will find a frame from a 16mm home movie shot at the game by Matt M. Kandle, a Chicago printer. It is allegedly the lone visual record of Ruth facing Root in the game's fifth inning.

Is Ruth actually pointing and predicting the homer he is about to hit? Or is he simply gesturing as he prepares for Root's pitch?

You decide.

YAZ

http://www.yaz.com/

This fine Web site is an homage to Carl Michael Yastrzemski, the beloved Red Sox Hall-of-Famer. His career is covered in detail and year-by-year. The site gives special emphasis on Yaz's Last Game (at Fenway Park, on October 1, 1983). The illustrations are fun—beginning with the card reproduction of young Yaz in 1959 garbed in a Carolina League Raleigh uniform and ending with the gallery of photos of Yaz in his last Fenway at-bat.

Off the subject of Yaz, a shining moment in Red Sox history is recalled in the "Game 6" link. (If Game 6 needs to be explained, you probably will have little interest in this site.)

When you log onto this site, an array of exclamations flashes on and off screen.

The first: "Yaz, Sir! That's My Baby...."

The last: "Bucky F_____g Dent."

Mark Fidrych: The Bird

http://member.aol.com/dantonacci/thebird/markfidrych.html

This fun Web site is devoted to Mark "The Bird" Fidrych, the Detroit Tigers' 1976 American League Rookie of the Year. Although The Bird's career was short-lived, he is a baseball legend not so much for his on-field accomplishments as his lovable eccentricities. Most memorably, he would talk to the baseball and go to his knees and manicure the mound before commencing his wind-up.

The site features video of The Bird playing gardener and briefly conversing with the ball as he prepares to fire a pitch at an opposing hitter. And with the proper software (which you can download), you will be able to listen to 33.6 seconds of Fidrych talking about manicuring the mound; 6.6 seconds of him introducing himself on "ABC's Monday Night Baseball"; even 24.2 seconds of Tigers fans giving The Bird a standing-O.

Curt Flood 21

http://member.aol.com/dantonacci/centerfielder/curtflood.html

"Notch," who maintains the Fidrych site, also sponsors this homage to Curt Flood, the St. Louis Cardinals outfielder who in 1969 requested that he be declared a free agent upon his trade to the Philadelphia Phillies. His reasoning: "after twelve years in the majors leagues, (Flood) did not feel that he was a piece of property to be bought and sold irrespective of his wishes."

For this reason alone, every professional ballplayer should revere Flood whenever he checks his bank statement. Unfortunately, I suspect that too few players even know who he is.

Here, you will find what may best be described as a Curt Flood slideshow along with audio of Flood describing why he would not accept the trade, Bill White offering his views of the significance of Flood's action, and ex-teammate Joe Torre speaking of Flood.

Dizzy Dean Quotes

http://www.cmgww.com/baseball/ddean/quote.html

This nice little Web page consists of nothing more than some down-home wisdom, courtesy of Ol' Diz.

There are promises: "Paul and I will win forty-five games for the Cardinals this year." There is chest-thumping: "Anybody who's ever had the privilege of seein' me play ball knows that I am the greatest pitcher in the world. And them that ain't been fortunate enough to have a gander at Ol' Diz in action can look at the records." And there is wisdom: "It ain't what it used to be, Granny. But what the hell is?"

Ol' Diz surely would have said amen to this last declaration after scanning a Web site, maintained by his namesake, titled Welcome To The World of Dizzy Dean. This Diz is a *very* contemporary-looking musician/songwriter from Melbourne, Australia.

I'd Rather Catch

http://www3.theatlantic.com/atlantic/unbound/flashbks/baseball/tebbetts.htm

Across the years, many outstanding baseball articles have been published in non-baseball magazines. Many are online, hidden away in the publication's archives; in fact, a large portion of this book easily could be devoted to Web pages in which they are featured.

This entertaining, anecdote-filled feature, authored by then-Boston Red Sox catcher Birdie Tebbetts, was printed in the September, 1949, issue of *The Atlantic Monthly*. In it, Tebbetts recalls his Nashua, New Hampshire boyhood; his early years in baseball; how ballplayers are treated by fans and the press; and, in particular, the ins and outs of catching and handling pitchers.

All-Time All-Stars

http://www.phillynews.com/packages/allstars96/

In 1996, the Major League All-Star game was played in Philadelphia. At the time, the *Philadelphia Daily News* polled its readers to determine an all-time-best baseball players list. The results can be found on this Web page, which includes voting results and extensive information on each winner.

The team consists of Lou Gehrig (first base); Rogers Hornsby (second base); Cal Ripken (shortstop); Mike Schmidt (third base); Johnny Bench (catcher); Babe Ruth, Willie Mays and Hank Aaron (outfield); and Nolan Ryan (right-handed pitcher). Inexplicably, no left-handed pitcher is cited. Ruth was voted "the greatest of them all."

My initial response to the list was: *Where is Ted Williams???* Philadelphia fans are not fools: Teddy Ballgame comes in fourth place among outfielders, earning a little more than 100 votes less than Aaron.

Crossing the Color Barrier

http://www.aafla.com/aafbb.htm

Although Jackie Robinson was the first black man to play major league baseball in the twentieth century, he was quickly followed by other pioneering athletes. In fact, four other blacks debuted in the bigs during the 1947 season. The most celebrated was, of course, Larry Doby, who came to Cleveland (and integrated the American League) in July. The others were infielder Henry "Hank" Thompson and outfielder Willard Brown, whose contracts the forever-struggling St. Louis Browns purchased from the Kansas

City Monarchs in July; and pitcher Dan Bankhead, who was brought by Branch Rickey to the Dodgers in August.

The purpose of this Web site is to note how each of these men fared in the big leagues and acknowledge their contributions to integrating baseball. The colorful baseball card reproductions make for a nice visual touch.

6 Baseball History: Negro Leagues

Black Baseball's Negro Baseball Leagues

http://www.blackbaseball.com/

This Web site, which is "edited by James A. Riley, Director of Research at the Negro Leagues Baseball Museum in Kansas City, Missouri," is the equivalent of an introductory survey on the Negro Leagues.

The site provides links to the history of the Leagues—"What they were, why they were founded, and why they no longer exist"; players (including information on Negro Leaguers already in the Hall of Fame and, on a more subjective note, "players who should be in" and "the best of the rest"); teams (offering further links to information on dozens of specific ballclubs); books (featuring a general list of publications on the subject); a calendar of upcoming events in the Negro League community; League collectibles and memorabilia; and additional links to other Negro League Web pages.

Negro Leagues Baseball

http://users.aol.com/skshivers/index.html

This A-plus Web site is jam-packed with Negro League history and visuals.

At the top of its home page is a nice four-part illustration of "Satchel Paige at work." The site provides links to the subjects of "Negro League History," "Hall of Fame Players," "Books," the "Pittsburgh Crawfords," "Segregation of Baseball," the "Negro League Baseball Museum," and the "Monte Irvin Story."

You can spend hours exploring the dozens of sublinks. And the images are a nice mixture of vintage photos and original art.

The site is maintained by Signe K. Shivers "in the hope that more people will discover the Baseball Greats who were forced to play in the shadow of the Major Leagues."

Sam Lacy

http://www.afroam.org/history/Robinson/sam.html#lacy

Ninety-something Sam Lacy has been writing about baseball for decades...and decades...and decades. Most recently, he has been penning columns for the *Baltimore Afro-American*, and he might be the world's oldest active sports scribe.

But more to the point, Lacy played an active role in the integration of baseball. Back in the 1930s, as a young sportswriter for the *Washington Tribune*, he commenced a letter-writing campaign to baseball commissioner Kenesaw Mountain Landis and other notables to correct the "terrible injustice" of segregation in the National Pastime.

Lacy's story is told on this Web page, which is a link on the Web site maintained by AFRO-America's Black History Museum (and is part of a series of links relating to blacks in baseball).

An index of Lacy's most recent *Baltimore Afro-American* pieces can be found at *http://www.afroam.org/information/lacy/lacy.html.*

Wendell Smith Papers

http://www.baseballhalloffame.org/library/aids/msb1.html

Sam Lacy was not the lone black sportswriter to be actively involved in the integration of baseball. He was joined in his advocacy by Wendell Smith of the *Pittsburgh Courier*. In 1996, Smith's papers were donated by his widow, Wyonella Smith, to the Baseball Hall of Fame.

This Web page, a link on the Hall's official site, features a biographical sketch of Smith and a description of his papers. Regardless of whether you are interested in doing further research on Smith, it makes for wonderful reading.

Negro Leagues Baseball Online Archives

http://www.nc5.infi.net/~moxie/nlb/nlb.html

Here is another thorough Negro League-oriented Web site, sponsored by Moxie Internet Galleries. The home page features links to league history, teams, and players. Currently, the site gives special emphasis to the most celebrated Negro League ballclubs and stars.

The resource link features data on several other Negro League Web pages. A gift shop link not only offers merchandise for sale but also includes announcements of upcoming Negro League events.

Additionally, you can "talk baseball with other Negro Leagues fans at the NLB conference." Click on the appropriate link for further details.

Umpires of the Negro Leagues

http://home.earthlink.net/~johnmur/

This scholarly, extremely authoritative Web site maintained by John Murray features essays and information on Negro

League arbiters. Emphasis is placed on the manner in which league games were umpired, where the officials came from, and the struggles they faced.

You will find links to an alphabetical listing of umpires and brief biographical data. And you can spend hours exploring the links to primary sources—mostly ancient newspaper articles—regarding Negro League umps.

Shadowball

http://www.negro-league.columbus.oh.us/

Shadowball, as defined on this site's home page, is "a term for Negro League baseball—black players and teams barred from competing in the big leagues. So-named for having to play in the 'shadows,' out of the limelight." It is also a term for "a warm-up practice of some Negro League teams. Players would pretend to hit, throw, and field, doing it so convincingly that fans often thought they were playing with a real ball."

What follows is a basic, solid, nicely designed site maintained by Harlan S. Williams and featuring links to "Teams & Players," "History & Analysis," "Arts & Culture," and "Jackie Robinson."

The spirit of this site is summed up in one of the "Player" link page subheadings listed under "Women in the Negro Leagues." The page's focus is on Toni Stone, Indianapolis Clowns and Kansas City Monarchs second baseman who in 1953 became the first of three women to play in the Negro Leagues.

The subheading: "She Made it a League of Her Own."

Satchel Paige & the Negro Leagues of Baseball

http://www.students.uiuc.edu/~dunkel/baseball/

"I have been fascinated by stories and tall tales about (the Negro Leagues)," writes Rob (Alex) Dunkel, who maintains this visually striking Web site, "(and) especially about the man named Satchel Paige, since I first read about them in a small article in a baseball magazine. These amazing legends even inspired me to base my senior term paper on this rich slice of history."

The crux of this Web site is a modified version of Dunkel's paper, and it makes for lively reading. "He not only battled racial discrimination during his legendary career, he also fought against the unstoppable effects of age," Dunkel notes. "When Paige finally made it to the major leagues at forty-two years of age, he was still capable of dominating good and great hitters alike...(and) could easily be called the timeless wonder of the baseball world."

Get That 'Negro' Off the Field

http://www.webcom.com/~blessed/negro.html

Here is another well-constructed, nicely illustrated Web site that spotlights Negro League history. The final paragraph of the introduction sums up the essence of this Web site: "Just as in American society in general, baseball lost or ignored many brilliant achievements and contributions of African-American citizens because of its racist structures and traditions. And as America has since reluctantly discovered and reveled in its newfound participants and their achievements, so too has baseball. Although African-Americans have made phenomenal strides in baseball and in society at large, discrimination persists."

Of special note are reproductions of two ancient posters. The first advertises the last two games of the Negro World Series, a "Big Four Team Double Header" held at Yankee Stadium and pitting the New York Cubans against the Nashville Elite Giants and the Philadelphia Stars opposite the Pittsburgh Crawfords. The second is for a "Summer Extravaganza" featuring "The Mound Magician" Satchel Paige and "Legendary Pitching Star" Dizzy Dean.

The Hill District: Homestead Grays

http://www.clpgh.org/exhibit/neighborhoods/hill/hill_n219.html
and

The Hill District: Pittsburgh Crawfords

http://www.clpgh.org/exhibit/neighborhoods/hill/hill_n255.html

These pages are links on a Web site titled Bridging the Urban Landscape, an online hypertext exhibit of Pittsburgh neighborhoods created by the Carnegie Library in collaboration with Common Knowledge: Pittsburgh.

At the top of each page is a vintage photograph of the respective teams, two of the most celebrated in the Negro Leagues. At the bottom of each page are further links, accompanied by humorous illustrations, that will take you to additional photographs and information on the Grays, the Crawfords, and other aspects of Negro League baseball in the Steel City.

Although you will find no detailed history here, the cumulative effect is to portray the manner in which the Grays and Crawfords blended into Pittsburgh's black community.

The Negro League Collector's Site

http://ourworld.compuserve.com/homepages/spaige/

Upon downloading this Web site's home page, you are greeted by a nineteenth-century illustration from an "advertising trade card" of two black schoolchildren playing catch in a field. The site is described as "non-commercial," and "designed to serve as a forum for collectors of vintage Negro Leagues memorabilia, autographs and artifacts....We believe that collectors play an important role in preserving the artifacts and heritage of this important institution. In doing so they help keep the history of the Negro Leagues alive and tangible."

Included are reproductions of ballplayer signatures, information on where to find Negro League collectibles, and an extensive price guide.

Negro League Baseball Stars

http://marin.k12.ca.us/~parkweb/NegroLeaguesHome.html

This sweet little Web site consists of drawings created by Joe Martini's third grade class at the Park School in Mill Valley, California in honor of Negro League stars. Links are provided to each illustration along with observations penned by the children.

You may find slicker sites and sites that outdistance this one from the point-of-view of content. But Negro League Baseball Stars serves as a shining example of the need to pass history down to younger generations and make them aware that, had Frank Thomas, Ken Griffey, Jr., and Albert Belle (not to mention Willie Mays, Ernie Banks, and Frank Robinson) been born decades earlier, they would not have been allowed to play major league baseball.

7 Baseball History: Museums and Halls of Fame

The National Baseball Hall of Fame and Museum

http://www.baseballhalloffame.org/index.html

The National Baseball Hall of Fame and Museum, located in Cooperstown, New York, "was dedicated on June 12, 1939 to honor the game's greats and to present the exciting history of the sport through the display of artifacts, photographs and memorabilia."

Nothing beats a trip to Cooperstown and hours spent exploring the Hall of Fame and Museum, and this Web site whets your appetite for a visit. It features links to current and special Museum exhibits; the Hall of Fame Library; the Hall of Fame Museum Store; Hall of Fame press releases and "news & notes"; and the whens and hows of Hall of

Fame membership. There are lists of inductees (cited alphabetically and by year of induction and voting percentages); information on the latest inductees; lists of eligible candidates for future Hall elections; and information on upcoming Hall of Fame induction weekends.

Two other links are of special interest. The first connects you to frequently asked questions regarding controversial non-Hall members Pete Rose and Shoeless Joe Jackson (which first appeared as a guest editorial in the February 18, 1991, issue of *The Sporting News*). The second is an "official statement" regarding the reasons why these two ballyard legends are ineligible for induction and the criteria that must be met for the situation to change.

This Web site has one flaw: There are not enough visuals of those Hall of Fame and Museum "artifacts, photographs and memorabilia."

National Softball Hall of Fame and Museum

http://www.softball.org/hall/index.html

Softball also has its very own Hall of Fame. This Web page, a link on the site maintained by the Amateur Softball Association, offers basic information on the Oklahoma City-based museum, which opened in 1973 and is "a permanent shrine to the men and women who played the game so well."

The page is not extensive, and it essentially serves as a museum appetizer. However, on it you will learn that Hall of Fame members include Bertha Tickey, who won 757 games during her career; Don Rardin, one of two individuals to play on championship squads in slow-pitch and industrial slow-pitch divisions; Joan Joyce, an 18-time All-American; and Sam Elliott, whose 21-year pitching record was an amazing 1,133–87.

By the way, the very first inductee—in other words, the Ruth/Cobb/Mathewson/Johnson/Wagner of softball—is one Harold "Shifty" Gears.

Canadian Baseball Hall of Fame and Museum

http://www.baseballhof.ca/

Frankly, before discovering this Web site, I had never heard of the Canadian Baseball Hall of Fame and Museum, located in St. Marys, Ontario. The site serves as a reminder that the United States holds no monopoly on the sport and that the World Series truly became an international event upon the entry of Montreal and Toronto into the major leagues.

Among the Hall members are top Canadian-born major leaguers (including Ferguson Jenkins, Jeff Heath, George Selkirk, Rocky Nelson, Reno Bertoia, and Terry Puhl), amateur players, and "builders of the Canadian game and honourary members who have helped popularize the sport in Canada."

You are welcomed to the site with the words, "Thanks for joining us. Watch as the Hall of Fame grows." Just below the welcome are links to an introduction (which tells you that the museum was founded in 1983 and is "dedicated to preserving Canada's baseball heritage"), a list of Hall of Fame inductees, several other baseball sites, and a Canadian baseball trivia quiz.

The home page is handsomely designed with the repeated image of a hitter dropping his bat and scampering for first base after bashing a pitch. Most pages on this site are similarly artistically enhanced.

Babe Ruth Museum

http://www.baberuthmuseum.com/

This Web site is sponsored by the Baltimore-based Babe Ruth Birthplace & Official Orioles Museum. On it, you will learn the whos, whens, and wheres of the Bambino's life and career and find a general history of the modern-era Baltimore Orioles.

The site is beautifully designed and includes several nifty visuals. I especially liked the dazzling Orioles montage on the main Orioles page (which includes decade-by-decade links covering the 1950s through 1990s) and the combination of familiar and not-so-familiar Ruth stills found throughout the site. The information included on the Bambino amounts to a mini-biography.

Other Web site features are information on museum membership, events and exhibits, and several links to other baseball-related Web sites.

Louisville Slugger Museum

http://www.slugger.com/museum/index.htm

This Web site features information on events, programs, and exhibits at this museum located in Louisville, Kentucky, the home of Louisville Slugger bats. On its home page is a photo of the front of the museum with an imposing bat—the world's tallest, it is claimed—perched in front of the entrance.

A brief "Sneak Preview Tour" of the museum and an extensive and informative history of the Hillerich & Bradsby Company are provided.

Peter J. McGovern Little League Museum

http://www.littleleague.org/museum/index.htm

This Web page, a link on the Little League Baseball Web site, offers an introduction to the South Williamsport, Pennsylvania–based museum that is "all about the excitement and sport of Little League Baseball" and serves as "a tribute to Little League Baseball, past and present."

The site works as a preliminary introduction to the museum as it presents a history of Little League baseball via pictures, displays, films, and exhibits. Its primary feature is a "Hall of Excellence," whose members are Little League graduates who have "demonstrated a commitment to excellence in their chosen profession and exemplify the values learned as youngsters in Little League Baseball." Inductees include major league baseball stars (Cal Ripken, Dale Murphy, Nolan Ryan, Mike Schmidt, Jim Palmer, Tom Seaver); athletes who went on to excel in other sports (Hale Irwin, Kareem Abdul Jabbar); non-professional athletes (from actor Tom Selleck and columnist George Will to Dr. Robert F. Sloan, Baylor University president and Little League coach, and Dr. Story Musgrave, NASA astronaut); and those who have excelled in more than one profession (United States Senator/basketball star Bill Bradley).

The Negro Leagues Baseball Museum

http://www.negroleaguesmuseum.com/default.asp

In November, 1997, the Negro Leagues Baseball Museum opened the doors of its newly constructed facility at 18th and Vine in Kansas City, Missouri—right across the street from the temporary quarters in which it had been housed for the previous four years, and blocks away from where the Negro Leagues were founded in 1920.

It will be fun to observe the manner in which the museum's spanking new Web site expands and evolves. For now, it offers a taste of Negro League history via lists of league teams, ballplayers enshrined in Cooperstown, and the first African- Americans to play for each major league club. Via RealAudio, you can hear James Earl Jones talk about the museum and the Negro Leagues.

You will find information on current exhibits, as well as a map of the neighborhood and driving directions on how to reach the museum.

Greenwood Baseball Club Hall of Fame

http://www.emeraldis.com/~lollis/club.html

"From mill teams at places such as Mathews, Ware Shoals, Panola, Grendel and Ninety Six, to independent Negro League teams in Ninety Six, [Greenwood County] has produced its share of stars on the diamond." This interesting little Web site honors baseball in this South Carolina county.

All the original Hall inductees "played as members of the Ninety Six Blue Jays." Among them are the colorfully named Bumpie Goode, Dad King, Derigo Logan, Crack Harris, and K.C. Lark. The Hall was founded by Robert Rosel Williams, whose uncle, Zeke Butler, managed the Jays. Williams also played for the team as well as for the Birmingham Black Barons.

This Web site is an example of how obscure sections of baseball history can be given their due on the Internet.

However, there is one omission on this site: it fails to tell you in which state Greenwood County is located! To find out, I had to e-mail the site.

Internet Baseball Hall of Fame

http://www.baseball.org/baseball/Net.Hall/

Here is one Baseball Hall of Fame that cannot be found in Cooperstown (or, for that matter, in any other city). Rather, it exists in cyberspace and serves as an alternative to Cooperstown in two ways. First, of course, the only way you can visit it is by logging onto the Net. Second, members are selected by "the fans on the internet."

This Hall of Fame is extremely selective. During its first decade in existence, only 38 players and 9 non-players have been inducted. You can download a members roll, and it is intriguing to see who is and isn't listed.

Ironically, the most eye-opening member is a non-player: Bill James, who is cited between Alexander Cartwright and Kenesaw Mountain Landis!

Forget Cooperstown

http://www.njmonthly.com/issues/Jun97/articles/Cooperstown.html

This Web page, consisting of an article written by Bob Klapisch and published in *New Jersey Monthly* magazine, is listed here because what it describes might easily be considered a museum—even though it is not open to the public.

Forget Cooperstown is a profile of Barry Halper, the owner of one of the world's largest collections of baseball memorabilia. In five rooms in his suburban New Jersey basement, Halper stores bats, uniforms, caps, baseball cards—and autographs, autographs, autographs. In fact, his collection has been valued at approximately $40 million.

The page is illustrated with photos of Lou Gehrig's cap, Joe DiMaggio's uniform, and a ball autographed to Halper by Babe Ruth.

Halper's collection is as celebrated as it is vast. He was present at a press conference given by Mickey Mantle several weeks after undergoing liver transplant surgery. Upon noticing Halper, The Mick inquired, "Barry, what did you pay for my old liver?"

Baseball History: Miscellany

http://www.sportsline.com:80/u/baseball/bol/chronology.today.htm

This Web page, one of the free links on the CBS SportsLine site, is so much fun to peruse that it earned its own separate entry.

The site is updated daily and, as advertised, consists of a lengthy list of baseball-related events that occurred on that specific date.

For example, on October 8, Mariano Duncan's three-run homer helped Cincinnati best Pittsburgh in Game Three of the National League Championship Series (in 1990); Earl Weaver signed a one-year contract to manage the Baltimore Orioles (1985); Dodgers coach and former player Jim Gilliam died (1978); the Braves traded pitcher Denny Lemaster and shortstop Denis Menke to the Astros for shortstop Sonny Jackson and first baseman Chuck Harrison (1967); Don Larsen pitched his classic World Series perfect game against the Dodgers (1956); the city of Birmingham, Alabama, barred Jackie Robinson's integrated all-star team from playing there (1953); The Cards' Paul Dean outdueled the Tigers' Schoolboy Rowe, 4-3, in the World Series (1934); 27-year-old Joe Cronin was named manager of the Washington Senators (1932); Boston's Babe Ruth pinch hit for pitcher Ernie Shore in the World Series (1915); one fan was on hand for a Pacific Coast League game between the Oakland Oaks and Portland Beavers (1905); Cleveland bested Baltimore for the fourth time in five contests to win the Temple Cup (1895); left-hander Lady Baldwin won his 42nd game of the season, beating Philadelphia, 11-0 (1886); and Chris Von der Ahe signed the ballplayers from the independent St. Louis Browns team, an act that would help lead to the establishment of the St. Louis Cardinals (1881).

If this page doesn't fulfill your appetite for baseball trivia, check out A Timeline of Amazing Days in Baseball (*http://www.trms.ga.net/~jtucker/lessons/sc/curveball/365days.htm*)

Chronology

http://www.sportsline.com:80/u/baseball/bol/chronology/index.html

This page, also a CBS SportsLine freebie, features an exhaustive year-by-year/month-by-month chronology/timeline of baseball history from 1839 to the present.

As you scan the site, you will learn that on October 6, 1845, the first recorded baseball game using Alexander Cartwright's rules was played between members of the Knickerbocker Club, which had just been organized by Cartwright; on October 21st, the *New York Herald* printed an announcement of a game set to be played that afternoon between "the New York Club and the Brooklyn Club" at the Elysian Fields in Hoboken, New Jersey; on October 22nd, the *New York Morning News* reported on the results of that contest, with New York besting Brooklyn by a 24-4 score in a "friendly match of the time honored game of Baseball"; and on October 25th, New York beat Brooklyn 37-19 in a rematch.

On this page, you can pick a year, a month, or a specific date and learn all kinds of baseball history lessons.

All-American Girls Professional Baseball League

http://www.dlcwest.com/~smudge/index.html

This women's baseball league existed between 1943 and 1954 and was the inspiration for the 1992 movie *A League of Their Own*. This detailed Web site is devoted to the league and in fact is dedicated to the women who played in the AAGPBL.

It features links to the league's history. Worth reading are Jack Fincher's "The 'Belles of the Ball Game' were a hit with their fans," published in the July, 1989 *Smithsonian*; a player roster; league teams; and other related material.

One interesting link is to "League Memorabilia." Here, you will find digitally scanned images of mementos, photos, and autographs provided by league players and fans.

Those who want additional information on women in baseball might want to check out the Web page maintained by the SABR Women in Baseball Committee (*http://www.well.com/user/hazen/WBBC/WBBC.html*), which includes a bibliography of published articles on the subject and a lengthy list of research requests.

The Book of Baseball Literacy

http://ng.netgate.net/~bbliteracy/

Dozens of baseball book-related Web sites exist just to advertise their product. They offer praise for the book, a bit of content, and a "how to order" link.

This Web site offers quite a bit more. Although it does hype *The Book of Baseball Literacy*, written by David Martinez and published by Penguin/Plume, it also features extensive book excerpts. These include profiles of players (from Henry Aaron to Satchel Paige), managers, executives, and media personalities (including the often-forgotten Lee Allen, who began working as Historian at the Baseball Hall of Fame in 1958 and "spent thousands of hours compiling detailed biographical data about every major league ballplayer"). There are chapters on teams, leagues, and other groups (from the All-American Girls Professional Baseball League to the Washington Senators); dates and events (the 1981 strike, the Black Sox Scandal, longest games, the George Brett pine tar controversy); places (the Green Monster, the Polo Grounds, and Wrigley Field); folklore, literature, and diversions (which range from the exclusion of blacks from the majors to the 1845 Knickerbocker baseball rules); records, statistics, and awards (including essays titled ".367," "56," and "61"); and rules, game terms, and baseball business (in which you will learn about baseball mud, "the reddish-brown mud used by umpires to rub into new baseballs," along with the designated hitter, gloves, umpires, free agents— and free agency).

This site serves as a rock-solid primer for anyone interested in learning the basics of baseball history.

The Federal League

http://world.std.com/~smark/fed00.html

Back in the second decade of the twentieth century, the Federal League declared itself a major league—and major competition to the American and National Leagues as it set out to lure away players from the established teams. However, the Federal was only in existence for two seasons.

This potentially intriguing Web site (which was still under construction during my visit) includes basic data and league-related visuals.

The reproduction of the Brooklyn Tip-Tops scorecard alone makes the site worth a visit.

Townball

http://www.sirius.com/~cmonser/Townball.html

This Web page, maintained by Chris Monser, serves as a compact history of Townball, described as "the nineteenth century version of a bat and ball game that can be traced back at least as far as the 16th C. In theory, it is a descendant of the bat and ball games played by our 'cavemen' ancestors. This theory is a result of the observation that there is no culture in the world that does not have some form of a bat and ball game."

On the page, you will find a diagram of a Townball field and a list of official and unofficial game rules. The "Rounders" link will take you to the description and rules for the bat-and-ball game that was "a popular pastime" in 16th-century England.

Halsey Hall Chapter of SABR

http://www.skypoint.com/~ashbury/hhhomepage.html

The Halsey Hall Society for American Baseball Research chapter is based in Minneapolis-St. Paul. Its Web site is cited here for two of its links: "The Quicksteps (19th Century Recreation Baseball Team)" and "Who Was Halsey Hall?"

The Quicksteps, who are sponsored by the Chapter, play by the "New York" baseball rules, which were promoted in the late 1850s. A list of rules and description of baseball (or base ball) as it existed at the time make for enjoyable reading.

There even are lyrics to the team's "Club Song," which is crooned before and after each game.

The site provides a biography of Halsey Hall, the Phil Rizzuto and Harry Caray of the Upper Midwest: "one of the most beloved sports and media personalities this area has ever known" and the first man ever to use the expression "Holy Cow!" on a baseball broadcast.

Eat your heart out, Scooter!

(At the SABR's Arizona Chapter Web site—the URL is *http://members.aol.com/fdelhichpt/index.html*—you will learn that the chapter is named for Flame Delhi. (Lee William "Flame" Delhi was the first Arizona-born ballplayer to make it to the majors.) He barely sipped his cup of coffee in the bigs, playing in just one game for the 1912 Chicago White Sox.

The Survival of Professional Baseball in Lynchburg, Virginia, 1950s–1990s

http://www.lib.virginia.edu/journals/EH/EH37/Nagy.html

This Web page consists of a lengthy, mind-massaging essay written by John Nagy that deals with the history of baseball in one specific American community. However, the significance of that history is national in scope.

"The story of professional baseball in Lynchburg illustrates ways in which baseball shaped community identity and how baseball managed to maintain its place in a society that threatened to find other amusements," Nagy writes near the top of the piece. After exploring the subject, he concludes, "Baseball would always occupy an important role in the shaping of certain aspects of American life, but unless it could update its reasons for existence, it would live in the museums and die in the ballparks. The survival of professional baseball in Lynchburg is not the story of a radical reawakening or baseball euphoria, but a redefinition of its place in contemporary American society."

Big Wiffer

http://www.ma.ultranet.com/~kuras/wifferh.htm

This informative Web page, a link on the site maintained by the Buffalo Head Society, offers a history of wiffleball. It opens with a quote from Kevin Mitchell (formerly of the Reds, Mets, and several other major league teams): "Hitting a Wiffleball is one of the hardest things to do in sports.... It's the reason I was able to hit the breaking pitch so well in the big leagues. You have to have complete concentration as a hitter to keep up with it...."

You will learn the origins of the wiffleball, how it was marketed, and how it "gave (kids) the thrill of being a great hitter or a great pitcher, without the draggy and difficult aspects of real baseball."

A related site is World-Wide-Web Wiffleball: "The Ruining of America's Backyards" (*http://www.wiffleball.com*). As you log on, there is an observation that can be contrasted to Mitchell's comment: "'Wiffleball ain't a sport,' my buddy stated. 'Anything that you get better at as you consume alcohol is NOT a sport.'"

Vermont Only: Coolidge, Grace, and Baseball

http://www.vtonly.com/hstynov6.htm

Baseball memorabilia is on display at the Calvin Coolidge Birthplace in Plymouth, Vermont, designated as a state historical site. But the point of this Web page, an excerpt from the Autumn, 1996, issue of *Vermont Life*, is to inform you that the former President was known as "The Reluctant Fan."

When on hand to throw out the first pitch to inaugurate the baseball season, Cal sometimes had to be compelled to remain at the ballpark by his wife, Grace—the real fan in the family and perhaps the most celebrated female baseball enthusiast of her time.

Back in 1925, Grace Coolidge received an acknowledgment from the owners of the Washington Senators and Boston Red Sox in which she was labeled "First Lady of the Land, First Lady of Baseball."

Wilmington Baseball History

http://pages.prodigy.com/wilm/baseball.htm

Here you will find an extensive and well-researched "look back at the baseball history of Wilmington, Delaware." The author is John H. Duffy, who takes the sport back to the 1860s, when the first local amateur teams came into existence. The site provides some nice photos and illustrations, including stills of the 1875 Wilmington Quicksteps and

1929 Wilmington Chicks, the entrance to Wilmington Park in 1942, a 1948 Wilmington Blue Rocks program, and an 1893 map of the "Baseball Grounds" located at the "southwest corner of Front (Lancaster Ave.) and Union Sts."

This site is a reminder that baseball in America is not only baseball in the major leagues and that a rich history of the sport exists in towns and counties across the country.

9

Fans' Player Sites

The Internet is flooded with fan-maintained player and team-oriented Web sites. Most are unabashed in their adoration; the team sites are especially notorious for their blind loyalty. Among Baltimore Orioles pages, the opening paragraph at the top of Adam Meister's photo-packed homage (*http://students.olin.wustl.edu/meister/orioles.htm*) is a blanket statement: "Of all the teams in professional sports today, there are no others that are as great as the Baltimore Orioles. Not even the Great Baltimore Ravens can rival the Orioles. No team has such a history or a worldwide recognition like the Orioles....Cal Ripken is by far the greatest all around player in baseball history....Roberto Alomar...is of course the greatest second baseman in the history of the sport."

If you love the Orioles, you have to despise the Yankees. So one of the links on Matt's Baltimore Orioles Page (*http://www.geocities.com/Colosseum/4413*) is Matt's "I Hate the Yankees Club." As you are logging onto Balto's Orioles Page (*http://www.greenapple.com/~balto/orioles.html*), the following JavaScript Confirm

"WARNING!" appears on your computer screen: "If you are a Yankee fan, entering this site may cause severe pain...it has been proven to convert even the most diehard Yankee fans to Orioleism!!"

Those who maintain team Web sites are not fair-weather fans who come to the ballpark only when their favorite nine is battling down the wire for a pennant. They are the proud bleacher bum-types who remain loyal even when their team is a cellar-dweller, and even though it has not played in a World Series since roughly the Taft administration. Their spirit is captured in a declaration found on Nathaniel Grow's Unofficial Detroit Tigers Homepage (*http://www.seorf.ohio.edu/~ab375/tigers.html*): "Even though the Tigers aren't the greatest now, they are still my team, and I follow them through every last game."

The downside of these sites is that, although heartfelt, few are exceptional. Beyond the boosterism, most do little more than duplicate data found elsewhere. They might offer ticket information, stats, player profiles, links to their team's coverage on the super Web sites, and last night's scores—that is, if the sites are kept up-to-date.

Among the player sites, many are skimpy and seem like works in progress: they barely extend beyond a photo or two, a stat list, and a declaration that "Joe Ballplayer is the greatest third-sacker ever"—even though Joe Ballplayer is 23 years old and has spent barely a half-season in The Show.

Additionally, endless player sites exist solely to sell baseball cards, autographs, jerseys, game-used equipment, and perhaps, if you look hard enough, even locks of hair.

There are, however, enough quality player sites to deserve a chapter. Not every current superstar is represented because not every current superstar has an A-1 fan site. In fact, some of the most intriguing pages are dedicated to second-line ballplayers or guys who struggled for years in the stix and finally made it to the majors around age 30, which is ancient for a rookie—and which is precisely what makes these sites so charming.

In addition to being enthusiastic, the pages listed here are generally solid, fact-filled, and intelligently put together homages to contemporary ballplayers. Even if you think you know everything t about the player in question, you probably will glean some nugget of new information from reading one of these top sites.

One of the frustrations of using the Internet is, if you happen to be seeking data on an individual with a common name, you invariably will come up with long lists of completely unrelated URLs. A search engine Joe Carter query, for example, will yield Web sites featuring Joseph G. Carter, invertebrate paleontologist; Joseph Carter, a student who made a presentation to Microsoft CEO Bill Gates; and Joe Carter, employee of a global management and technology consulting organization. But I could locate no extraordinary Joe Carter, Baseball Player sites.

Imagine what you would download if you were seeking Web sites dedicated to John Kennedy or Jimmy Stewart, not the assassinated president or beloved movie actor but the middle infielders whose major league careers spanned the mid-1960s and mid-1970s!

Barry Bonds

http://www.imagixx.net/~bondssf/

This well-done Web site, maintained by Jon Louden, is a shrine to Barry Bonds, "the star of the San Francisco Giants." The highlight is the lengthy "Info" link, which reads like a mini-Bonds biography. Upon scanning it, you come away with the impression that Bonds is a combination Babe Ruth-Lou Brock-Ted Williams-Mother Teresa—which is a completely appropriate view of a favorite baseball hero.

There are stats, photos, and the like, along with links to other Bonds sites. The selected articles, culled from various sources, are headlined "Bonds is NOT a jerk," "Bonds joins Canseco in 40-40 club," "Cover Report: Barry Bonds," and "Who is better: Bonds or Griffey?" In the latter, the answer—in the opinion of the author, Nick Peters, a *Sacramento Bee* reporter—can be gleaned from the following statement: "Bonds, 32, is regarded as *the best* left fielder in the game and Griffey ranks *among the top* center fielders...." (The italics are mine.)

Ken Griffey, Jr.

http://www.uhu.com/junior/index.html

There are dozens—no, scores—of Ken Griffey, Jr. Web sites on the Internet. This is one (maintained by John Tanouye) of several that merit inclusion. Its colorful and handsomely designed home page (which includes a repeated image of Junior making a leaping catch) covers categories such as "Biography," "Statistics," "Multimedia," and "Memorabilia" links (as well as one to links to other Griffey pages). The site is loaded with facts and especially trivia.

Among the latter: Junior hit a three-run homer in his initial professional at bat and a double in his first time swinging in the majors. It would "cost over $12,000 to collect all of his 540+ (baseball) cards listed in the Beckett (guide)." To date, Junior has made several television and movie appearances (in "The Fresh Prince of Bel Aire," "The Simpsons," "Little Big League," and "Harry and the Hendersons"), but his budding acting career was thwarted when the 1994 baseball strike ended, and he had to cancel appearances on "Lois and Clark: The New Adventures of Superman" and "New York Undercover."

The Roger Clemens Web Site

http://www.shaysnet.com/~bsjclark/rogerclemens/rcmain.htm

"Red Sox Nation," the maintainer of this site, apparently is not at all miffed that The Rocket abandoned the Sox for the Blue Jays at the end of the 1996 season. At the top of the home page, just above a photo of Clemens firing a fastball at some hapless hitter, it is noted that "Roger holds the Blue Jays club records (for) Ks in a game and wins in a season!"

On perusing this site, you will learn that Clemens played center on his college basketball team, and the NBA

Seattle Supersonics and Boston Celtics expressed interest in drafting him.

His Red Sox uniform number, 21, was previously worn by Tex Hughson, Mike Torrez, and Juan Marichal. In 1986, he became the only player ever to win a Cy Young Award, an MVP, and an All-Star MVP in the same season.

And Roger even has met the last three United States presidents!

My Ultimate Derek Jeter Web Page!!!

http://www.gis.net/~rokeefe

Jeter is, of course, the New York Yankees' 1996 Rookie of the Year and pin-up boy. This Web site, maintained by 16-year-old Jeanette O'Keefe, exudes a refreshing adolescent sweetness.

On the home page, O'Keefe writes, "This page is dedicated to Derek Jeter, my favorite Yankee, because there really aren't too many home pages about him. This page is gonna have LOTS of pictures... OK, hope you like it. And remember, this page will be CONSTANTLY changing so keep coming back!!!"

On the site, O'Keefe reveals Jeter's "fav player" (Cal Ripken); "fav music" (Mariah Carey and Toni Braxton); "fav movie" (*Seven*); "fav ice cream flavor" (chocolate); "fav food" (chicken parmesan); and "fav away-game city" (Toronto). Jeter dislikes cats and is afraid of dogs. And his best friend is Alex Rodriguez. For those who care, O'Keefe even debunks a rumor that Jeter is dating Mariah Carey.

Allison's A-Rod Page

http://www.halcyon.com/dougf/allison/alex/a-rod.html

A-Rod is Alex Rodriguez, and this Web site, maintained by Allison Fawcett, rivals My Ultimate Derek Jeter Web Page!!! (shown earlier) in its unbridled enthusiasm.

At the top of its home page is a cute-as-a-button picture of A-Rod. Scroll down, and you will find the following: "You gotta love Alex! You gotta love the way he could gun a guy out at first, from his knees, facing the other way, with both eyes shut! You gotta love that while most kids his age are busy asking if you want fries with that, he's out there making future Hall of Famers consider early retirement. More over Omar. Move over Cal. Alex is going places!

"Take me with you A-ROD!"

Oh, yes, the site also includes A-Rod facts and reproductions of magazine covers on which he has appeared. Some of the "Cool Info on Alex" reveals that he is an exceptionally well-rounded individual. His favorite book as a kid was John Steinbeck's *Of Mice and Men*. His hobbies are golf, traveling, and reading. His favorite band is the Rolling Stones (whose members seem old enough to be his grandfather). The places he would like to visit are Australia and London. He expects to meet his wife in church or at a supermarket. His secret ambitions: "I want to get a degree in broadcasting from the University of Miami. I'd also like to play golf on the Senior PGA Tour or own a pro sports team." His best advice comes from his mother: "Be respectful to others, save your money, and stay humble."

And his best friend is Derek Jeter.

Cal Ripken: One for the Ages

http://patriot.net/~rbarthle/cal/index.html

As you might expect, there are quite a few Ripken-related Web homages. On this snazzy site's home page, its maintainer, Rob Barthle, writes, "Cal Ripken has been one of my biggest idols for as long as I can remember.... Being from the Washington D.C. area, I have had the thrill of watching the Orioles win the World Series in 1983, gone through the years of Eddie Murray, Al Bumbry, Jim Palmer, John Lowenstein, Doug DeCinces, Ken Singleton, Rick Dempsey, Earl Weaver, Cal Ripken, Sr., Tippy Martinez, Mike Boddicker, Storm Davis, Brady Andersen (sic), Mike Devereaux, Billy Ripken, Rafeal (sic) Palmeiro, Chris Hoiles, Ben McDonald, Mike Mussina, Bobby Bonilla, and throughout it all, Cal Ripken, Jr.... I am 23 years old, and my life has been centered around baseball, both as a pitcher up through the college level, and through the Orioles and my personal hero, Cal Ripken, Jr."

The site is loaded with links, to a Ripken poll, stats and facts, photos, a Ripken trivia game, and links to other Ripken sites.

An especially nice touch: six photos, placed side-by-side, of Ripken swinging a bat and belting what I presume is a base hit. They can be found halfway down the site's home page.

Nolan Ryan Tribute Page

http://www.ghgcorp.com/mingster/

"All Aboard THE RYAN EXPRESS" flashes in red lettering at the top of this colorful Web site, which is maintained by Ming Cheung. The route and destination, of course, are "Nonstop to Cooperstown."

Links marked "New York Mets," "California Angels," "Houston Astros," and "Texas Rangers" will take you to pages that highlight Ryan's career on each team. Additional links feature everything from stats to major league records to a reproduction of the tickets and programs for the Angels game of June 16, 1992, the Rangers contest of September 15, 1996, and the Astros game of September 29, 1996—the dates the teams retired Ryan's numbers.

The Unofficial Wade Boggs Page

http://www.buffnet.net/~rmp12/wade.htm

The background of this Web site's home page features an attractive pattern of repeated New York Yankee insignias. The appropriately named "Hitting Machine" link will take you to a number of stats that reflect on Wade Boggs' batting prowess. The largest image on this page (beyond a head-shot of Boggs) is his current hit total. Another link is titled "Java Powered Preview of the 3,000 hit celebration."

The site also includes Wade Boggs factoids, records—and, of course, a pair of photos of the ballplayer horseback-riding on the Yankee Stadium turf just after his team copped the 1996 World Championship. If you have the proper sound capabilities, you even can hear what he had to say after the Series' final game.

Rickey Henderson: Man of Steal

http://www.sisna.com/users/rickey24/RICKEY.htm

Jeff (you really have to explore this Web site if you want to know his surname) maintains this homage to baseball's all-time stolen base king. The information on it is culled from Oakland Athletics, New York Yankees, and Toronto Blue Jays media guides, *Sports Illustrated*, *The Baseball Encyclopedia*, *USA Today*, and the ballplayer's own book, *Off Base, Confessions of a Thief.*

Despite his talents and records, Henderson has long been regarded as one athlete who does not go 100 percent every time the umpire yells "Play ball!" However, if you are a true fan of a player, you will overlook that player's flaws. And so, on his site, Jeff stresses Henderson's accomplishments.

Jeff observes, "Following stolen base 939, Rickey made a now infamous speech proclaiming that he 'was now the greatest.' Rickey received much criticism for these words, as many thought he meant he was now the greatest baseball player ever." What follows is a link to the entire "I am the greatest!" speech, which Jeff requests you read to "see what he really meant."

One of the site's links includes the following quotation: "In our sun-down perambulations of late, through the outer parts of Brooklyn, we have observed several parties of youngsters playing 'base,' a certain game of ball.... Let us go forth awhile, and get better air in our lungs. Let us leave our close rooms.... The game of ball is glourious."—Walt Whitman, 1846.

A Tribute to Mark McGwire

http://cwws.com/~schubert/mm.htm

Upon logging onto this Web site, your computer screen is dominated by a striking image of McGwire swinging a bat and looking skyward, following the path of one of his Ruthian clouts. The background is black, with the words "A Tribute to Mark McGwire" standing out in bright green.

The site includes McGwire-related video clips, a slide show, stills, stats—with emphasis on the ballplayer's pursuit of 500 career dingers—a collection of McGwire memorabilia, and several features/interviews.

Hideo Nomo

http://www.pacificu.edu/up/as/bb/nomo.html

There are many Hideo Nomo-related Web sites on the Internet. Appropriately, quite a few are written in Japanese. This bright page (whose background is Dodger-blue) actually is a link on a Web site established by a Pacific University Asian Studies Class (which is listed elsewhere in this book).

The information included here is brief but to the point. Nomo, of course, is not the first Japanese native to play major league ball. That distinction belongs to Masanori Murakami, who in 1964 and 1965 pitched for the San Francisco Giants. So, until the 1995 season, when Nomo debuted with the Los Angeles Dodgers, "there had been no other Japanese of influence in the Majors, but Hideo Nomo has changed all that in dramatic fashion..."

Another Nomo Web site, Tornado Boy (*http://www.st.rim.or.jp/~k_ono/tornado/*), is simply too good to overlook. It is maintained by Koichi Ono, who examines Nomo's career with a microscope. On one of this site's links, you even can download the lyrics of the ditty "Day-O, Heh Day-Ay-Ay-O....Hideo Nomo True Dodger Blue."

Air Chiu's Jeff Bagwell Fan Page!!!

http://www.geocities.com/Colosseum/Track/8850/index.html

Adoration of a ballplayer transcends team loyalties. Such is the case with Air Chiu, maintainer of this homage, who declares, "Jeff Bagwell is my favorite baseball player of all-time even though I'm a die-hard Mets fan. Still, he deserves recognition because I feel he is one of the most underrated baseball players today. He's a superstar who is a good and humble guy. This is my tribute to him."

Some baseball experts say that Boston-born minor leaguer Bagwell's trade from the Red Sox to the Astros for pitcher Larry Andersen during the 1990 season—because the Sox were in a pennant race and needed relief pitching—is one of the biggest steals in baseball history.

This may well be, judging by the stats, articles, and other material included here. If you knew nothing about Bagwell before downloading this site, you would come away with the impression that he is, indeed, one of the top players of his generation.

The Unofficial Larry Walker Home Page

http://www.infoshare.ca/travis/walker/

The home page of this Web site, maintained by Travis Webb, includes headlines spotlighting the Colorado Rockies outfielder's latest feats of on-field heroism. On the site, you will find reproductions of magazine covers featuring the ballplayer, personal information, stats, a picture archive, and audio and video on Walker. Most impressive is the compilation of Walker-related articles from the national and Colorado media and the Web.

The Pat Hentgen Page

http://users.aol.com/hentgen/hentgen1.htm

This adoring Web page, whose maintainer is anonymous (however, he can be e-mailed at argunc@ucla.com), is dedicated to "one of the most fiery and intense players in baseball today... PAT HENTGEN." It is jam-packed with data on the 1996 Cy Young winner, from game-by-game logs to newspaper articles and from audio clips to a Pat Hentgen Page Chat Room.

Click on the "This person reminds me of Pat" icon, and you will be taken to the Official Site of Cy Young (*http://www.cmgww.com/baseball/young/young.html*).

You even can sign the Pat Hentgen Page Guestbook, which includes—start the drum roll—"a confirmed entry from PAT HENTGEN HIMSELF. (Thanks Pat)."

Deion Sanders: Poo-head

http://www.macatawa.org/~greyjack/deion.html

Some player-related Web sites are not authored by blindly reverential fans. This one is sponsored by the "National Campaign to Make it a Federal Requirement to Refer to Deion Sanders as 'Poo-head.'" Perhaps it belongs in the humor chapter. But after further consideration, I concluded that the creator of this Web site makes a pretty convincing case.

The site's home page opens with a welcoming statement from Andrew D. Myers, chairman of the NCtMiaFRtRtDSaP-H. Links from the home page answer the following earth-shattering questions: "Uh, what's the point?"; "Which federal agency would be responsible for this, anyway?"; "What's the proper pronunciation of NCtMiaFRtRtDSaP-H?"; "How many people have joined the NCtMiaFRtRtDSaP-H so far?" (The membership "continues to surge upwards, our ranks are now solidly in the double-digits...") And finally: "How can I join?"

Among the links: A Kabalarian analysis of the name "Deion."

The site's one flaw, from a baseball perspective: the Deion photo on it features him in football regalia.

Don Mattingly Tribute

http://www.inforamp.net/~drb/donnie.htm

Many Mattingly fan sites are on the Internet, which attests to the popularity of Donnie Baseball. This Web page is perhaps the best.

Darrin R. Brooker, who maintains the site, describes Mattingly as "the greatest Yankee of my Generation!!!"—and who's to argue. "Is there any better memory on those lazy Sunday afternoons?" Brooker asks. "Memories of a tied game in the bottom of the 8th, Don Mattingly hitting one of his routine line-drive doubles into the gap, and Willie Randolph or Steve Sax or Wade Boggs coming around third to score easily and break the tie. I remember those games. Those were the days when I truly loved the game of baseball... This webpage is my humble attempt to capture those memories for the fans who appreciated Don's unmatched desire for the game he loved."

On this page, you will find everything from excerpts from articles on the ballplayer to career stats, career highlights, and Mattingly-related links. And there is a nice array of photos.

This Is Chipper Jones

http://www.geocities.com/~philipfromga/

Atlanta Braves fans are apparently not into the Web. Considering the team's eye-popping success during the 1990s and the proliferation of stars and stars-to-be on its roster—beginning with Greg Maddux, John Smoltz, Tom Glavine, Kenny Lofton, and Chipper Jones—Web sites for Braves ballplayers are fairly hard to find. One, The Greg Maddux Shrine (*http://www.macshack.com/johns/greg/greg.html*), a fan page "dedicated to the Professor of Pitching," was briefly considered for inclusion here. The information contained on the site may have been impressive, but the site was in dire need of updating. Meanwhile, a number of individual sites spotlighting Lofton featured photos of him in a Cleveland Indians uniform, as if his pre-1997 season trade to Atlanta was a mirage.

This Web site, on the other hand, includes up-to-the-minute stats at the top of its home page. It is maintained by Philip Rodgers and is colorful and well-designed.

Among its best features are articles on Jones, the Braves' star third baseman whose all-American name rivals that of Mickey Mantle. One, headlined "Old Timer" and written by Scott Freeman, begins, "In this cynical age of baseball as business, Chipper Jones may be just the kind of throwback player that fans, disenchanted by the Dow Jones version of the national pastime, have craved. A scrapper. Full of hustle. Wears his stockings up high like the old-timers. Plays like he actually loves the game."

Dale Murphy: Forever a Brave

http://users.aol.com/braves3/murphy.htm

This exhaustive and visually dazzling Web site, maintained by Matthew Crowder, is a model for fan-sponsored pages. It is fun to look at and is loaded with endless Murphy-related links.

Crowder captures the spirit of his site when he observes, "At a time when athletes shun their role model status and are routinely suspended and banned from their respective sports for unlawful conduct, Dale Murphy shouldered the burden of being a role model to thousands of children and generously gave of his time and money to numerous charities. Dale is a man of extraordinary talent and character."

He then brings baseball politics into the arena when he adds, "Unfortunately, many baseball fans suspect that Murphy will be the next victim of the Baseball Writers' oversight when he is not voted into the Hall of Fame. Apparently 400 home runs is pretty much a free ticket to Cooperstown but 398 home runs, back-to-back MVP awards, 5 straight Gold Gloves, and 740 consecutive games, not to mention his unsurpassed community service record, is another story. "Whether or not Murphy is given his due by the BBWAA, I figure the least I can do is salute him with this page."

The Wizard: Ozzie Smith

http://www.i1.net/~alchu/ozzie.htm

The Wizard of Oz flies through cyberspace at the top of this Web site. It is maintained by Al Chu, who explains that "here in St. Louis, Ozzie Smith is almost a god. He's the sports icon of St. Louis, much like Jordan is in Chicago and Joe Montana was for San Fransisco (sic).... He's in all likelihood the greatest defensive shortstop in the history of the game as well as just a class act. I've grown up practically my entire life watching him in a Cardinals uniform (he came in 1982, I was born in 1979) and wish him well in his retirement. Cardinals baseball just won't be the same."

On the site, you will find a list of Oz's own personal-favorite defensive plays and a nice selection of Ozzie photos.

Bernie Williams Fan Club

http://www.cheshire.net/~erivera/bwfc/bernie.html

Eli Rivera, who maintains this Web site (and describes himself as "a personal friend of Bernie Williams"), is a true-blue Bernie believer. For one thing, on the home page, he invites you to "Visit Bernie Williams' Hometown: Vega Alta, PR." Only a fervent fan-atic would consider journeying to a player's hometown. What would you do there? Take photos of his high school? Stare in awe at the ballfield he played on as a kid? I don't think the Williams family would appreciate your showing up for lunch.

If you are a Williams fan, stick to Rivera's loving tribute to his hero. "Bernie has been an example of dedication, talent, affection and above all pride to sports," he observes. "Good son, good brother, good father, good student, good friend, excellent guitar player and an all-star baseball player."

Paul Molitor: A Tribute

http://www.geocities.com/CollegePark/1904/molitor.html

After logging onto the home page of this Web site, which is maintained by Nathanael Barnes, you are greeted by a large autographed picture of the Ignitor. What follows are up-to-the-minute statistics and links (which are jam-packed with data on Molitor and his accomplishments during his 20-year major league career).

On perusing the site, you come away with the feeling that Molitor's career has been hampered by his having spent it playing mostly in small-market cities and not being a home run hitter. When you think about solid and consistent contemporary players, Molitor's name does not immediately come to mind. Yet if you click on this site's "All-Time Leaders" icon, you will learn that he is in the all-time top 20 in hits, doubles, steals, and at bats and is nearing the top 20 in total bases and runs scored. In these categories, his name is mixed in among the likes of Mickey Mantle, Al Kaline, Tris Speaker, Al Simmons, Ernie Banks, Charlie Gehringer, Rod Carew, Cap Anson, and Paul Waner.

Shrine to John Kruk

http://mason.gmu.edu/~corr/kruk.htm

"Why do I wear #29 for my summer league softball team?" asks the anonymous maintainer of this Web site. "You can have your Hall of Famers, you can have your Griffeys and Rodriguezes and guys named 'Chipper'...my favorite baseball player ever is John Kruk, first baseman for the Padres, Phillies and White Sox. He swung a mean bat, had deceptive speed, gave his all for the team, and always came through in the clutch. More than anything, though, it's just that he's so NORMAL. He looks like that guy from the machine shop you always see in the neighborhood bar. As he himself said, when admonished for being a professional athelete (sic) and yet smoking, 'I ain't an athelete (sic), lady, I'm a baseball player.'"

This laid-back site goes on to include everything from career stats to Kruk-related articles and reminiscences to an e-mail from "a guy who says he knows the Krukker personally," which brings you up-to-date on what the ballplayer has been up to since his 1995 retirement. Then there is a photo of a slightly annoyed Kruk, with the following caption: "Probably thinking either 'I ain't hittin' worth a spit,' or 'If this game goes into extra innings, we won't get back to the hotel in time to get room service.'"

"Anonymous" also puts out a call to anyone having transcripts of Kruk's appearances with David Letterman.

Bert Blyleven: Dutch Treat

http://www.midwest.net/scribers/cbconly/bert.htm

This simple, sincere Web site is an ode to "Rik Aalbert Blyleven, better known as Bert," who won 287 games and struck out 3,701 batters in his 22-year major league career. It features a thoughtful analysis of Blyleven's career, penned by site maintainer Cindy Birk Conley, along with the hope that someday soon he will be considered for the Hall of Fame.

As proof of his meriting admission, Conley offers a statistical comparison between Blyleven and Robin Roberts (who, of course, is already in the Hall).

Tribute to the Hawk

http://www.netpoint.net/~sparodi/dawson.htm

"The Hawk" is not Ken Harrelson or Bob Taylor but Andre Dawson, and this anonymously written Web page (which is a link on a personal Florida Marlins site) is a combination mini-bio/loving tribute to the ballplayer, who retired after the 1996 season.

At a time when so many of the jocks who make the biggest headlines are boors, it is a pleasure to read this page and learn about Dawson. At the conclusion is the following: "I received an e-mail from a lady in Canada about a young man (who) was very sick, recovering from a brain tumor... (She wanted to know) if there was any way that Andre Dawson could call him for his birthday. I was fortunate (in) that I had a way to contact his uncle and forward this request on to him. Several days later, it was so special to receive an e-mail from the same lady telling me how much it meant to this young man that Andre had taken the time to call her young friend to tell him happy birthday. It meant a lot to me that I could be the one to help deliver the request... that's just the kind of guy (Dawson) is and he will surely be missed."

Manny Ramirez

http://www-scf.usc.edu/~nyveen/manny/manny.html

This nice little Web site, maintained by Jeff Nyveen, features a solid selection of Ramirez-related photos and articles. Nyveen explains that the Cleveland Indians flychaser "is my favorite ballplayer. After noticing his 1.000+ high school slugging percentage on the back of a baseball card, I became a Manny fan.... Since Day One, I have been predicting greatness for Manny.... Manny has one of the most beautiful swings in baseball. He has unbelievable power, a quick swing, and an amazing eye. The scary thing is that he's just a kid. And he can only get better."

Ramirez' stats reveal that his slugging percentage was over 1.000 for three straight years in high school—and was an incredible 1.619 his senior year. So one can understand why Nyveen became enamored of Ramirez.

Nomar Garciaparra

http://www.geocities.com/Colosseum/3600/NOMAR.html

This neat little Web site consists mostly of a loving tribute to the Boston Red Sox infielder—the consensus American League rookie-of-the-year for 1997. It includes all the basics regarding Garciaparra's brief amateur and professional career.

You also will learn that the ballplayer's real name is Anthony Nomar Garciaparra—and that his "unique middle name is actually his father's name (Ramon) spelled backwards."

My Mo Vaughn Page

http://www.geocities.com/Colosseum/Track/4242/

This Hit Dog homage is maintained by teenager Justin Rayburn, who resides in Monument, Colorado but originally is from Wakefield, Massachusetts and describes himself as "a big fan of New England sports." On his home page are links to pages dedicated to other Red Sox stars, as well as "My Mo Vaughn Page."

Included on the site are a brief bio, stats, a thorough baseball card checklist, and list of Vaughn-related links. If you did not know that Mo played shortstop while in high school, that he and teammate John Valentin attended Seton Hall together, that Mo appeared on "Saturday Night Live" in 1994, and that major leaguer Greg Vaughn is his cousin, you will be so informed before leaving this site.

Jim Edmonds Home Page

http://www.geocities.com/Colosseum/6860/JEdmondsHome.html

This visually dazzling Web site is crammed with information on the multitalented Anaheim Angels outfielder. However, its anonymous maintainer is not blindly adoring of his hero. He may declare, "Edmonds is a prototype center fielder. He covers ground, catches what he gets to and shows no fear of the wall or the turf. On top of that, he's got a good arm. He has made only one error in each of the last two seasons." But he is quick to add, "As a baserunner, he's surprisingly poor. He doesn't get good jumps on base hits, which makes it a struggle to score from second on sharp singles."

One of the site's outstanding features, found on its home page, is a video replay of "THE CATCH by Jim Edmonds!...Some say it is the BEST catch of the YEAR, some say it was the BEST catch of the DECADE, and some say it was the BEST catch EVER!!"

One can only watch the play (made during the 1997 season) over and over and marvel at Edmonds' pure athleticism!

Matt Williams Hot Corner

http://www.macatawa.org/~gornie/sports/williams/williams.html

A bit of humor marks the top of this Web site's home page, which features two head shots of Williams. In one, he wears a San Francisco Giants cap. The other has been ever-so slightly retouched, in a way that is better seen than described, to signify his joining the Cleveland Indians between the 1996 and 1997 seasons.

"Gornie," the site's maintainer, explains, "I created this webpage for people like me—die-hard Matt Williams fanatics who are tired of finding millions of pages devoted to the world's most overrated underachievers and not one devoted to the most underrated overachiever."

Later on, Gornie adds, "This site is always under construction. Please send ideas ASAP to the e-mail address listed below. I will try to implement all good ideas as quickly as I possibly can. Criticism is also welcome, unless you're one of those idiot Dodgers fans or a fan of Ken Caminiti, Travis Fryman, Robin Ventura, Wade Boggs, or Chipper Jones. Thank you."

Humdeki's Hideki Irabu Page

http://members.aol.com/Humdeki/index.html

Will he develop into a solid starting pitcher? Or is he just an overrated and temperamental egomaniac who conned George out of millions?

The verdict is not yet in on Hideki Irabu and more than likely will not be for quite a while. At least this Web site, which describes itself as "the first Irabu site ever!," does not fawn over the ballplayer. His defeats and embarrassing outings are duly reported along with his successes.

Additionally, there are several reproductions of Irabu baseball cards. The Japanese ones are quite interesting.The linking of celebrities and products is unintentionally reflected in two Irabu photos, appearing one on top of the other, in which the hurler is practically posing under banners or signs promoting Wendy's and Toyota.

Springer Nation

http://www.neptune.net/com~kmchf/SN

Springer Nation (not to be confused with Woodstock Nation) will keep you up-to-date on the exploits of Dennis Springer, an Anaheim Angels hurler who deserves a Web site all his own just for perseverance. Springer was a 30-year-old career minor leaguer when he made his major league debut during the 1995 season with the Philadelphia Phillies. That year he compiled an inglorious 0-3 record in four games. The following season, he was 5-6 for the then-California Angels.

So it is no surprise that Springer Nation admittedly has "had its ups and downs... From the miraculous 'Springer' Training '96 where Dennis started off the spring pitching 14 and 1/3 consecutive scoreless innings... To the heartache when Springer surprisingly did not even make the Angels' opening day roster in '96... To when Springer got his first call up from Vancouver and became a part of the Angels' bullpen... To when he got sent back down to Vancouver after a miserable outing out of the pen in Seattle."

Included on the site are a "Springer Nation mailing list," a "Springer Nation trivia challenge," a "Springer Nation Archives," even a list of the "Citizens of Springer Nation."

The Dickie Thon Fan Club

http://www.inetnow.net/~ferenczy/thon.com/

Scroll down this Web site's home page, and you will be informed that the "DTFC welcomes all baseball fans that have a genuine love of the game and at least enough knowledge to put up a good argument if anyone wants to start one. It also helps to know who Dickie Thon was."

Actually, Thon was a solid major leaguer who enjoyed a 15-year career playing shortstop for California, Houston, San Diego, Philadelphia, Texas, and Milwaukee and compiled a .264 lifetime batting average.

All you ever could hope to know about Dickie Thon the ballplayer is contained here.

One of the links on this site is "Hairface's Major League Baseball Wall O' Shame," which earned its own entry in this book's baseball humor chapter.

The Jeff Huson Home Page

http://members.aol.com/edijkelly/index/jeff.huson.html

The key to this Web page is its "Why Jeff Huson?" link. It recounts the manner in which Edith Kelly, its maintainer, came in contact with Huson, a utility infielder who has played for several teams since his 1988 major league debut.

On several occasions, the ballplayer was kind to Edith by sending her an autographed baseball card and signed postcard. Once, when Kelly attended an Orioles/A's game, Huson even spoke with her and gave her a bat he had cracked while taking BP.

For Kelly, the result was a meaningful bond—and the creation of a nice little Web page.

Beth's Tribute to Chris Gomez

http://members.tripod.com/~Gomie/

Every ballplayer has at least one die-hard fan.

If you do not believe me, check out this Web site maintained by Beth McIntyre.

Even though McIntyre dutifully reports that, in 1996, Chris Gomez batted .262 with 86 hits, 29 RBIs, and three homers—statistics that do not have him on the path to

Cooperstown—she reverentially refers to him as "the star shortstop" of the San Diego Padres. And she adds, "When most people think of great shortstops they think of players like Derek Jeter, Alex Rodriguez or Ozzie Smith. However, the steady play and dedication of hard-working, unsung heroes like Chris are what really wins baseball games. He deserves just as much recognition as the so-called 'superstars' that are paid millions."

The site is divided into such sections as "The Detroit Years" (Gomez' former team), "More Chris Gomez Pictures," and "ChrisGo Speaks." (McIntyre likes to call Gomez "ChrisGo.")

The initial quote in the latter category: the ballplayer's reaction upon "striking out after Chris Gwynn doubled in the winning runs in LA."

I repeat: *Every* ballplayer has at least one die-hard fan.

Some even have their own clubs. The Web site maintained by The Rich Amaral Appreciation Society (*http://www.uidaho.edu/~kuec9454/personal.html*) pays homage to the Seattle Mariners sub. It is stated on the home page that Amaral is, quite simply, "one of the most versatile utility players in all of Major League Baseball."

However, the society has not been appreciating Amaral lately. On several visits, the "Personal History," "Career Highlights," and "Career Statistics" links were as dead as a baseball in the pre-Ruthian era.

The Keith Foulke Page

http://members.aol.com/jfgindin/foulke.html

The Keith Foulke page is dedicated to the young pitcher who made his major league debut during the 1997 campaign after having toiled in the San Francisco Giants minor league system and who at mid-season was traded to the Chicago White Sox. The site, which is maintained by Jim Gindin, reads like an entry from *Current Biography.*

At the top, Gindin writes, "Every Major League ballplayer should have a home page. Or at least an unofficial home page written by someone who has never met him, or has any real reason to follow his career.... I'm not a big White Sox fan, nor am I otherwise related to Foulke. I'm just someone who's really into baseball. About two years ago, I noticed that a pitcher for the San Francisco Giants' Class A team in San Jose was posting great numbers. I wanted to find out a little more—was this a major league prospect? I had never before heard Keith Foulke's name...." This Web site serves as an excellent example of the manner in which a true baseball fan can become enamored of a non "flavor of the month" ballplayer.

Bartolo Colon

http://www.geocities.com/Colosseum/Arena/5435/

Here is another case of a fan attaching himself to a ballplayer while the latter is still a prospect. In this case, the player is Cleveland Indians pitcher Bartolo Colon.

"I first learned about Bartolo in the 'organizational reports' in one of the winter editions of *Baseball Weekly*," writes Ben Carterette, the site's maintainer. "I noticed a pitcher called 'Colon, Bart' in the Indians' report with excellent stats at Class AA. At the time, I thought, 'Bartholomew Colon? What a cool name...' A couple of weeks later, *BBW* printed stats from winter league ball. I again noticed Mr. Colon; this time his name was correctly listed as 'Colon, Bartolo' and he had pitched 20-some innings and not allowed a run. I thought, 'Bartolo Colon? That's an even cooler name.' Thus I became his biggest fan."

The result is this nicely done Web site, which works best as Carterette's diary of Bartolo Colon's career to date.

Bye, Bye Joey!

http://www.en.com/users/jeffh/ab.html

I wonder if Jim Gindin would include Albert (formerly Joey) Belle in his statement about all major leaguers deserving Web sites?

After all, more than any other contemporary ballplayer, Albert Belle is the Man You Love to Hate. Certainly, this talented but surly and deeply troubled athlete does little to offset his image as a jerk.

It is not surprising, then, that you will be hard-pressed to find any Albert Belle fan page valentines on the Internet. In fact, among the first 20 URLs listed for Belle on the Excite search engine, a majority reflected on the ballplayer's ongoing troubles: "Belle ordered into counseling for recent outburst"; "Indians' Belle proudly wears a scowl"; "Belle's car dealings at issue in Halloween lawsuit"; "Fan arrested for confronting Belle"; "Belle hits rare slump during controversy"; "Belle passes on workout"; "Belle skips All-Star workout"; and "Belle ordered to undergo counselling" (again).

Bye Bye, Joey! is a link on a Web site maintained by the Hansen family of Lodi, Ohio. It consists of a brief essay, written during the 1996-97 off-season by a Hansen who describes himself as a "die-hard Cleveland Indian fan," and its content reflects not only on Belle but on what is wrong with the baseball industry in the 1990s.

It reads in part, "I have kept my mouth shut for a long time now, gladly living with Mr. Albert Belle's tirades, tempers and slumps, in return for the fabulous numbers he has put up, sometimes single-handedly. Albert Belle is a wonderful batter, a so-so fielder, and a lousy role model.... I want everybody to know I love the sport of Baseball, but I hate the path it has gone down. Just like Football, Basketball and Golf, it's become a sport for the rich fan. A man with children can no longer afford to take the kids out to the ballpark for a Sunday outing.... All to pay the outlandish salaries of modern ballplayers. Now, here comes Joey, wanting the highest salary.... So, good bye, Joey. Good bye, and I won't hold my breath for your Hall of Fame induction."

10

Major League Team Official Sites

Most major league ballclubs sponsor and maintain their own Web sites. In general, these Web sites spotlight a team's stars, hot prospects, and on-field exploits along with what/when/where data on schedules and ticket purchases. The best sites are fun to explore, particularly by the team's fans. And if you are an out-of-towner planning to catch a game in Atlanta or Philadelphia or San Francisco, the sites offer useful information that will help you in your pre-visit planning.

However, be forewarned: these sites are also public relations extensions of the individual ballclub. Their reason for being is to promote the team and present the club in the most positive corporate light. You will find no Steinbrenner-bashing on the Yankees site, no anti-Duquette scribblings on the Red Sox URL, no Reinsdorf expletive-deleteds on the Chicago White Sox site. If there is any kind of controversy regarding the club's on-field play or the manager's status, a player's boorish behavior or an owner's view that the local taxpayers *must* pay for a new stadium so that he can enhance his profits by selling luxury boxes, it will not be discussed here.

For a more objective view of your favorite team, check out its coverage on the up-to-the-minute sports news sites (the best of these are reviewed in Chapter 1), sites maintained by local newspapers (the best of these are reviewed in Chapter 2), or the national sporting press.

Incredibly, not every major league club has an official site. As of this writing, the Anaheim Angels, Colorado Rockies, and New York Mets were minus Web sites.

Get with it, guys! Even the Arizona Diamondbacks (*http://www.azdiamondbacks.com/main2.html*) and Tampa Bay Devil Rays (*http://www.devilrays.com/*) had Web sites (or sites in development) months before they drafted major league players, developed their rosters, and opened their inaugural seasons. The Devil Rays page was still under construction when I logged on. The Diamondbacks site served as a teaser of things to come. One of its home page links deserves to remain online after the site fully evolves. It allows visitors to "take a virtual flight through Bank One Ballpark," the team's home stadium.

Because their flaws far outweigh their assets, four official sites have been excluded from the main body of this chapter. The green-and-orange Baltimore Orioles "Online Sports Page" (*http://www.theorioles.com/*) spotlights the results of the team's latest game, the manner in which it has recently performed, and its upcoming schedule. The various links ("Roster," "Press Box," "Group Sales," "Schedule," "Make-Up Dates," "Transactions," and "Ticket Info") are self-explanatory. And there are links to each of the Orioles' minor league affiliates.

On the whole, however, this site is unusually sparse. Beyond a statistical comparison of the 1997 and 1969 squads, there is a surprising lack of acknowledgment of Orioles tradition and history—including its World Series triumphs and Hall of Famers.

The Pittsburgh Pirates site (*http://www.pirateball.com/*) could celebrate its young players or its past heroes from Kiner to Clemente to Mazeroski. However, at first glance, it seemed to be intent on appealing to 12-year-old boys with underdeveloped minds. The main visual on its home page is the Pirate insignia over mostly yellow lettering informing one and all that "It's a Freak Show."

Since when are major league ballgames and ballclubs supposed to be freak shows?

The Orioles and Pirates sites are inoffensive compared to those maintained by the Chicago White Sox and Kansas City Royals. Both are marred by shamelessly crude and offensive commercialism.

Before logging onto the White Sox site (*http://www.chisox.com/*), I wondered whose photo might dominate the home page: Frank Thomas, Albert Belle, or Jerry Reinsdorf. Instead, there is a colorful but somewhat abstract outline of the New Comiskey Park. Flashing icons at the top simulate fireworks. And smack-dab in the center is a bright red-and-yellow McDonald's logo! Also prominent on the home page—not at its top or bottom but right in the middle—are logos for Miller beer, Coca Cola, Armitron, Ameritech, and United Airlines.

I suppose that one can rationalize that Reinsdorf does have all those big salaries to pay.

In fairness, some of the page's links are fact-filled and entertaining. The "History" page includes a detailed timeline of significant dates and franchise highlights, from November 20, 1893 (the roots of the team's inception) to the present. Others, however, seem merely manipulative. The "Ask the Pros" link—"Here's your chance to 'Ask the Pros' detailed baseball questions"—is more market research/demographics-oriented than informational. In addition to your question, you are asked to fill out a form requesting your age and gender.

Worst of all is the Royals site (*http://www.kcroyals.com/*). It features the usual: links to schedules and ticket information;

"Royals News" (including recent player transactions, draft picks, and the like); trivia ("Correctly answer the trivia questions and you will be entered into a drawing to win $20 in Big Blue Bucks"); "The Team" (including profiles of players, manager, and coaches); "The K" (which is, of course, Kauffman Stadium); and "Kids Zone" (which is hosted by Sluggerrr, the official Royals' mascot).

The latter is the commercial equivalent of a fastball zooming at top speed at a batter's forehead. There are no child-oriented activities here. Instead, just after Sluggerrr finishes introducing himself, he commences hawking "my new line of Sluggerrr merchandise...including the cutest Sluggerrr stuffed dolls...." Then there is a solicitation to "let the Kansas City Royals' Sluggerrr bring more excitement to your next event." At $250 an hour ($125 for charity events, and travel charges may apply), you can hire Sluggerrr to appear at picnics, parades, parties, store openings, executive sales meetings, hospitals, nursing homes, or churches.

It is noted that "all proceeds from Sluggerrr's appearances go to support Royals Charities." Yet if the Royals organization is so magnanimous, why charge for Sluggerrr's presence at charitable functions in the first place?

"Kids Zone" deserves some kind of award for combining crass commercialism with sheer audacity.

Atlanta Braves

http://www.atlantabraves.com/

Tomahawk chop-lovers will enjoy this thorough Web site. An "overview" link explains the ins and outs of the site. At the left of the page are colorful icons that will lead you to the site's various features.

"Ballpark" features descriptions and a diagram of Turner Field and ticket information. "Hank Aaron" pays homage to the all-time home run leader. "History" is one of the most impressive links. It includes all-time team records, rosters, statistics—even a list of team names (where you will learn that, at different times, the franchise was known as the Boston Red Stockings, Boston Beaneaters, Boston Doves, and Boston Rustlers). "Kids Korner" is a child-oriented link featuring a "Test Your Baseball Knowledge Crossword Puzzle" and a "Come to Turner Field Maze." "Lineup" includes extensive player profiles and current statistics. "Merchandise" is "your complete online resource for Official Braves Clubhouse Merchandise." "Minors" includes links to all the team's bush league affiliates. "Multimedia" consists of "pictures, movies and sounds of the Atlanta Braves." "Newsstand" includes information on ordering team media guides, programs, fan magazines, and merchandising catalogs. "Pressbox" links to team press releases and a search engine "for daily and archived news off the wire." "Schedules & Tickets" features ticket ordering information and allows you to either select a premade schedule or customize one based on your individual plans. "Scoreboard" includes basic most-recent-game data.

The "Community" link lists the organization's charitable activities within the Atlanta community. But it also features a picture of a corporate-looking Ted Turner and includes blather about how it "takes dedication and responsibility from the entire organization to become a true champion. But most importantly, champions are inspired by self sacrifice and collective commitment—simply put, teamwork...." Although the essence of this sentiment is noble, it comes off as a hollow cliche.

Boston Red Sox

http://www.redsox.com/

Each time you log onto this Web site, there is a different crisp, black-and-white photograph at the top of the home page. On one occasion, it was of Carl Yastrzemski. Underneath was a quote from Yaz: "Ted Williams was my baseball hero when I was growing up, he and Stan Musial." Another time featured a team shot and a quote from Bill Dickey: "If I were catching blindfold, I'd always know when it was (Jimmy) Foxx who connected. He hit the ball harder than anyone else." A third occasion featured an even older team shot and former team owner John I. Taylor declaring, "It's in the Fenway section (of Boston), isn't it? Then call it Fenway Park." A fourth visit displayed the same team shot and a quote from Joe Cronin: "Boston is one of the greatest sports towns in the world. A fellow with an Irish name like mine ought to get along there."

Four major links are available here. "News & Info" includes links to organization press releases and promotional features on players; "'97 (or '98) Club" is essentially a press release on the team's season aspirations; "Yesteryear" spotlights the team's storied past; "Going to the Game" is a mini-homage to Fenway Park. On each page, additional links are provided to everything from "Manager's Notes," "Pre-Game Notes," and "Current Roster," to "The Green Monster" and "Fenway Faithful," to a Fenway Park seating chart and an interactive CyberSox Challenge game.

Among the other links on the home page are links to the team's minor league affiliates, an online chat room, and a child-oriented "Fenway Funzone."

Chicago Cubs

http://www.cubs.com/

Log onto this snappy Web site, and you will be greeted by the familiar image of the "Wrigley Field Home of Chicago Cubs" sign, which is found outside the ballyard, and a "WELCOME" on its message board.

History and the modern era mix nicely on this site. You will find the latest game summaries, rosters, and statistics along with a spotlight on what many consider the team's greatest asset: Wrigley Field and its storied ivy. There is a "journey through decades of Cubs memories"; a spotlight on all-time great Cubs players, from Grover Cleveland Alexander and Cap Anson to Billy Williams and Hack

Wilson; and a "where are they now" look at Cubs players of seasons past. Lest we forget, there is an audio message from Mr. Cub (and we are not talking about Glen Hobbie).

Refreshingly, this site does not blindly glorify its sponsor. For years, the Cubs have not been serious pennant contenders, and site visitors are queried as to "what area of need is the most important for the Cubs to address in the off-season?" You could vote for starting pitching, relief pitching, power hitting, middle infield, and outfield—and the more cynical (not to mention those yearning for a World Series in Wrigley Field) might be tempted to check all five.

Cincinnati Reds

http://www.cincinnatireds.com/

Upon logging onto this brightly designed Web site, you will be greeted with a friendly introduction: "Welcome to the Cincinnati Reds' Web Site. It is our pleasure to provide a place where you can come and get information on the very first major league baseball team ever."

You will find the usual data on this site, from scores and news and notes to player profiles and contests designed for children and adults, and much of it is colorfully presented. One of several visual highlights is the previous day's game totals displayed on a dazzling green scoreboard. But in no way is this site all glitz and no content. For one thing, the player profiles are unusually extensive. On my visit, the question posed in the "Kids' Zone" essay contest was thoughtful: "What will Reds Baseball be like in the year 2500?"

Given the emphasis on history in the site introduction, you would expect to find considerable space devoted to the era when the Big Red Machine was known as the Red Stockings. You will not be disappointed; there is an extensive team history, an A-to-Z all-time player roster (which begins with Ted Abernathy and Cal Abrams and ends with

Billy Zitzmann and George Zuverink), and a timeline. The latter begins on June 1, 1869, when "in the first game ever played by a professional baseball team (all paid players, no amateurs), the Cincinnati Red Stockings beat the Mansfield Independents, 48-14."

Cleveland Indians

http://www.indians.com/

As you log onto the "official home of the Cleveland Indians on the World Wide Web," you are greeted by a nice collage of a glove, bat and ball, an Indians insignia, and a long shot of Jacobs Field.

The site is loaded with features. When I logged on, you could e-mail questions to Sandy Alomar; other ballplayers are featured throughout the season. You could take a "virtual trip to the (Jacobs Field) ballyard"; before doing so, however, you will have to download software. You could play various trivia games. You could view illustrations of team jerseys, dating from the 1908-1909 season. You could learn all about the history of baseball in Cleveland. And, of course, you could read Indians' press releases, download statistics, check up on last night's action, peruse schedules, and even order tickets for postponed Indians games (because, more than likely, all the regular season contests will be sold out).

Detroit Tigers

http://www.detroittigers.com/

This is one of the newer official major league Web sites, and the dominating image on its home page is state-of-the-art: a nicely-designed scoreboard combining a mixture of past (flags signifying the team's World Series accomplishments) and present (the previous day's box score/game highlights and the starting time for the club's next scheduled contest).

From the home page, you can download Tigers schedule and ticket information, statistics and player profiles, farm team scores, and details on how to join the team's Kids Club. There is an A (Animals, ATM, and Autographs) to W (Wheelchairs and Will Call/Gate 7) guide to Tiger Stadium along with a history of the "aging and venerable old park" and data on the team's new facility, scheduled for completion in 1999.

Florida Marlins

http://www.flamarlins.com/

I especially liked the "we-are-the-world" image at the top of this Web site's home page: animated, high-fiving hands of anonymous black and white Marlins teammates.

Otherwise, this site features game notes, schedules, contests, messages from the team's president, and other Marlins features mixed in with flashing advertising visuals.

There is no focus on team history here. But that should not be surprising, given the short time the franchise has been in existence.

Houston Astros

http://www.astros.com/

This Web site's home page gets right down to the most recent Astros game recap along with links to press notes, team stats, roster/bios, and tickets. On my visit, I enjoyed reading the chatty "letter" from minor league pitcher C.J. Nitkowski; in fact, this site gives special emphasis to the exploits of the team's farm team players.

The team history link is extensive and impressive. It includes a historical slide show, year-by-year results and recaps, season and career hitting and pitching leaders, a section on how the Astros have fared in the postseason, managerial win-loss records, and an all-time roster.

Another highlight is a link to "Baseball Fitness Tips," consisting of a program of special exercises, designed by Dr. Gene Coleman, the Astros' strength and conditioning coach, "for all athletes who want to improve some of their basic skills."

Los Angeles Dodgers

http://www.dodgers.com/

This solid Web site is handsomely designed and jam-packed with information. Among the links available to peruse on my visit were "Dodgers Begin Multi-Language Live Radio Broadcast"; "1997 Dodgers Schedule & Game Archive"; "The Stars Come Out at Dodger Stadium" (a spiffy page including photos of Billy Crystal, Jon Lovitz, Tony Danza, Jonathan Silverman, and others who attended "Hollywood Stars Night"); "Dodger Family Game Highlights" (a nice feature consisting of photos of players' and coaches' families); a heartfelt and colorful "Tribute to a Hall of Fame Manager"—Tommy Lasorda; an "On-Line Interview With Vin Scully"; information on an upcoming Dodger Fantasy Camp; and details on how to "Get Plug-ins In Our Hot Links Section."

However, this site is not flawless. For one thing, there were too many typographical errors on "The Stars Come Out at Dodger Stadium" page—beginning with a date listing for the event as *1977*, rather than 1997!

For another, you had to search with a magnifying glass to find the word "Brooklyn" on this site!

Milwaukee Brewers

http://www.milwaukeebrewers.com/

No, the smiling face peering out of this Web site's home page is not Bud Selig, inviting you to share a cold one with him as you blow dust off the furniture in the baseball commissioner's office. It is the Brewers' announcer Bob Uecker, (of the Mendoza line lifetime batting average) who acts as "your online guide."

Included on the site are updates on the construction of the team's new ballyard, Miller Park; ticket information; news and notes; schedules; and other standard fare. Also available are interactive games fashioned to "challenge baseball fans both young and old"; a helpful "A-Z Fan

Guide" featuring a history of County Stadium, a seating guide, and promotional schedule; and a "Down on the Farm" link leading to information on the team's minor league affiliates.

Minnesota Twins

http://www.mntwins.com/

This Web site's home page features a large, impressive Twins logo over a baseball and a pair of game tickets. The links here include history, game notes, tickets, schedule, players, farm report, and pro shop.

You also can "Travel Through Twins History" and examine the team's past decade-by-decade from the 1960s on, review World Series and American League Championship Series highlights, and scan the team's all-time roster. You can "Follow the Twins Tracker," which allows you to chart the club's game coverage throughout the season.

When I logged on, there was a link to a special feature, presented by *Readers Digest* and devoted to baseball in America.

Montreal Expos

http://www.montrealexpos.com/

This "le site officiel" includes a nice visual at the top of its home page. Featured are two of the organization's biggest assets: manager Felipe Alou and pitcher Pedro Martinez. The links that get you further into the site are named "Play Ball!" and "Au Jeu!" (This is the lone official Web site with versions in English and French).

On the site, you can download information on "everything you need to know about your Expos" (including data on players and coaches, a team history, and a section on the franchise's greatest players) and "where, when and how to see your Expos" (featuring data on Olympic Stadium, an overview of season giveaways and promotional events, and an interactive schedule). Also provided are "box scores and stats for the current season" (which consists of a game summary index for the previous month), "fun and games for everyone" (which mainly includes information on joining the team fan club), and "collectibles and publications" (which is the team's online boutique).

New York Yankees

http://www.yankees.com/

When you log onto this Web site, you are greeted by a handsome and colorful visual of the Yankees' fabled logo. This segues into a beautiful blue-and-white image of the logo in front of a long shot of the House That Ruth Built.

The links here are the usual ones involving player profiles, schedules, ticket information, and minor league reports. But several features make this site unique. One is a replica of the Yankee Stadium scoreboard. If you visit when a game is in progress, the inning-by-inning numbers are posted just as they are at the ballpark! If you hang around the site long enough, it is fun to watch the numbers appear on the scoreboard. (This is one of several Web sites to feature this extra.)

Another is "Yankee Slugger," an interactive Internet game in which "you control the actions of a real, live motion Yankees game. The game is based on actual video footage of a Yankees game." (However, the game takes about 20 minutes to download and requires special connection configurations.)

You would expect a team with such a storied history as the Yankees to spotlight that past. If you click on the "Time Machine" icon, you can download photo, audio, video, and text archives relating to the team's history and records. If the intent here is to make the likes of Mickey Mantle, Don Mattingly, and Babe Ruth come alive, that purpose is fulfilled.

Overall, this is one dazzling and classy Web site.

Oakland Athletics

http://www.oaklandathletics.com/

The initial image on this Web site is one of the most striking on any official major league URL: a baseball, with the A's logo on it, furiously spinning and then literally coming apart at the seams.

This segues to the home page, which also is nicely conceived. A flashing image at its center informs you of the team's upcoming opponents. You can download appropriate information regarding tickets, schedules, game notes, rosters, recaps, links to minor league clubs, and an A's archive. The latter is particularly fact-filled; you will even find an entertaining mini-history of the A's famous White Elephant mascot.

But what makes this site distinctive are its design and images. The color scheme is dominated by stark black, yellow, and green. Throughout are pointillist views of a dugout scene, a ballplayer swinging big lumber, and a team photo dating from when the franchise still was located in Philadelphia. All might have been painted by a modern-era Georges Seurat.

Philadelphia Phillies

http://www.phillies.com/

This Web site covers the basics from Phillies schedules to tickets, rosters to stats, minor league teams to franchise history. The latter section is unusually well done. There is data on nineteenth-century baseball in Philadelphia, early ballyards, and team highlights and lowlights.

If you are the New York Yankees, it is easy to extensively focus on franchise glory. But this is not so simple with a team like the Phillies, which in its less-than-storied past has suffered through decades of second division obscurity. So it is refreshing to see an element of candor in the first line of the "History of the Philadelphia Phillies" introduction, where it is noted that what follows is "both good and bad."

The major visual portion of its home page, which does take a while to download, is a snazzy image: a ballpark photograph, taken from the outfield bleachers.

San Diego Padres

http://www.padres.org/

Whimsy dominates this Web site's home page. At its top is a cartoon drawing of a pudgy padre (played by Eugene Pallette or Charles Durning, perhaps?) swinging a baseball bat. He is Friar John, the Swinging Friar—the team's new mascot and the site's host. For a photograph of the padre as he appears at team games, click on the "Fan Fare" link. Here, you will find useful information on the Jr. Padres (a group fashioned for under-fourteens) and the Compadres Club (a "Frequent Flyer Club" for Padres fans) and a column written by Dr. Baseball (AKA Eddie Epstein, the team's director of baseball operations).

Beyond this, you can download the usual official major league team site features. The "Padres Almanac" (which includes everything from a historical timeline and team records to uniforms through the years) opens with a three-tiered statement by team owners John Moores and Larry Lucchino regarding their vision for the club. Thankfully, it does not read like a press release. The owners declare that they are committed to putting "a team on the field worthy of the fans' support," providing "new entertainment experiences at the ballpark and (marketing) the club to a new, broad region," and being "active participants in the community."

Finally, Friar John offers a "Daily Diary" that features homey comments on the Padres' on-field plight and team-related news and notes.

San Francisco Giants

http://www.sfgiants.com/

The initial image on this Web site is of an enlarging, spinning "Virtual Dugout" newspaper featuring a headline that is heaven for all Giants fans: "GIANTS WIN." Next, you are taken to the site's home page, which is designed as if it were a periodical. There are headlines; on my visit, the top story was "GIANTS REBOUND IN NEW YORK," so on that day, at least, the team indeed was victorious.

In addition, there are scoreboards, survey results (the topic of the hour was how participants feel about realignment), and a children's link (featuring a biography of and interview with the team mascot, Lou Seal, and information on joining the Giants' Kids Club).

Happily, the "Giants' History" link acknowledges not only "40 Years In San Francisco" but "The New York Years" as well. They date from 1883 to 1957; after all, John McGraw and Bill Terry are as much a part of the franchise as Willie McCovey, Juan Marichal, and Bobby Bonds.

If you are unfamiliar with pre-Giants baseball in San Francisco, you will learn that "before the Giants moved out west, Joe DiMaggio, Lefty O'Doul, Joe Cronin, Lefty Gomez, Tony Lazzeri and Fred Crosetti all played ball in The City before going on to the majors." Never heard of Fred Crosetti? Obviously, they mean Frank, the San Francisco native and former New York Yankees shortstop/longtime coach. Do not believe everything you read on the Internet.

Seattle Mariners

http://www.mariners/org/

Guess whose photo dominates this Web site's home page? Lou Piniella? Edgar Martinez? Jay Buhner? A-Rod? How about Rob Ducey? Andy Sheets? Lee Tinsley?

If you say Junior (otherwise known as The Franchise), you win the prize.

Among the site highlights (beyond the usual stats 'n stuff) are a solid array of audio and video clips; a "Fan's A-Z Guide to Kingdome Baseball" (which actually should be A-W, as it begins with "Advanced Tickets" and concludes with "Water Fountains"); and extensive player profiles (along with information on how to contact your favorite Mariner). Also here are all-time Mariners records and a list of everyone who ever played for the team. Stat freaks should savor the "Last Time It Happened" link (found on the "Records & Stats" page), which will tell you the last time a Mariner pitched a no-hitter, hit back-to-back home-runs, hit for the cycle, or stole home.

Another handy feature—one that similar Web sites might consider adding—is a search engine that allows browsers to quickly download data on any Mariners-related subject or individual.

St. Louis Cardinals

http://www.slcardinals.com/

The dominating image on this Web site's home page is a colorful red, orange, and green real-time scoreboard featuring pennants blowing in the wind, loads of bats and balls, and, of course, several renderings of the St. Louis Cardinal. Scroll down, and you will find the latest scores, standings, links to minor league affiliates, and a Busch Stadium seating guide.

You also can "play CyberSkipper and manage the 'Birds. Compete against other fans and win prizes throughout the season." And, if you are 15 years old or under, you can join the IronKids Cardinals Crew and get loads of goodies.

Texas Rangers

http://www.texasrangers.com/

The first image seen on this Web site is a Rangers logo with two ballplayers. One is a faceless hurler firing a ball. The other is Ivan Rodriguez, who is quickly becoming this team's version of Ken Griffey, Jr.

Using the "Dugout" link, you can peruse stats and Ranger biographies and find further links to farm teams from the Oklahoma City 89'ers to the Gulf Coast Rangers. At the "Ballgame" link, there are schedules, ticket information, broadcast listings, and live audio. At the "Ballpark" link, you will find a Ballpark in Arlington seating map and information on the Rangers' Legends of Baseball Museum and Learning Center, located in the stadium. The museum includes a visiting exhibit of baseball memorabilia from the National Baseball Hall of Fame. The learning center features interactive educational exhibits on "history, geography, science, math and communications, all with a baseball spin."

If you click on the "e-mail" icon, you will be taken to a page loaded with related links. From here, you can send "general questions or requests" to the Rangers staff, purchase tickets online, participate in a fan survey, and even e-mail Rangers players.

Toronto Blue Jays

http://bluejays.ca/

This Web site is a nice mixture of the present and past. It features news and updates; a current roster; and television, radio, and promotional schedules. Yet at the top of its home page there is a "flashback," the focus of which is not necessarily the team's glory days and world championships. On the day I visited the site, there was a photo, from 1979, of Alfredo Griffin. That year, he smacked 179 hits, scored 81 runs, made 21 steals, hit .287, and was Rookie of the Year.

Another home page link is to a "History of the Blue Jays Uniform," offering a detailed chronology of the evolution of the team's home and road jerseys.

If a ballclub does not cultivate its younger fans, it will have no paying customers in future decades. One way to accomplish this is by having a lively kid-oriented Web site link—and not one that views children as little more than pint-sized consumers. (See the Kansas City Royals Web site description in this chapter's introduction for a distressing example of this.) On the Blue Jays site, the children's link is both entertaining and educational. There are essay contests; kids' trivia; a player e-mail (allowing youngsters to contact their favorite Blue Jay); a Kidzone Contest Fridge (which includes names of contest winners and their respective entries, along with kids' e-mail); and Baseball Math (which poses mathematics questions relating to the manner in which baseball statistics are derived).

11

Minor and Independent Leagues

In recent years, minor league baseball has become extremely popular across America for many reasons. For one thing, ticket prices are not exorbitant. You still can purchase seats right behind home plate in a minor league ballyard for less than it would cost to see a first-run movie.

Also, the ballplayers are often accessible to the fans. Particularly in the lower minors, the young Barry Bonds and Roger Clemens wannabes actually walk among those who have paid their way into the ballpark. It is generally easy to chat with them and get their autographs.

Best of all, minor league games are great venues for watching young ballplayers as they develop. Many never get beyond playing for Portland in the Eastern League or Kissimmee in the Florida State League or Visalia in the California League. But you never know when you will be seeing a star in the making. Watching Albert Belle play for Canton-Akron way back when he still was known as Joey Belle, Derek Jeter on the day after he was called up to the Albany-Colonie Yankees, and Jeff Bagwell holding down third base for the New Britain Red Sox are among my favorite baseball memories.

Most minor league franchises are affiliated with major league ballclubs and exist primarily to develop young talent. However, the 1990s have seen the emergence of a new type of contemporary minor league ball: independent leagues, which are separate entities in no way affiliated with the majors. These leagues may be far from settled; each year, new franchises emerge with regularity while "old" ones—those that played out the previous season—disband. And personnel connected to affiliated minor league teams have been known to brag that independent league players are washouts, long-faded big leaguers (like Oil Can Boyd) or bushers who sported .220 batting averages and 5.00 ERAs in Class A.

But many in the independent league movement are fiercely proud of their sovereignty in what they believe has become a corporate-dominated industry, rather than a mom and apple pie tradition. Much of this feeling is apparent on independent league Web sites. Typically, near the top of the official Prairie League site are the words "PROFESSIONAL BASEBALL—INDEPENDENT AND INTERNATIONAL." (The league fields teams in Canada as well as the United States.)

Many—but not all—minor and independent league teams have official Web pages. Some are included as links on their major league affiliate's official site. In general, they feature large color illustrations of the team logo and offer basic information that will be useful to fans planning a ballyard trip: schedules, player rosters and stats, ticket information, and, most helpfully, directions to the stadium. The more ambitious and elaborate pages feature reports from most recent games; Fan Forums, soliciting comments on the team and its players; links specially designed to appeal to children; even archives featuring information on franchise and stadium histories, season-by-season records, and lists of all-time teams and managers.

Some fans have established their own unofficial minor league pages that usually feature little more than schedules, ticket information, and special events dates. Cari

Bloodworth, in one example, maintains a site for the Nashville Sounds (*http://www.nashville.net/~sounds/*). Yet on the home page, she emphasizes that this is "not official. The author has attempted to publish public information on the WWW with permission from the Nashville Sounds, but the Sounds organization is in no way responsible for the information published on these pages."

Minor League Baseball (National Association of Professional Baseball Leagues)

http://www.minorleaguebaseball.com/

If you follow minor league baseball in general or the specific teams associated with your favorite big league ballclub, this site is a must-view.

Its most valuable feature is links to complete schedules for all the current season's minor league games, from Triple-A down through the various Rookie leagues. Also useful are links leading to basic information on all minor league teams. If you want to know the name of a team's radio announcer or directions to the home playing field, this is an excellent one-stop source. Another asset is a player database on which you can search for the current statistics of any minor leaguer.

This Web site also features press releases and news items relating to the business of minor league baseball, lists of current Minor League Players of the Week, present league standings, line scores for yesterday's games, scheduled starting pitchers for today's games—even game attendance reports.

FanLink

http://www.fanlink.com/

This thorough, nicely designed Web site describes itself as "the home of Minor League Baseball and Independent

Professional Baseball on the Internet....Unlike the majority of Minor League information on the web, FanLink sites and pages have been individually contracted by minor league teams. These sites are all 'official' in nature."

For openers, click on the "Breaking News" icon, and you then can download news-oriented minor league items from the Associated Press and other sources. Links include "Team Indexes," which will take you to subindexes for minor, independent, winter, and miscellaneous leagues; "League Index," which includes historical and other information on specific leagues; "Infield Chatter," featuring surveys and discussions in which users are polled on such subjects as interleague play and attending major versus minor league games; and "Fanlink Features," made up of minor-league-oriented articles.

Also on "FanLink" are links to current and back issues of *Baseball America*.

RealBaseball

http://www.realbaseball.com/

This Web site, maintained by Steve Lorenze, is "dedicated to the independent minor leagues of professional baseball. On this site you'll find information about all the independent leagues."

Included are links to league standings, team directories, player transactions, and local newspaper articles. These links are fun to peruse, and not just because they allow you insight into life in the independent minors. They also offer data on the present whereabouts of major league blasts-from-the-past. During the 1997 season, for example, Oil Can Boyd, Charlie Kerfeld, Darryl Motley, Bret Barberie, and Wally Ritchie were involved in independent baseball as players or managers.

RealBaseball is the official Web site of the Prairie League champion Minot Mallards.

If you are at all interested in the independent minor leagues, this site is essential viewing.

Prospects, Projects and Suspects

http://www.dmlco.com/pps/

This Web site (which also may be of use to fantasy/roto players) is operator Daniel Levine's "attempt to make sense of young baseball talent."

Levine offers considered opinions on the abilities of minor league prospects included in trades, lists the year's top young talent, and adds midseason updates on established minor leaguers and "new names to keep in mind." He explains, "Most notably, I consistently find that prospect lists ignore the one factor that nobody can outrun: time. What makes Andruw Jones such an amazing prospect? Simple: 4/23/77. That's his date of birth. Making him, for example, 5 years younger than Chipper Jones, who isn't exactly a grizzled veteran. 5 years. Conservatively speaking, that's probably an extra 750 hits over the course of his career. Maybe 100 HR's, 400 RBI's. Significant impact...."

Whether you agree with or fault Levine's logic, his site does make for stimulating reading.

A not-dissimilar Web site is Baseball First...Everything Else Second (*http://members.aol.com/gammonsjr/index.html*). The site is described by its maintainer, Josh Boyd, as "a unique page full of analysis, commentaries and entertaining columns focusing on Major League Baseball Prospects." Although I would not go so far as to call it unique, given the staggering amount of data available on the Web, this page does offer several lists and analysis that are worth considering.

New England Baseball Guide

http://www.klx.com/guide/index.html

If you are traveling through New England and contemplating a visit to a ballgame, this handy Web site will assist you in your plans.

Although the Boston Red Sox are covered here, the focus is on the area's dozen or so minor league teams from the AAA Pawtucket Red Sox to the Northeast (Independent) League Bangor Blue Ox, Massachusetts Mad Dogs, and Waterbury Spirit. In addition to schedules and ballpark information, there is a ballyard picture gallery featuring a nice selection of stills and even a New England map with locations of cities with teams.

Colorado Silver Bullets

http://www.lifetimetv.com/sports/SilverBullets/index.html

The Silver Bullets, which began play in 1994, is "the first and only all-female professional baseball team to be officially recognized by the National Association of Professional Baseball Leagues." This handy Web site is a one-stop reference for Silver Bullets information, schedules, rosters, player profiles, and team history.

Additionally, links are available to "Women In Baseball," which offers a mini-history on the subject, dating from 1866; and "Women's Sports World," a page spotlighting women's sports and fitness. The latter is sponsored by the Women's Sports Foundation, "a national nonprofit, educational member-based organization dedicated to promoting the lifelong participation of all girls and women in sports and fitness."

International League

http://www.ilbaseball.com/

Many minor leagues have their own Web sites. This handsomely designed site is loaded with features involving everything from present-day player exploits and rosters to league history.

A particularly enjoyable link offers a detailed recap of the longest professional game ever played, an International League affair between Rochester and Pawtucket on April 18, 1981. The contest was suspended after 33 innings and lasted almost eight-and-a-half hours. Numerous professional records were set, from time-of-game and innings played to number of at bats, put-outs, and strikeouts (for one and both teams).

Seeing on-field action in this historic contest were some familiar names: Floyd Rayford, John Hale, Chico Walker, Rich Gedman, Bruce Hurst, Bob Ojeda, Marty Barrett, Cal Ripken, Jr., and Wade Boggs.

Carolina League

http://www.cl.org/baseball/

The Carolina League, a Class A-Advanced league, also maintains its own Web site. Its highlight: excerpts from Jim L. Sumner's *Separating the Men from the Boys: The First Half-Century of the Carolina League*, which charts the league's history from its inception during World War II.

Features are devoted to such legendary Carolina Leaguers as Leo "Muscle" Shoals (who hit .337, belted 362 homers, and drove in 1,529 runs in the minors without ever playing a game in The Show) and Woodrow Clark "Woody" Fair (another career minor-leaguer who batted .306, hit 275 homers, and stole 263 bases in 17 seasons). And you will learn that there really was a Carolina League ballplayer called Crash Davis (which was the name of the character played by Kevin Costner in *Bull Durham*).

California League

http://www.californialeague.com/

Another Class A-Advanced Web site worth noting is maintained by the California League. This one features a nice "History" link, which charts the manner in which the league came into being. Every seven days during the baseball season, one California League ballplayer is profiled in a lengthy "Top of the Week" feature. There also are links to previous profiles.

Other minor league (as opposed to minor league team) URLs

A Fan's Guide to the Midwest League: (http://www.wp.com/JOWO/Guide/introduction.html);

The Official Frontier League Homepage: (http://www.bright.net/~paints/frontier.html);

Official Site of the Northeast League: (http://www.northeastleague.com/index.shtml);

Prairie League Professional Baseball (http://www.hotcaesar.com/prairlg/);

Liga Mexicana de Beisbol, or **Mexican League**: (http://www.lmb.com.mx/), which is en espamx/e

The Arizona Fall League

http://www.infoshare.ca/travis/findex.htm

For several years, the Arizona Fall League has showcased cream-of-the-crop prospects specially selected to continue playing past the end of traditional minor league seasons. It is owned by Major League Baseball Properties, the licensing department of Major League Baseball. Talent from Mike Piazza to Michael Jordan have played there; 1960s baseball buffs will relish knowing that, upon the league's formation, Lou Klimchock (.232 batting average in 12 big league seasons, beginning in 1958) was hired as the league's director of marketing.

This no-frills Web site features rosters, schedules, league leaders, and players of the week. There also is a link to the appropriate page on the Major League Baseball site, from which you can download additional league information.

Indianapolis Indians

http://www.indyindians.com/

This Web site, maintained by the Indianapolis Indians, the Cincinnati Reds' AAA affiliate, is above average in that it is a solid blend of yesterday and today.

For example, everything you could ever want to know about the Indians' spanking new ballyard, Victory Field, can be found, from "Animals" and "Autographs" to "Tours" and "Water Fountains."

Yet there is an emphasis on the team's past. Download the "Franchise History" and "Stadium History" links, and you will find nice essays on baseball in Indianapolis, the Indians' franchise, and Bush Stadium, which housed the team from 1931 to 1996. Download the "All-time Managers" link, and you will learn that Napoleon Lajoie, Donie Bush, Al Lopez, Luke Appling, Don Zimmer, and Felipe Alou helmed the team. The "All-time Roster" link was under construction when I visited but, given the site's overall quality, it promises to be a winner.

Omaha Royals

http://www.omaharoyals.com/

This Web site, maintained by the Kansas City Royals' AAA team, merits inclusion for its outstanding selection of historical images. They encompass vintage programs, team and individual photos, and newspaper clippings, with the end result being a collage of baseball history in Omaha.

However, keep in mind that the images take forever to download.

Minor league baseball is noted for its on-field, child-oriented contests held between innings, from dizzy-bat races to scoots around the bases with the team mascot. Although having little to do with the game, they lend an aura of sweetness and fun to the proceedings. This spirit is captured on the Royals' home page, which features a cleverly designed black-and-white photo of smiling ballplayers; in their midst is an animated team mascot playing a piano.

Pawtucket Red Sox

http://pawsox.com/

The Pawsox are the Boston Red Sox's AAA affiliate. Two features help raise this Web site above the norm: an "All-

Time Pawsox Team," as voted by the fans (and which reads like an all-star Red Sox squad of the recent past); and, in particular, a "Top Ten Moments in Pawsox History" link.

At Number Ten is Roger Clemens's 1993 return to McCoy Stadium, the Pawsox home field, when the Red Sox placed him on the disabled list and he was sent down to the minors on rehab. Number One is the longest game in professional baseball history, with the Pawsox hosting Rochester at McCoy in 1981.

There are plenty of surprises in between.

Phoenix Firebirds

http://www.primenet.com/~firebird/

When I logged onto this Web site, maintained by the San Francisco Giants' AAA affiliate, it was sponsoring a "chance to pick the All-Time Phoenix Baseball Team." Selections could be made for each position, with the votes cast via e-mail.

Suggestions were offered in each category. At first base, you could vote for Willie McCovey, Dave Kingman, Mike Laga, Rich Murray, or Rich Lancellotti. At third base, there were Matt Williams, Jim Ray Hart, and Tom Heintzelman. Among the outfielders: Felipe Alou, Bobby Bonds, Jack Clark, Chili Davis, Jesse Reid, Horace Speed, and Bob Taylor. It will be interesting to see who is elected. The winners should be announced by the start of the 1998 season.

This contest, and these names, serve as a jarring reminder that some all-time all-star minor leaguers become major league stars and Hall of Famers. Others, meanwhile, become little more than answers to trivia questions.

Rochester Redwings

http://www.redwingsbaseball.com/

Not only were the Rochester Red Wings, the AAA affiliate of the Baltimore Orioles, the 1997 International League champs, but they maintain a classy, championship-calibre Web site.

Their site is exceptionally well-designed. At the top of the site's home page is an attractive rendering of the team's new ballyard, Frontier Field, with animated fireworks exploding overhead!

However, to obtain the full effect, your browser must be Java-enabled.

Other Official Class AAA URLs

Buffalo Bisons:
http://www.bisons.com/

Charlotte Knights:
http://www.aaaknights.com/

Colorado Springs Sky Sox:
http://www.skysox.com/

Columbus Clippers:
http://www.clippersbaseball.com/

Iowa Cubs:
http://www.iowacubs.com/

New Orleans Zephyrs:
http://www.zephrysbaseball.com/

Norfolk Tides:
http://www.pilotonline.com/ tides/index.shtml

Ottawa Lynx:
http://www.ottawalynx.com/

Richmond Braves:
http://www.rbraves.com/index.asp

Scranton/Wilkes Barre Red Barons:
http://www.redbarons.com/

Syracuse Skychiefs:
http://SkyChiefs.com/skychiefs/

Toledo Mud Hens:
http://www.mudhens.com/

Arkansas Travelers

http://www.travs.com/

The Travelers are the AA affiliate of the St. Louis Cardinals. Their Web site earns inclusion here for three noteworthy features:

- The gritty black-and-white action photo that dominates the home page
- The "Scrapbook" link, which offers (for the uninitiated) an explanation of the meaning of "AA," along with a team history illustrated with vintage photos
- The description of baseball as the "greatest game on dirt"

Birmingham Barons

http://www.quicklink.net/barons/

Two eye-opening features are on this Web site, maintained by the Chicago White Sox's AA affiliate.

The first is an informative "History" link that traces the team's past to 1885.

The second is a link that will take you to everything you ever could want to know—baseball-wise, that is—about the Baron's most famous contemporary ballplayer: Michael Jordan, who chased down flies for the team during the 1994 season. For the record, in his first at-bat for the Barons, Air Jordan skied out against John Courtright. He collected his initial base hit, in his eighth at bat, against Joe Ganote. It was a single. His first home run came in his 345th at bat, against Kevin Rychel. His final statistics: 127 games played; .202 batting average; three homers; 51 RBI; 30 stolen bases.

Jacksonville Suns

http://www.jaxsuns.com/

The Web site maintained by the Suns, the AA Detroit Tigers' affiliate, includes a nice team history along with reminiscences of former players who are current major leaguers.

While exploring this site, you will learn that the Suns (which have been in existence since 1904) count among their ex-managers King Kelly, Rube Marquard, Mickey Owen, Sibby Sisti, Dixie Howell, Harry Walker, Solly Hemus, Bill Virdon, Clyde McCullough, Billy Gardner, Gene Lamont, and Jack Robinson (not *the* Jackie Robinson, but a chap with the same name who shared managerial duties during the 1904 season with Kelly and Robert Black).

Memphis Chicks

http://www.socomm.net/chicks/

This Web site, maintained by the Seattle Mariners' AA affiliate, is unusual in that it stresses baseball lore above all else.

Upon logging on, you are immediately informed that baseball is "A Memphis Tradition." The first organized games in the city date from 1877; the Chicks have been in existence since 1901; and Pete Gray, Luis Aparicio, Luke Appling, and Bo Jackson are among those who wore Chicks uniforms.

Oh, yes, information on the current team can be downloaded via the various home page links.

Shreveport Captains

http://www.shreveportcaptains.com/

From this Web site's smartly designed home page, you can link to a nicely done essay, penned by Scott Ferrell, on 100 years of baseball in Shreveport.

Then there is the all-time roster, which begins with Harry Ables ('04), Ivan Abromowitz ('56), and William Abstein ('05-'06) and ends with Albert C. Youngblood ('23), Edwin L. Youngblood ('47) and Faustino Zabala ('68-'70). In between are Dusty Baker, Rod Beck, Royce Clayton, and plenty more.

The Captains are the AA affiliate of the San Francisco Giants.

Other Official Class AA URLs

Akron Aeros:
http://www.neo.lrun.com/AkronAeros/

Binghamton Mets:
http://www.spectra.net:80/mall/bmets/

Bowie Baysox:
http://www.hgnet.com/baysox/baysox.htm

El Paso Diablos:
http://www.diablos.com/

Huntsville Stars:
http://www.huntsvillestars.com/

Knoxville Smokies:
http://www.1stresource.com/~ksmokies/

Midland Angels:
http://www.midlandangels.org/

Mobile BayBears:
http://www.mobilebaybears.com/

New Britain Rock Cats:
http://gs1.com/rock/cats.html

New Haven Ravens:
http://www.ravens.com/

Norwich Navigators:
http://www.gators.com/

Portland Seadogs:
http://www.ime.net/seadogs/

Reading Phillies:
http://www.readingphillies.com/

Trenton Thunder:
http://www.trentonthunder.com/

Wichita Wranglers:
http://www.wichitawranglers.com/wwhome.html

Lake Elsinore Storm

http://www.pe.net/storm/

Because the team, an A-Advanced affiliate of the Anaheim Angels, has only been in existence for a few years, there is no extensive team history. However, unlike many official team sites that ignore their pasts, this page features extensive essays on the team's previous seasons along with audio and video archives.

Given the team's location, you should not be surprised to discover that its mascot is named Hamlet. He has his own special child-oriented link on the site.

Finally, the visual that dominates the home page—a baseball collage featuring bat, glove, balls, tickets, photos, and Hamlet—is unusually well-designed.

Lynchburg Hillcats

http://www.cl.org/baseball/lynchburg/

The Hillcats are the A-Advanced affiliate of the Pittsburgh Pirates. Their Web site merits inclusion for its list of former Lynchburg players, managers, and coaches, from 1940 to the present, who made the majors. Some (Frank Carpin, Buck Guth, Bob Habenicht, Danny Lazar, Emmett Mueller, Mike Poepping, and the immortal Skeeter Scalzi) are obscure. Others (Don Buford, Dwight Gooden, Wes Ferrell, Johnny Klippstein, Whitey Kurowski, Roger

McDowell, Kevin Mitchell, Tin Naehring, Jeff Reardon, Darryl Strawberry, and the immortal Wayne Terwilliger) are not.

As you can tell from this list, the Hillcats once were a New York Mets affiliate.

In addition, there are essays titled "The 1894 Lynchburg Hill Climbers," "The 1895 Lynchburg Tobacconists," "The Bottom Line for the 1896 Tobacconists," and "The 1947 Lynchburg Cardinals." All are authored by Vince Sawyer.

Other Official Class A-Advanced URLs

Bakersfield Blaze:
http://bizweb.lightspeed.net/~blaze/

Durham Bulls:
http://www.dbulls.com/

Fort Myers Miracle:
http://miraclebaseball.com/

High Desert Mavericks:
http://hdmavs.com/

Kinston Indians:
http://www.cl.org/baseball/kinston/

Lakeland Tigers:
http://www.lakeland-tigers.com/

Lancaster JetHawks:
http://www.jethawks.com/

Modesto A's:
http://www.modestoathletics.com/

Prince William Cannons:
http://www.pwcannons.com/

Salem Avalanche:
http://www.cl.org/baseball/salem/salem.html

San Bernadino Stampede:
http://stampedebaseball.com/

San Jose Giants:
http://sjgiants.com/

Stockton Ports:
http://www.stocktonports.com/

Vero Beach Dodgers:
http://www.vero.com/ dodgers/

Wilmington Blue Rocks:
http://www.bluerocks.com/

Winston-Salem Warthogs:
http://www.warthogs.com/

Official Class A URLs

Augusta Greenjackets:
http://www.shopaugusta.com/jackets

Beloit Snappers:
http://www.snappersbaseball.com

Cedar Rapids Colonels:
http://www.kernels.com/

Charleston RiverDogs:
http://www.awod.com/riverdogs/

Clinton LumberKings:
http://www.clinton.net/~lkings/

Fort Wayne Wizards:
http://www.wizardsbaseball.com/

Greensboro Bats: http:
//www.spyder.net/bats/

Hickory Crawdads:
http://www.unifour.com/crawdads/

Lansing Lugnuts:
http://www.lansinglugnuts.com/

Peoria Chiefs:
http://www.chiefsnet.com/

Piedmont Boll Weevils:
http://www.co.rowan.nc.us/boll/

South Bend Silver Hawks:
http://www.silverhawks.com/

West Michigan Whitecaps:
http://www.whitecaps-baseball.com/

Pittsfield Mets

http://www.berkshire.net/~pittmets/

This Web site, maintained by the New York Mets' A short-season affiliate, is one of the rare lower minor league URLs that extensively spotlights team history. The Mets play their home games in picturesque Wahconah Park, built in 1919. It is noted that "odd outfield dimensions, plastic owls that hang from the rafters to scare away pigeons and the proximity of your seat to the action grab your attention as you settle into your seat.... Wahconah Park was built long before the advent of night baseball, thus the ballpark faces west, not east, as virtually all baseball parks do. When the sun sets, it glows directly over the centerfield fence, shining straight into the batter's, catcher's and umpire's eyes, thus putting a halt to the action. Time is called and the field is cleared while mother nature takes its course."

However, the city of Pittsfield may be building a new stadium. Although this will "allow fans and players the comforts of a new facility, Wahconah Park will always hold special meaning to those who played there."

On the site, you will learn that the two earliest Pittsfield teams were the Hillies (Eastern League) and Electrics (Can-Am League), and that former Pittsfield players include Edgardo Alfonzo, Greg Maddux, Mark

Grace, Rafael Palmeiro, George "Boomer" Scott, Pete Gray—and Lou Gehrig!

Other Official Class A Short-Season URLs

Erie Seawolves:
http://www.seawolves.com/

Eugene Emeralds:
http://www.go-ems.com/

Hudson Valley Renegades:
http://www2.hvrenegades.com/renegades.html

Lowell Spinners:
http://www.lowellspinners.com/

New Jersey Cardinals:
http://www.njcards.com/

Portland Rockies:
http://www.transport.com/~rockies/prhome.htm

Southern Oregon Timberjacks:
http://www.mind.net/tjacks/

St. Catharines Stompers:
http://vaxxine.com/stompers/

Vermont Expos:
http://www.vermontexpos.com/

Official Rookie-Advanced URLs

Bluefield Orioles:
http://ci.bluefield.wv.us/babybrd1.html

Great Falls Dodgers:
http://www.sportsmt.com/dodgers/

Princeton Devil Rays:
http://www.localweb.com/dcweb/PDR/Raywatch.html

St. Paul Saints

http://www.spsaints.com/

This outstanding Web site, maintained by the St. Paul Saints, presently in the independent Northern League, is a model for official minor league Web pages. It is colorful and loaded with links, and effectively combines present and past.

In addition to the usual press releases, schedules, ticket information, and rah rah boosterism, there is a lengthy and fact-filled history. It opens with a section on "Professional Baseball in St. Paul, 1885-1960." Then there is a spotlight on "Former St. Paul Saints," including Charles Comiskey, Miller Huggins, Bill McKechnie, Walter Alston, Lefty Grove, Duke Snider, Roy Campanella, Leo Durocher, and basketball great Bill Sharman (who played in the minors during the 1950s).

One of the site's treats: a photo of Saints manager Alston shaking the hand of Roy Campanella after the Brooklyn Dodgers catcher-to-be smacked a dinger during the 1948 season.

Another Northern League site worth citing, because of its acknowledgment of local history, is the one maintained by the Duluth-Superior Dukes (*http://www.dsdukes.com/*).

Other Official Independent League URLs

Big South League

Greenville Bluesmen:

http://www.tecinfo.com/~bluesmen/

Frontier League

Canton Crocodiles:

http://web.tusco.net/crocodiles/index.htm

Chillicothe Paints:

http://www.bright.net/~paints/

Evansville Otters:
http://otters.evansville.net/

Johnstown Steal:
http://www.surfshop.net/users/steal/Steal.htm

Springfield Capitals:
http://www.springfield-il.com/capitals

Heartland League

Altoona Railkings:
http://www.railkings.com/

Northeast League

Albany-Colonie Diamond Dogs:
httl://www.diamonddogs.com/

Allentown Ambassadors:
http://www.ambassadorbaseball.com/

Bangor Blue Ox:
http://www.bangorblueox.com/

Catskill Cougars:
http://members.aol.com/catcoug/index.htm

Elmira Pioneers:
http://www.elmirapioneers.com/

Massachusetts Mad Dogs:
http://www.maddogs.com/

Northern League

Fargo-Moorhead RedHawks:
http://www.fmredhawks.com/

Madison Black Wolf:
http://www.madwolf.com/

Sioux City Explorers:

http://www.siouxlan.com/explorers/

Sioux Falls Canaries:

http://www.iw.net/canaries/index.htm

Thunder Bay Whiskey Jacks:

http://www.jacks.ca/

Winnipeg Goldeyes:

hppt://www.xpressnet.com/goldeyes/

Prairie League

Grand Forks Varmints:

http://www.fargoweb.com/varmints/

Minot Mallards:

http://www.realbaseball.com/

Regina Cyclones:

http://www.hotcaesar.com/cyclones/

Southern Minny Stars:

http://fox.co.net/stars/

Texas-Louisiana League

Rio Grande Valley White Wings:

http://www.harlingen.com/baseball.html

Western League

Bend Bandits:

http://www.empnet.com/BendBandits/

Chico Heat:

http://www.chicoheat.com/

Grays Harbor Gulls:

http://gulls.techline.com/

Mission Viejo Vigilantes:

http://www.vigilantes.com

Salinas Peppers:

http://salinaspeppers.com/

Tri-City Posse:

http://www.cbvcp.com/posse/

12 Ballyards

Part of the delight of attending the games of many major and minor league teams is the chance to visit the ballpark. At the major league level, the most favored yards may be ancient, nostalgic monuments (such as Wrigley Field or Fenway Park), or new and state-of-the-art (the list begins with Jacobs Field and Camden Yards). A trip to such a ballyard becomes an event in and of itself; to some, the actual ballgame becomes secondary to enjoying a meal in a posh restaurant with a window on the ballfield, flaunting one's status in a luxury box, or just soaking up the atmosphere.

Newer ballparks are controversial in that they cost money to build—lots and lots of money. Where do those dollars come from? The bank accounts of multimillionaire team owners? Or the pockets of working- and middle-class taxpayers, who then will be unable to afford tickets to even the cheapest seats? In this regard, some ballpark-related sites are political/activist in nature in that they put forth agendas. They may be "dedicated to supporting Claude Brochu's plans for a new stadium in downtown Montreal"

(Bob's Montreal Expos Page at *http://qlink.queensu.ca/~6rhp/expos.htm*), or establishing "the case for building a new Cincinnati Reds ballpark" (Broadway Commons at *http://www.broadwaycommons.com*). After construction is approved (as is the case with the new ballyards in Seattle and Milwaukee), various Web sites joyously begin charting construction in countdown-to-completion style.

Meanwhile, other sites are dedicated to maintaining the status quo. The Fans For Yankee Stadium (*http//spectra.net/~ralphw/yankees.htm*), for one, is "an effort by the fans of the NY Yankees to keep this historic landmark and monument to the game of baseball from disappearing forever."

Beyond the build-me-a-new-ballpark-or-else controversies, other ballyard Web sites offer information about and photos of major and minor league playing fields or wax nostalgic about ballyards of the past. Some even are sponsored by the parks themselves. Typical is 3Com Park (*http://www.3com.com/3compark/index.html*). Although handsomely produced, its Web page is little more than an online press release.

The following is a sampling of the most solid and unusual ballyard Web sites. More information can be found at the various super-Web sites, or on those maintained by individual teams.

Ballparks by Munsey and Suppes

http://www.ballparks.com/

This exceptionally entertaining, fact-filled Web site, maintained by Paul Munsey and Cory Suppes, allows you to tour American and National League ballyards of the present and past. You even can learn about parks of the future—those that have been proposed but at the present remain uncompleted.

For example, clicking on the brown "AL" icon will bring up small images of old AL ballparks. A further click on the specific stadium image will lead you to several photos and data on anything you could ever possibly want to know about that park.

Without a doubt, Ballparks by Munsey and Suppes is the mother of all ballyard Web sites.

Stadiums and Arenas

http://www.wwwcd.com/stadiums.html

This handy Web site, sponsored by the *World-Wide Collectors Digest*, features listings for stadiums and arenas throughout the United States and Canada.

Easy-to-use links will take you to basic information regarding each stadium (address, stadium and ticket office phone numbers, seating capacity, year opened, type of surface, directions to the stadium, a seating chart). You also will find a schedule for the team or teams that use the facility and an exterior photo. In addition to ballyards from Anaheim Stadium to Toronto's Skydome, NBA, NHL, NFL, and college and university home fields or courts are also included along with racetracks and several "world" and "other" stadiums.

Missing, from a baseball point-of-view, are listings of the minor league parks.

A related site is Major League Baseball Stadiums (*http://www.geocities.com/Colosseum/5696/stadiums.html*). Although the information at this site can be gleaned elsewhere, it is worth a visit for the visual on its home page: a map of the United States and Southern Canada featuring the location of each major league ballyard.

The Ballpark Time Machine

http://pubweb.acns.nwu.edu/~dps004/Index.html

The tone of this friendly Web site is set at the top of its home page. There, you will find an image of Kevin Costner in *Field of Dreams*. Your host, Dan Skinner, welcomes you, and his effort works as a nice complement to the Munsey and Suppes site.

The emphasis here is on ballyards that no longer exist and thus qualify as fields of dreams: Baker Bowl (Philadelphia), the Polo Grounds (New York), Braves Field (Boston), Crosley Field (Cincinnati), Sportsman's Park (St. Louis), Shibe Park (Philadelphia), Ebbets Field (Brooklyn), Forbes Field (Pittsburgh), Griffith Stadium (Washington), and the old Comiskey Park (Chicago).

Of course, if the various lords of baseball had their way, the likes of Yankee Stadium and Fenway Park soon would be entitled to inclusion here.

Left and Center Field of Dreams

http://www.mebbs.com/dreams/

For the filming of *Field of Dreams*, a ballyard was in fact constructed in a cornfield near Dyersville, Iowa. It has become quite a tourist attraction, and this Web site offers information on everything from the Field of Dreams Festival held at the site each August to maps and directions to Dyersville to the Ghost Players (locals who were cast in the movie as extras and who appear at the Field and make personal appearances).

Brian Merzbach's Baseball Parks

http://www1.mhv.net/~merzbach/

Brian Merzbach attends lots of ballgames. In lots of ballyards. On his visits, he snaps away with his camera, and his photos can be found on this Web site.

Minor and major league parks are included, from Camden Yards, Comiskey Park, and County Stadium through War Memorial Stadium (Greensboro, North Carolina), Welland Sports Stadium (Welland, Ontario), and Yale Field (New Haven, Connecticut). In some cases, Merzbach offers reviews of the ballyards and rates them by appearance, atmosphere, and concessions.

Dustin's Minor League Ballparks

http://home.supernova.net/~dustin/

This solid Web site features a listing of minor league ballyards across America from those in the Appalachian League all the way to the Texas and Pacific Coast Leagues. The descriptions of individual parks range from bare basics to vivid and folksy.

Not every ballpark is cited. If you want to write about one not mentioned or add your opinion of one already on the site, click on the "Add a Ballpark" icon.

Baseball Across America

http://www.pc-professor.com/ballparks/marsh/

Back in 1995 Kevin Marsh took a baseball fan's fantasy vacation. During the course of ten weeks, he traveled across America and visited more than 60 different ballyards in such diverse locales as Lake Elsinor, California; Duluth, Minnesota; Binghamton, New York; and Zebulon, North Carolina.

The photos Marsh snapped along the way form the heart of his site. Click on the city, and you will download large, crisp stills of its yard, taken during game-time.

A similar Web site is Minor League Ballpark Photos (*http://www.pc-professor.com/ballparks/jarvis*), maintained by Gary Jarvis.

Ebbets Field Ventures, LLC

http://www.ebbetsfield.com/index.html

This stunningly designed Web site offers an idea that baseball nostalgia enthusiasts are sure to embrace: the rebuilding of baseball history through the construction of a replica of Ebbets Field in an Eastern United States city. The park then would be the home field of a minor league team.

In addition to presenting and explaining this proposal, the site includes links to a photo gallery, a trivia game, a biographical sketch of Charlie Ebbets (the man for whom the ballpark was named), and other goodies.

This site serves as a mini-Ebbets Field museum. Its pages do take a while to download, but they are well worth the wait.

Chucky in Fenway

http://www.5-star-web.com/fenway/

Chucky (AKA Charles Freedman) adores Fenway Park. In fact, to him, it is not just "the greatest baseball stadium in the world" but "the greatest place on earth."

On his Web site, Chucky offers a guided tour of the ballyard in pictures and words. He looks as if he has died and gone to heaven as he poses in the dugout and right by Pesky's Pole.

And he is even shown kissing the Green Monster!

13

Amateur Baseball: Youth/Instruction

On the Internet, you can view hundreds of Web sites relating to baseball as it is played in Little League and softball leagues, by high school and college teams, and in men's and women's adult leagues.

In the area of youth-oriented baseball, many Web pages are sponsored by a variety of organizations—from the Antelope Valley/California District 51 Little League to Bowling Green Youth Baseball. Others are maintained by individual teams, from the Austin Diamondbacks to the West Urban Cardinals and Wheaton Blue Warriors. These pages generally list rosters and schedules and feature stats, won-lost records, team pictures, and lists of team sponsors. The more ambitious pages offer mission statements and lists of parental responsibilities. All are united in that they consistently radiate community pride.

Because these sites are primarily local in appeal, they do not merit inclusion here. After all, only those involved with the Rutherford (New Jersey) Little League would want to note the date of its first annual golf outing and that it is "always in need of donations to keep its program running." Only those interested in the Fremont (California) Babe Ruth Bambinos would care to know that in "the T-ball division, the combined teams of Giants and Tigers destroyed the competition to win the moving up tournament." It only would matter to those who follow the Kenosha (Wisconsin) Kroakers that the team ended its season "with a real splash. It rained after the 5th inning Sunday (8/10) and it rained Monday (8/11) and it rained Tuesday (8/12) for a while too. Then Tuesday evening we finished Sunday's game against the Rochester (Minnesota) Honkers..."

Unfortunately, while evaluating amateur baseball sites, I came upon an occasional commercially oriented page featuring a relentless hard sell. Here, young ballplayers are viewed primarily as consumers with money to spare. A typical one is The Baseball Information Network (*http://www.baseballinfo.com/*), a database that lists the names of more than 15,000 baseball coaches, organization directors, and tournament hosts, and almost 2,500 tournaments geared to players between the ages of 5 and 18. These listings (as well as updates) are available for a fee. I guess that's fair enough if you really need this information.

However, if you click on the links listed under "Free Areas," you are taken not only to information but also to sales pitches for the company's services. High school ballplayers are advised that they can "be among the first 1,000 people to sign up (for a player profile database) and take advantage of our Grand Opening Special price of $15.00."

My inclination is that the $15.00 would be better employed as part of the cost of a new bat or glove.

Little League Baseball

http://www.littleleague.org/

This Web site is the "official home of Little League Baseball, the largest organized youth sports program in the world." It includes news from Little League headquarters in Williamsport, Pennsylvania; information for league administrators and volunteers; features on present and former Little Leaguers; "Parents Pages"; a "Just 4 Kids" page; summer camp information; reports on the Little League Baseball World Series; even a "Little League Reference Room" offering links to various aspects of Little League history.

If you are in any way active in Little League, as a parent, player, coach, or umpire, you will want to bookmark this site.

PONY Baseball/Softball

http://www.pony.org/

PONY Baseball/Softball is "an international youth baseball and girls softball program that offers an opportunity for local community league competition and international tournament play for youth ages 5-18. Since its inception in 1951, more than six million children have participated in the PONY program."

On this Web site, you can download everything from the history of PONY baseball to descriptions of PONY publications, game rules, and rule changes to information on PONY's umpire registration program.

Links also are provided to affiliated league Web sites. If you are at all knowledgeable about silent movie Westerns, you will enjoy the humor behind the name of one league: William S. Hart PONY Baseball/Softball.

Babe Ruth League

http://www.baberuthleague.org/

This Web site is maintained by the Babe Ruth League, which originated in a Trenton, New Jersey suburb "over 40 years ago." Today, more than 6,300 individual leagues exist (which are "independent within the guidelines provided by [the] Babe Ruth League International Board"), with 43,000 teams, and 868,000 players between the ages of 5 and 18.

On the site, you will find everything from a league history to lists of Babe Ruth graduates who made the majors.

And, as one might expect, you will find Sultan of Swat photos and illustrations throughout the site.

American Legion Baseball

http://iquest.net/~jquinlan/home.htm

American Legion Baseball is described on this fact-filled Web page as "the oldest and largest, nationwide, baseball program in America." Over the years, more than eight million teenagers have played legion ball.

The site features a timeline spotlighting the history of American Legion Baseball (which began in 1925 in South Dakota); lists of legion ballplayers in the Hall of Fame and "Graduates of the Year," current major leaguers honored for their "character, leadership, playing abilities and community service"; and information on how to form legion teams.

Other Little League, PONY League, Babe Ruth League, and American Legion Baseball-related sites are maintained by the American Amateur Baseball Congress (*http://www.voyager.net/aabc/*), which describes itself as "the largest amateur baseball organization in the United States for players above junior baseball age and the only amateur baseball program which provides progressive and continued organized competition—sub teens through adults"; and Dixie Youth Baseball (*http://www.dixie.org/*), formerly Little Boys Baseball, which is "primarily a youth baseball program of youth 12 years of age, and under, playing on a scaled-down diamond to meet the physical development of the growing child."

Junior League Baseball Magazine

http://www.jlbmag.com/

This solid Web site is a condensed version of *Junior League Baseball*, which describes itself as "America's youth baseball magazine." The links essentially are magazine features:

"When I Was a Kid" (which includes interviews with major leaguers who recall their childhood baseball experiences); "Skills Clinic" (involving game strategy); and "In the Stands" (focusing on the manner in which adults communicate with children). Also provided are tournament listings, baseball camps and schools, youth baseball organizations, and a "Fun and Games" page.

Sports Illustrated for Kids

http://www.pathfinder.com/

This is the perfect Web site for baseball-loving youngsters to visit between Little League games. They will have fun as well as bone up on their baseball history.

The site's graphics alone should entrance children. The spotlight may be on all sports, but sufficient baseball-related material is available. On one visit to the site, I found a portrait of Mark McGwire, a multifaceted look at Jackie Robinson, previews and predictions, a games page, and information on the magazine's free Bat-O-Matic Fantasy Baseball League. On another visit, I found quotes from Ken Griffey, Jr., and other black athletes on their experiences with racial discrimination. A third time, there was a "Pro & Con" kids' debate on the question "Should an athlete serve a suspension right away?"

This site is crammed with humorous illustrations that will appeal to its intended audience. And much of the material will not only entertain children but also massage their minds.

Baseball Parent Newsletter

http://members.aol.com/baseparent/index.html

This is the online edition of the Knoxville, Tennessee–based *Baseball Parent Newsletter*, which is "written exclusively for the parents and coaches of youth baseball players." The magazine is published six times a year and offers strategy, mechanics, confidence-building tips, and information on instructional camps, tournaments, and the youth World Series.

The highlights of this Web site: links to other youth-oriented URLs and helpful articles from current and recent issues of the magazine, including "Is Your Child's Baseball Field Safe?"; "Profile: T-Ball USA Association, Inc."; "Midseason Tips on How to Fine-Tune Your Child's Game"; and "Off-Season Training at Two Top High Schools."

John's Little League Baseball Home Page

http://www2.netdoor.com/~jtravis/

"Ever wondered if your child's Little League coach has even *seen* a baseball game, let alone *played* the game? Like to browse the Little League Baseball basics your child should be taught? Are you the 'Manager' or 'Coach to be' and want to brush up on the techniques of fundamental Little League Baseball?"

These questions are asked by John, who maintains this extremely helpful site and writes that he has spent "years... parenting, coaching and umpiring in Little League Baseball." "My goal," he notes, "is to share with you what I've learned and experienced in years of Little League Baseball."

And so he does, offering his personal views on surviving tryouts, impressing managers and coaches, and preparing practice drills. The text is filled with anecdotes and "war stories."

Tips for Little League Parents

http://www.halcyon.com/kat/partips.htm

Keith Taylor, who maintains this site, describes his son's Little League initiation: "I had heard the horror stories about the overbearing Little League parents and coaches, but last season was my first chance to see for myself. And I saw a lot... some bad, but mostly good. But what I did learn was important: how to make Little League more enjoyable, and a greater learning experience, for the kids.

And, after all, no matter how much we enjoy it, too, Little League is for the kids."

Amen to that!

What follows are Taylor's tips on parental involvement in Little League, different coaching philosophies, and plenty of perceptive commentary regarding the facts that Little Leaguers are children and Little League should be a positive, pressure-free experience.

Mudball!

http://www.halcyon.com/kat/mudball.htm

Mudball!, a link on the Tips for Little League Parents site, is so special that it deserves its own entry.

The page is maintained by Little Leaguer Austin "Mudball" Taylor. A highlight: a photo of "Mudball" in uniform, surrounded by those of Ty Cobb and Joe DiMaggio.

You never know. Perhaps in a dozen or so years, Mudball will be a hot prospect tossing them around in spring training with an aging Alex Rodriguez, a graying Ken Griffey, Jr., or a long-in-the-tooth Frank Thomas.

Aaron "Glue Glove" Lyon

http://www.mlsd.com/aaron/

Perhaps Austin "Mudball" Taylor should hook up with Aaron "Glue Glove" Lyon, who also has his own Web page. It features a photo of a confident "Glue Glove" choking up on his bat; he is garbed in a Pirates uniform, despite the fact that his most recent team is listed as the Cardinals! Nearby is an illustration of Elmer's Glue-All dripping into a glove.

"Glue Glove" reports that he is so nicknamed because "I always catch the ball at first base." And his stats—a .392 batting average and .431 slugging percentage during his most recent season—are good in any league.

National High School Baseball Coaches Association

http://baseballcoaches.org/

This organization was founded in 1991 "to provide services and recognition for baseball coaches and to help promote and represent high school baseball." On this Web site, you will find basic information about the Association and its annual convention, lists of tournaments and events, *Baseball America* top-25 high school rankings, and selections from "Extra Innings," the organization's newsletter.

Amateur Baseball Umpires

http://www.superaje.com/~brenmcla/

At the core of this Web site is the "personal home page" of Brent McLaren, who notes that it "will maintain the format of a growing collection of essays or electronic newsletter on umpiring....It is dedicated to ultimately provide an information base for anyone who strives to improve baseball officiating. As such this site is permanently under construction."

McLaren has compiled an outstanding array of articles involving umpires' mechanics, style, equipment, clinics, and the like. He also solicits "quality contributions."

Competitive Baseball Web

http://cbweb.com/spo/home.html

One of this Web site's home page links is a solicitation to join the title organization, which claims—incorrectly, I might add—to be the "Internet's Largest Baseball Site." It is unclear exactly what this organization is and who sponsors it.

On the upside, plenty of baseball-oriented information is available that youth league coaches may find helpful. Coaches can post such notices as "Beaver Valley Baseball Looking for Spring Scrimmages" and "Coaches Needed for National Tournament." You will find articles with titles such as "Changeup Most Underrated Pitch," "Dealing

With Pressure From Parents," and "Is There Really Ever a Must-Win Situation?" The "Pitchers Bible" link features a step-by-step list of hurler dos and don'ts. The "Coaches References" link will take you to a bibliography of training-related books.

Competitive Youth Baseball

http://members.aol.com/JonHoelter/Youthbaseball.html

This Web site, maintained by Jon Hoelter, exists "for the promotion of youth baseball." It includes hitting and pitching tips, contributions from parents and coaches, and such oddities as "20 Reasons to Coach Youth Baseball" and a glossary of Australian baseball terms.

WebBall

http://www.textras.bc.ca/webball/

This Web site, maintained by Richard Todd (neither the ex-NFL quarterback nor the British movie actor), is fashioned for "amateur baseball coaches and players." It features detailed instructional information on various aspects of the game from pitching to conditioning. A search engine allows you to look up specific data.

However, the highlight is an interactive strategy clinic that is both informative and fun to use. The site features more than 100 potential offensive and defensive game situations.

How to Coach Tee Ball Without Going INSANE

http://www.geocities.com/Colosseum/Loge/3775/

This thoughtful and thorough Web site, maintained by Rob Doss, actually is a who/what/when/where/why of Tee Ball. Not only are pages devoted to coaching the activity and dealing with players—with such self-explanatory headings as "Left-Handed Or Right-Handed?"; "How Responsive Are They At This Age?; "The Value Of A

Spirited Player"; and "Can Girls Play This Game?"—but you also will find a mini-Tee Ball history and a detailed explanation of "why this game can be so complicated."

If you coach Tee Ball, or if your child plays Tee Ball, this Web site is a must-see.

The Art of Catching

http://www.emporia.edu/N/www/athle/esusport/baseball/project.htm

This solid Web site is maintained by Jason Vittone, head baseball coach at Brescia College in Owensboro, Kentucky. Rather than simply list his team's players and stats, he offers online instruction on the fine art of catching.

In the "Introduction" link, Vittone observes that a catcher "needs to be the team leader. The role of a catcher is to be able to anticipate all situations before they occur and react appropriately. Catching is a very cerebral position. All beginning catchers should be made aware of the responsibilities that go along with the position.... The objective of this site is to take a beginning or experienced catcher through all the steps necessary in becoming a proficient, well rounded catcher."

Further page links include "Setting Up," "Throwing," "Drills," "Stance," "Bunts," "Sign Giving," "Framing," "Blocking," "Plays at Home," and "Bullpens." The information on each is intelligently written and thorough.

Hitting for Excellence

http://www.hitting.com/

Dave Hudgens is a professional coach, scout, and hitting instructor whose most recent job is Assistant Director of Player Development for the Oakland Athletics. He maintains this Web site in which he offers information on "improving your hitting and increasing your chances for becoming a 'Money Player.'" Such athletes, Hudgens adds, "are hitters who are either on scholarship or play for a professional team....

"The shame of it all is that most (of the players Hudgens evaluates) could be 'Money Players' if they had just been taught the proper mechanics. Just 2 practice hours a week of the PROPER TECHNIQUES can dramatically change a hitter's chances of getting to the big leagues. But the same 2 hours of practicing the WRONG TECHNIQUES can stop a potential hitting career—cold!"

Hudgens goes on to "expose" what he believes is bad advice on the art of hitting. He includes this on links titled "Discover Your Hitting Expertise With This Simple Test"; "Photo Analysis—Your Key To Developing Your Hitting Talent"; "The 'WORST Hitting Advice' I've Ever Heard—& How It Could Be DESTROYING Your Hitting Career"; "'Watching These Players' Could Dramatically Improve Your Hitting"; "The Truth of Why 'An Aluminum Bat' Could Destroy Your Hitting Career"; and "Why Coaches Don't Teach The Right Hitting Techniques." Most intriguingly, there is a link to "The Truth About 'Michael Jordan's Baseball Career' & Why You Have A Better Chance To Make It To The Major Leagues."

Although Hudgens does come on like gangbusters, and other professional instructors might disagree with his techniques—and all this is a teaser to order his training materials—his page still makes for provocative reading.

Dick Mills' All About Pitching

http://www.pitching.com/

In 1970, Dick Mills pitched in two games for the Boston Red Sox—which makes him every bit as much an ex-major leaguer as Yaz, Pudge, Tony C., or Teddy Ballgame. He is the host of this Web site, which is "designed to give parents, coaches and players instant access to proven information that will help each player become a better, more confident, stronger and healthier pitcher by following a proven big league plan."

Mills's teaching certainly has impacted on his son, Ryan, who was selected in the 1995 amateur draft by the New York Yankees and offered a $535,000 signing bonus. Ryan instead accepted a baseball scholarship to Arizona State. His father adds that, "in the May 11, 1997 issue of *Baseball America* magazine Ryan is projected by pro scouts to be the #2 college pick in the 1998 amateur draft."

Mills's pages are headlined "A Simple Yet Winning Pitching Philosophy," "The Pitchers Freeze-Frame-Photo-Clinic," and "Stop Teaching Pitchers To Push-Off The Rubber... If You Want Them To Throw Harder." There also is a discussion group, which is "open to coaches, dads and players with questions, comments and advice about what it takes to become a top pitcher."

My one quibble with this site: At a time when young ballplayers—girls as well as boys—are being raised in one-parent households, and that parent might be a mother or a father, why is the discussion group "open" to dads and not moms?

WK's Coach Box

http://www.wk20.com/

Wendell Kim is a pro: He is a longtime major league third base and infield coach, with his most recent affiliation the Boston Red Sox. In the off-season, Kim teaches baseball in Korea, works at the San Francisco Giants baseball fantasy camp, and conducts instructional clinics specifically designed for Little League and youth baseball league coaches. His extremely helpful and thorough Web site is useful both in gaining an understanding of a professional coach's responsibilities and in offering extensive coaching tips.

A site highlight: "You Be the Coach," a "place where you can get a chance to be a Big League coach and put yourself in a real game situation. Take a look at the situation and send me your answer. Let me know why you made your decision and what factors you considered.

Remember—in giving me your answer—this is the Big Leagues. Sometimes answers may be different in the same situation in a different setting or at a different level!"

Kim also publishes the best answers on his site.

Coaching Youth Sports

http://www.chre.vt.edu/~/cys/

This literate and extremely helpful electronic newsletter for coaches, athletes, and parents is edited by Richard K. Stratton, Ph.D., and is a public service of the Health and Physical Education Program at Virginia Tech.

Its purpose is to "present information about learning and performing sport skills. The information comes mostly from the motor skill learning and sports psychology areas of the sport sciences. While the primary focus will be on athletes in the 6-16 year age range, topics related to high school athletes may also be discussed."

The articles on the site do not specifically deal with baseball but focus on general athletic activity. They cover a wide range of issues: "Stress in Youth Sports"; "Motivation: Why Participate?"; "Coaching Youths With Disabilities"; "Integrating High Skilled and Less Skilled Athletes"; "Coaching Your Own Child"; and "Dealing With a Worried Child."

You also can link to previous newsletters. Additionally, the "other web sites" link will take you to a fine array of related Internet resources.

CPSC Releases Study of Protective Equipment for Baseball

http://www.kidsource.com/CPSC/baseball.6.10.html#Study

This Web page is essential reading for coaches and parents of young ballplayers. It is a press release that was issued on June 4, 1996, by the United States Consumer Product Safety Commission (CPSC).

Its essence is explained in the opening paragraph: "(The CPSC) announced today that safety equipment for baseball could significantly reduce the amount and severity of 58,000 (or almost 36 per cent of) baseball-related injuries to children each year."

This determination was made after the commission conducted a year-long study "on the ability of safety equipment to reduce baseball injuries and deaths."

The page features the fundamentals of the study and stresses that children should not play baseball, softball, or Tee Ball without proper safety equipment.

However, the page could do without the self-serving quote from Ann Brown, the CPSC chairman, found at the top of the page.

Another helpful, related site is 10 Health Tips Every Youth Baseball Coach Should Know (*http://www.kidsource.com/kidsource/content/news/baseball.3.11.html*).

Jim's Slow-Pitch Softball

http://www.staff.uiuc.edu/~j-danner/

This handy, link-loaded Web site is maintained by Jim Danner, who has spent nine years coaching women's fast-pitch softball. He has umpired baseball and both fast- and slow-pitch softball, and has operated his own softball league. "I have seen a whole lot of softball, and made many mistakes, but have helped many people," he writes. "I feel I know this game as well as anyone."

The key home page link is "'HIT THE BALL' For some tips." Click on the speeding ball, and you will be taken to practice drills; workout ideas; batting, pitching, fielding, and baserunning advice; coaching hints; and equipment information.

Louisville Slugger

http://www.slugger.com/

I logged onto this Web site expecting to find little more than ad copy for the company's product. Although the site is not hype-free, I was pleasantly surprised to discover some helpful information aimed at young people who are learning the game.

One of the site's best features is "Louisville Slugger Online," which allows you to e-mail questions on "how to improve your game through playing tips and the selection of performance-enhancing equipment" to members of the company's advisory staff (who include fast-pitch softball star Lisa Fernandez and Miami Hurricanes baseball coach Jim Norris). Kids are encouraged to join Louisville Slugger Team TPX for free and receive an instructional newsletter and a chance to win an aluminum bat.

However, keep in mind that this is a commercial site with a commercial agenda.

Amateur Baseball: College/Olympic

College baseball program and team-related sites spotlight both powerhouses whose best players will graduate to the pros and less renowned programs like Baldwin-Wallace College in Ohio, Chapman University in California, Neosho County Community College in Kansas, and Tyler Junior College in Texas.

Some sites are maintained by the schools or athletic departments; others are fan sites. They are characterized by rah-rah boosterism and feature press releases, schedules, rosters, polls, season results, ticket information, and player profiles (with a spotlight on second basemen or centerfielders named players-of-the-week or all-conference or all-American, or those signing letters of intent).

Other sites are sponsored by conferences and offer more gung-ho enthusiasm along with standings and schedules, links to member teams, and press releases. They also feature football, basketball, tennis, and volleyball as well as baseball.

Some college baseball coverage, particularly during the College World Series, can be found on the various super-Web sites. However, conference Web pages are the best sources for generic college baseball information and team links. Their URLs are:

Atlantic Coast: *http://www.theacc.com/*

Big East: *http://www.bigeast.org/*

Big Ten: *http://www.bigten.org/sports/baseball/index.htm*

Big 12: *http://www.big12conf.com/*

Conference USA: *http://www.c-usa.org/*

Ivy League: *http:/www.ivyleague.princeton.edu/*

Pacific-10: *http://www.pac-10.org/*

Southeastern: *http://www.sec.org/*

Western Athletic: *http://www.wac.org/*

NCAA Online

http://www.ncaa.org/

Here is the official Web site of the NCAA (National Collegiate Athletic Association), a "voluntary association of more than 1,200 institutions, conferences, organizations and individuals devoted to the sound administration of intercollegiate athletics."

This information-rich site features links to "NCAA News," "Membership Information," "Championships" (which includes information on how NCAA champions are determined and lists team champions and tournament dates and locations), a "Sports Library" (listing NCAA publications), and "College Bound" (which is designed for high school athletes and stresses the incredible odds against scholastic athletes ever playing pro ball).

The "Statistics" link is of special note. It includes a search engine that allows you to research individual and team batting, pitching, and fielding records.

The site is extremely valuable for those interested in downloading basic NCAA-oriented data. However, you will have to look elsewhere to find information on NCAA controversies or the opinions of those who feel that the rules for collegiate athletic eligibility are riddled with hypocrisy.

Omaha...Home of the College World Series

http://nbdc.unomaha.edu/cws.htm

Just as the highlight of each major league campaign is postseason play and the World Series, the NCAA-sponsored College World Series is the main event for college baseball.

On this Web site, you will learn the ABCs of the College World Series: who gets to play, how it all operates, and how it culminates in the finals, held in Omaha, which determine the series champ.

Links are provided to the previous four tournaments, which highlight the competing teams, the final results, and the all-tournament squads. The "CWS History" link will take you to lists of past College World Series winners, runner-ups, and championship game scores, dating from 1947; series MVPs (who have included Mark Kotsay, Todd Walker, Phil Nevin, Calvin Schiraldi, Terry Francona, Bob Horner, Dave Winfield, Sal Bando, and Bob Garibaldi); and the all-time series team (whose members include Kotsay, Walker, Winfield, Steve Arlin, Burt Hooten, Barry Bonds, Will Clark, Robin Ventura, Spike Owen, and Pete Incaviglia). The "CWS Records" link includes lists of dozens of individual and team records. Here, you will learn that J.D. Drew of Florida State holds the series home run record, hitting five dingers in six games in 1995-96; the RBI leader is Stan Holmes of Arizona State, with 17 in six games in 1981; and Bob Garibaldi of Santa Clara struck out 38 batters in five games back in 1962, a figure that has not been topped.

Another related site worth checking out is the Unofficial College World Series Page (*http://www.novia.net/~mossimo/cws.html*).

FANSonly

http://www.fansonly.com/

This information-packed, colorfully designed Web site covers all of college sports. The "News" icon will take you to game previews, team reports, and scores. "Insider" includes opinion pieces and FANSonly polls. "Voices" includes message boards, live chat, and AudioNet cybercasts. "Recruiting" features facts and rumors regarding which athletes will be attending what schools. "Road Trip" spotlights individual teams. From "Schools," you can link to the official Web sites of two dozen university athletic programs.

During the fall, when I explored this site, it was dominated by football. In the spring, however, baseball is in the spotlight with extensive coverage of conference tournaments, regionals, and the College World Series.

You also can subscribe to a free FANSonly newsletter, which is e-mailed each week.

International Olympic Committee

http://www.olympic.org/

On this Web site (which comes in English and French versions), you will find the official line of "The Olympic Movement." You will be greeted by a "welcome from the President"; you can read the Olympic Charter; you can download the latest plans for individual upcoming summer and winter games; and you can peruse news and press releases dating from the previous two years.

This site is not specifically focused on baseball; to download any Olympic baseball information, you will have to extensively search the site. There is, however, a treasure trove of information for those who follow Olympic activities.

USA Baseball

http://www.usabaseball.com/

This well-rounded Web site is maintained by USA Baseball, the "National Governing Body of amateur baseball in the

United States and a member of the United States Olympic Committee." It "selects, trains and supports the USA Baseball Team and USA Baseball Junior Team, which participate in various international competitions."

The page features a history of Olympic baseball, USA Baseball schedules and results, current rosters with player and coach biographies, stats, records, and all-time rosters (including lists of Olympians who made the majors).

Among the latter are many elite active players: Mark McGwire; Will Clark; Barry Larkin; B.J. Surhoff; Andy Benes; Tino Martinez; Robin Ventura; Charles Nagy; Charles Johnson; and Michael Tucker.

Others, such as Gary Green, John Hoover, Pat Pacillo, Mike Milchin, Ted Wood, and Joe Slusarski, are, at best, answers to trivia questions.

A notable related Web site is the one maintained by the United States Olympic Committee (*http://test.olympic-usa.org/sports/az_3_3_2.html*).

Amateur Softball Association

http://www.softball.org/

The Amateur Softball Association (ASA) is "the national governing body of amateur softball in the United States." More than 260,000 teams are registered, including more than 73,500 junior Olympic (youth) clubs whose rosters include more than one million boys and girls. The ASA also works in conjunction with the United States Olympic Committee to "insure (sic) that our national team has the best possible chance of winning."

This Web site includes information on the ASA and its programs and activities, a profile of the organization's umpiring program, official softball rules, and excerpts from *Etched in Gold*, which chronicles the United States' first-ever Olympic gold medal-winning softball team.

A related site worth checking out is Softball Canada (*http://home.sprynet.com/sprynet/softblca/*).

Anchorage Bucs

http://www.alaska.net/~enigma/bucs/

Not all college baseball is played on college campuses. The Anchorage Bucs, for one, describe themselves as "America's #1 summer collegiate baseball team, containing players from major universities throughout the United States." Their logo consists of a pirate who might be the long-lost brother of the Pittsburgh Pirates' buccaneer, and they play in the Alaska League, whose other teams include the Anchorage Pilots, Fairbanks Goldpanners, Mat-Su Miners, Kenai Oilers, and Hawaii Island Movers. (The league actually extends beyond Alaska's borders.) Other opponents have ranged from the Japan Aichi All Stars and Moscow Red Devils to the Colorado Silver Bullets.

This Web site includes information on the Bucs present and past. The team came into being in 1980 when they were known as the Cook Inlet Bucs; their history is charted on a nicely illustrated page that spotlights a 1982 photo of Buc Wally Joyner (then a Brigham Young sophomore). Other ex-Bucs include Bobby Jones, Mike Macfarlane, Reid (son of Nolan) Ryan, and Jeff Kent. And on the site, you can even hear the Bucs theme song!

Another plus is the Alaska Baseball Pictorial Archive, which includes photos dating from the first decade of the twentieth century. Of special note is the shot of the Lightning Strikers, a 1914 women's team.

On the home page, you will find what I assume is an "Alaska joke." It comes in the form of a quote from Yogi Berra, in which he exclaims, while turning down mousse for dessert while visiting the Frozen State, "the meat's too tough and the horns get stuck in my teeth."

The Sport Source

http://wylie1.com/source/base.html

How many colleges have baseball programs? Where is reliable basic information on them?

If you are a high school ballplayer and are thinking about going on to play in college, you may be asking these questions, and this Web site will be worth a look. It serves to hype The Sport Source, which publishes annually updated guides (which also cover sports other than baseball) listing NCAA, NAIA, and NJCAA programs; tuition cost and scholarship information; entrance requirements; baseball program history; the style of play the team favors; and advice from coaches and college faculty.

Links on the home page will take you to sample entries, which give you a feel of the guide's content.

USC Trojans

http://www.usctrojans.com/sports/m-basebl/usc-m-basebl-frame.html

Most college athletic Web sites only spotlight present-day teams and players; if they at all recognize previous squads, it is by listing alumni currently playing pro ball.

However, you will occasionally find a site that acknowledges the school's past. This one in particular has a more than adequate emphasis on USC rituals and folklore.

Click on the "Traditions" link, and you will find an impressive list of history-related pages. On them, you can learn everything from the origin of USC's nickname, to Trojan songs and when they were composed, to the history of Tommy Trojan, "the statue of the bronzed Trojan warrior (that) has been a symbol of the university's fighting spirit."

15

Amateur Baseball: Adult

Athletic activity is not restricted to the young, though it wasn't too long ago that a post-adolescent who jogged or went one-on-one in the schoolyard might be considered an eccentric clinging to childhood games.

Along with a marked rise in health club memberships and sales of adult-size sneakers and sweatshirts, there has been an increase in men's and women's participation in baseball. Adults today are not just New York Yankees or Cleveland Indians or St. Louis Cardinals fans; not every over-twenty something is a stereotypical beer-bellied couch potato whose physical activity consists of ambling to and from the refrigerator. Adult baseball, softball, and townball leagues run the gamut from the self-explanatory Atlanta Men's Adult and Senior Baseball Leagues to the Thirty-Plus Baseball League, a California-based "non-profit player-run association" that operates "in a competitive but friendly atmosphere with a further mission of contributing in a positive fashion to the communities in which we play."

Men's Senior Baseball League

http://www.msbl.com/msbl/index_1.htm

This is the official Web site of the Men's Senior Baseball League (MSBL) and Men's Adult Baseball League (MABL). The former is "a national organization with over 250 local affiliates, 2500 teams, and more than 40,000 members who play organized amateur baseball in local leagues." The latter is "a national organization of baseball leagues for adults 18 and over." Both "are committed to providing adult players the opportunity to play real baseball at a competitive level on a regular basis." Every autumn, there is a league World Series in Arizona and a Fall Classic national tournament in St. Petersburg.

On the site, you can download a league history and learn all you need to know about how the MSBL and MABL work.

Baseball Fantasy Camps

http://www.dennismc.com/baseball/basfnpg1.html.ssi

Have you ever longed to don the uniform of your favorite major league team and "become a kid again...(as well as) rub elbows with some of (your) childhood or adult heroes?" If you answer a wholehearted yes and have a few thousand dollars to spare, you were born to attend a baseball fantasy camp. The concept was devised in the 1980s by Randy Hundley, father of New York Mets catcher Todd and a major league backstop in his own right for the Chicago Cubs.

This helpful Web site lists all the necessary information—dates, location, and price—of all major league-affiliated fantasy camps. Further information on each can be obtained by downloading its link.

Dennis McCroskey, who maintains the site, already has attended 18 separate camps. He also hosts a number of other Web pages, including Dodgertown West (*http://www.dennismc.com/baseball/dtw/dtwhmpg1.html-ssi*), the home page of an organization composed of Los Angeles Dodgers Adult Baseball Camp alumni; and International Baseball for the Middle Aged Jock (*http://www.dennismc.com/baseball.basinpg1.html-ssi*), in which he reminisces about his baseball experiences in Russia, New Zealand, and Australia.

A Look at Women's Baseball

http://www.rabble.com/xpress/1997.03.01/baseball.html

This modest Web page introduces the Women's National Adult Baseball Association (WNABA), which was established in 1994 in the wake of the success of the film *A League of Their Own*. More than 100 teams and 2,000 players are affiliated with the league, which sponsors a National Championship of Women's Baseball tournament.

The page is maintained by Richard Hopkins, who helped organize the WNABA and is president and general manager of the Arizona Cactus Wrens team. "The enthusiasm displayed by the women was incredible," Hopkins writes, of the Wrens' beginnings. "They were eager to learn, eager to play, and eager to win. Unlike the men players I've managed, the women did not have the notion that they knew it all already."

Hopkins also rails against the fact that "Major League Baseball, that bastion of manliness that also banned another group of players from admission for a long time before Jackie Robinson broke through, refuses to allow women to play baseball," and that "women, and men everywhere need to rise up against this injustice. Write to your congressman and senators, voicing your disapproval of Major League Baseball's stance against women."

More information on the WNABA can be found on the Web site maintained by the organization. The URL is *http://www.von.net/wnaba*.

The B & N Softball Page

http://idt.net/~mbeth19/softball.html

The Internet is loaded with Web sites featuring softball equipment for sale. This page is sponsored by Dr. Mark McDowell and Dr. Ronald D. Noebe, who describe themselves as a "pair of avid softball players, who also happen to be very curious engineers. We have been following the debate raging over softball equipment for the last several years and decided to do a little searching on our own as to the truths behind much of the hype that is now associated with the sport."

This site is worth a look because of the docs' thoughtful softball bat evaluations, comparisons, and content analysis.

New Jersey Wiffleball Association

http://wiffleballusa.com/

"Wiffleball is played by all ages," states this Web site's home page. "It seems though that it's played more serious (sic) as players get older." For this reason, this page focuses on the game as experienced at the adult (as well as competitive) level.

Wiffleball tournaments around the country are listed along with national competitions hosted by the NJWA. Also helpful is a link leading to "official Wiffleball rules" as interpreted by the organization. If you follow them, it is promised that you will have the "Ultimate Wiffleball Experience."

16

International Baseball

Baseball may be known as America's Pastime, but it certainly is played across the globe. On the Internet, you will find baseball Web sites from Australia, Austria, Belgium, Canada, Croatia, the Czech Republic, the Dominican Republic, England, Finland, France, Germany, Ireland, Italy, Japan, Mexico, Namibia, the Netherlands, Norway, Portugal, Puerto Rico, Scotland, South Africa, Spain, Sweden, Switzerland, Taiwan, Venezuela—and points in between.

Scores of teams and leagues from around the world maintain their own Web pages. Like their American counterparts, they feature stats, scores, standings, and plenty of rah-rah boosterism. Many are available only in native languages; a few are cited in this chapter.

Some international team names are humorous. An Austrian ballclub is known as the Vienna Lawnmowers. Would the American contingent of their roster include Billy and Larry Gardner, Randy and Donie Bush, Jim Greengrass, Jake Flowers, Pete Rose, or Ron Gardenhire?

You've heard of the Boston Red Sox and Chicago White Sox. How about Germany's Dusseldorf Dead Sox!

Are Billie Holiday, Bessie Smith, and B.B. King the starting outfield of the Sydney (Australia) Blues?

Are Alvin, Simon, and Theodore the Tinker-to-Evers-to-Chance of the Hagen (Germany) Chipmunks?

One only can imagine the type of player on the Wesseling (Germany) Vermins.

International Baseball Association

http://monviso2.alpcom.it/digesu/

The International Baseball Association is a governing organization whose membership includes 108 national baseball federations. The IBA organizes tournaments and awards an International Cup and World Cup of Cups; it also is recognized by the International Olympic Committee.

At this Web site (which was under heavy construction during my visit), you can sense the global nature of baseball as you check out links to the "African Baseball & Softball Association," "Confederacion Panamericana de Beisbol," "Baseball Federation of Asia," "Confederation Europeenne de Baseball," and "Baseball Confederation of Oceania."

The World Sport Center

http://www.worldsport.com/

This Web site is sponsored by the General Association of International Sports Federations, which "is made up of 88 International Federations and organizations governing world sport."

Baseball and softball are world sports, and they are among the activities found in an A-to-Z list on the site's home page. Click on the "Baseball" icon, and you will be taken to a page maintained by the International Baseball Association, a GAISF member. (See the preceding entry.) From the "Softball" icon, you can download the International Softball Federation's page. Here, you will find official international softball rules, a history of worldwide softball and slow-pitch, softball-related news and notes from across the globe, and the inductees in the federation's Hall of Fame (whose members are named Rhonda Boyd, Marilyn Marshall, Paul Rogers, and Eugene McWillie rather than Babe Ruth, Mickey Mantle, Rogers Hornsby, and Willie McCovey).

Japanese Baseball

http://www2.inter.co.jp/Baseball/

If you are in any way interested in Japanese professional baseball, this is the Web site for you. It is maintained by the Professional Baseball Organization of Japan's Baseball Information System Administrative Office. On it, you can link to data on the most recent baseball seasons, final standings from 1936 to the present, yearly batting and pitching leaders, all-time leaders, and a baseball register that enables you to search for both Japanese and non-Japanese players.

Japanese Baseball

http://www.pacificu.edu/up/as/bb/baseball.html

Here is another excellent Web site dedicated to Japanese baseball present and past. It is presented by Pacific University's Fall, 1995, Asian Studies Class and features a general history of baseball in Japan; a brief essay on the differences between baseball in America and Japan; a revealing profile of Hidemi Tanaka, a Japanese student studying at Pacific University; and an excellent critical bibliography of books and articles on the subject.

Jim Allen's Japanese Baseball Page

http://www2.gol.com/users/jallen/Jimball.html

If you visit the preceding sites and still are hankering for data on baseball Japan-style, this solid Web page should fulfill all your needs. Allen, the author of *Jim Allen's Guide to Japanese Baseball*, includes loads of information on such links as "Japanese Baseball News," "Brief History of Japanese Baseball," and "General Information About Japanese Baseball."

Of special note is the link to "The English Bibliography on Japanese Baseball," which includes an extensive list of books, guides, newsletters, and newspaper and magazine articles on the subject.

Fantasy Sports Japan

http://www.fsjsports.com/

This Web site is a for-a-fee fantasy baseball game in which the players are not American major leaguers. Instead, starting lineups consist of players from any of the 12 Japanese professional baseball teams.

However, by clicking on the "Japanese Baseball" link, those simply interested in the subject will find information on players, schedules, and player/manager interviews.

This site is worth perusing if only for its "Foreign Players Archives" link, which allows you to download a list of "imported" players (from Kyle Abbott and Jerry Adair to Ray Young and Don Zimmer) who appeared on Japanese rosters between 1936 and 1996. Plus, the "Foreign Players in Japan" links will allow you to catch up on the major leaguers (or career minor leaguers) currently on the roster of the Nippon Ham Fighters, Yakult Swallows, Chiba Lotte Marines, or Yomiuri Giants.

Croatian Baseball Association

http://oliver.efzg.hr/~denny/

This is the official site of the Croatian Baseball League. Although its English translation is awkward, it nonetheless is a fascinating page for those curious about baseball 'round-the-world.

On the "About Croatian Baseball" link, you will learn that American sailors first brought the game to Croatia in

1920. The initial Croatian games ever played were "between Marjan and Hajduk and Hajduk and Borak. First one Hajduk lost 8:6 but in the second one they beat Borak 12:5." The information that follows traces the evolution of baseball in Croatia to the present.

The site also includes lists of Croatian teams, champions, and statistics. For the record, in 1996 Damir Karin (playing for the Olimpija Karlovac) not only was the Croatian League's leading hitter with a .469 average, but also sported a 6–2 record on the mound, with a 3.45 ERA.

Are you listening, George Steinbrenner!

International Baseball and Softball Statistics

http://utopia.knoware.nl/users/hwede/

This exceptional Web site is maintained by Harry Wedemeijer, who describes himself as a "baseball and softball statistician from Delft." It includes links galore to stats for international tournaments, Dutch competitions, and the like, as well as information on Olympic baseball and softball, rules for umpires, and addresses for international and national baseball federations.

A special link, to "Baseball and Softball Clubs in the Netherlands," includes names, locations, and telephone numbers for dozens of ball teams—proving, again, that baseball's popularity knows no boundaries.

The SABR UK Homepage

http://www.mhoerch.demon.co.uk/index.html

This Web site easily might belong in one of the history chapters because its primary focus is baseball in Britain's past. Given all the available evidence, only a stubborn and blindly patriotic flag-waver would insist that baseball was "invented" in America.

"We're doing a great deal of research to crack open the idea that baseball is just a descendant of rounders;

we've discovered that baseball is most likely the older and more venerable of the pair," it is noted on the home page. "The first reference to baseball in England was in 1700, and almost a century later, Jane Austen mentioned it in one of her novels. Rounders, on the other hand, first appeared in the Oxford English Dictionary in 1856. We have more supporting evidence—read on!"

You may do so by perusing a dozen or so articles with such titles as "Baseball—Made in Britain" (in which Geraint Johnes and Bob Thornton trace the sport through British history); "The Chicken or the Egg?" (which offers evidence that baseball predates rounders); "The Last Game" (in which Patrick Morley describes the final baseball game played at the Baseball Ground in Derby); and "Footprints in the Snow" (in which Martin Hoerchner discusses the pitfalls of researching the roots of baseball).

The British Baseball Federation

http://www.bbf.org/

Cricket, rugby, and soccer are not the only sports played in the United Kingdom. The British Baseball Federation consists of a number of baseball leagues in the UK. On this Web site, you will learn that one of them is the British Baseball League (which, interestingly, is sponsored by Coors rather than a local brewery). It consists of two conferences: the Northern (whose teams include the Kingston Cobras, Menwith Hill Patriots, Birmingham Bandits, Nottingham Stealers, Lancashire Tigercats, Leeds Luddites, Hessle Warriors, and Liverpool Trojans) and Southern (London Warriors, Enfield Spartans, Hounslow Blues, Brighton Buccaneers, and Essex Arrows).

The four teams in Scotland—the Dundee Dragons (formerly the Dodgers), Glasgow Comets, Edinburgh Reivers, and Livingston Wildcats—also are federation members. The organization also sponsors regional conferences; PONY and Bronco youth baseball leagues; a Tee-Ball program; and a pitch, hit, and run schools program.

South Manchester Softball League

http://www.ccl.umist.ac.uk/staff/harold/softball.html

As baseball is played in the United Kingdom, so is softball. This Web site offers all you would need to know if you lived in the area and were in any way interested in the sport.

But it is worth a brief visit just to peruse the names of the teams in the local league. They include the Jammie Dodgers, Ringway Ringers, Fog Lane Foghorns, Didsbury Bats, Rusholme Funsters, Manchester M 16s, and my favorite, the Insight Blaggers.

Newcastle Baseball Umpire's Association

http://users.hunterlink.net.au/nbua/

On this handy Web site, you will find much more than information on the Newcastle Baseball Umpire's Association, an "independent body of umpires which has served (Australia's) Newcastle Baseball Association...for over 60 years."

You'll find a nice essay on the whos, hows, and whats of baseball in Australia, and links to such organizations as the "Newcastle Baseball Association," the "Sydney Baseball Umpire's Association," the "Australian Baseball League," and several teams in the latter.

On this site, as you will see, the Wizard of Oz is not necessarily Ozzie Smith or a classic film starring Judy Garland.

SSV Dornbirn Sharx and Indians

http://www2.vol.at/Baseball-Softball/

This is the "official homepage of the SSV Dornbirn SHARX and INDIANS," Austrian baseball and softball teams.

Although team schedules and the fact that a new baseball coach has been appointed in Dornbirn may be of little interest, this site is worth a visit for the opportunity to note the manner in which baseball terminology is integrated into a foreign language. In this instance, that language is German.

In a detailed account of the results of a "Softball Mixed Turnier in Dornbirn siegt das Team der Dornbirn Indians vor den Rankweil Braves und den Gotzis Unforgetables," you will find such sentence fragments as "die Indians hatten 2 Out und lagen 5 Runs hinten"; "Florian Fassler ging durch ein Fielders Choice out"; and "Marion Mittelberger kam durch ein Single und zwei Stolen Base ans dritte und machte bei einem Passed Ball ein gelungenes Homestealing." Then there is the following reportage: "Die nachsten beiden Batter kamen durch Base on Balls auf die Bases. Bases Loaded, 2 Outs, 1 Run hinten. Kathraina Wustner kam ans Schlagmal 2 Balls, 1 Strike und jetzt nahm der Coach der Rankweiler sein zweites Time in diesem Inning und ging wiedermum zum Pitcher-charged conference."

What a way to learn a foreign language!

While exploring international baseball Web sites, I became familiar with two other oft-used phrases: "Beste resultate mit Netscape 2.0" and "Objekt nicht gefunden" (or, in Italian, "Pagina non trovata").

Die Baseball-Homepage der Dormagen Typhoons

http://ourworld.compuserve.com/homepages/typhoons

This Web site, which is completely in German, is maintained by the Dormagen Typhoons baseball team. It grabbed my attention for two reasons: the vivid illustration of a batter bashing a baseball at the top of the home page, and the name of one of its links, "Sex, Drugs und Baseball?"

You do not have to speak German to understand the words "Die Moral der Typhoons," which are printed in large black letters at the top of the page, and the words of wisdom, printed in bold to stand out, which end the page's initial paragraph: "No Sex before de Spiel!"

Bavarian Baseball and Softball Federation

http://members.aol.com/bbsvhome/english.htm

The material found on this Web site (which is in German and English) reflects the extent upon which baseball is played in Germany. Among the links are schedules for men's, women's, and youth leagues. The team names run some sort of gamut, from clones of major league monikers (Ansbach Red Sox, Erlangen White Sox, Furth Pirates, Munchen Tigers, Poing Rangers) to a potpourri (Eching Centurions, Deggendorf Dragons, Ruhpolding Rabbits, Baldham Banshees, Mitwitz Rebels, Memmelsdorf Barons, Grunwald Jesters, Steinheim Red Phantoms, Grobenzell Blue Caps, Pocking Bumble Bees).

Of special note is the "Baseball Quotes" link. Here, you will find (in English) a fine selection of remarks from the likes of Earl Weaver, Roger Angell, Tommy Lasorda, Wally Pipp, Whitey Ford, Cal Ripken, Al Rosen, Ron Luciano, Pee Wee Reese, Sadaharu Oh, Dwight D. Eisenhower, and Dick Stuart (who is referred to as "Stonefingers," rather than "Dr. Strangeglove").

My favorite, from Tallulah Bankhead: "There have been only two geniuses in the world: Willie Mays and Willie Shakespeare."

In addition, entire sections are devoted to Casey Stengel, Yogi Berra, Bill Lee, Bob Uecker, Lefty Gomez, and Rocky Bridges.

Challengers Baseball Club

http://www.challengers.org/

A general overview of baseball in Switzerland can be gleaned from this Web site, which is sponsored by Zurich's Challengers ballteam. There are schedules, stats, official rules, and data on the country's national team and two baseball leagues, the National League-A (NLA) and National League-B (NLB). The Barracudas, Flyers, Frogs, Eagles, Hawks, and Cardinals join the Challengers in the NLA; the Rainbows, Devils, Submarines, Lions, Red Barons, and Unicorns are among the teams in the NLB.

The "Players Profile" link will take you to mini-biographies of the top ballplayers in Swiss baseball. Among their surnames are Blickenstorfer, Labhart, and Eisenring (as opposed to Spahn, Sain, and Pray-for-Rain), and they hail not only from Switzerland but also Hong Kong, Mexico City, and Karachi, Pakistan.

Leones del Escogido Baseball Club

http://www.escogido.do/

On this Web site, you will find up-to-the-minute data on the Dominican Winter League as well as an informative history of Dominican baseball in general and the Leones del Escogido (Escogido Lions) team in particular.

Across the years, such native Dominicans as Ozzie Virgil Sr., Juan Marichal, Pedro Guerrero, Mario Soto, Joaquin Anduja, and Felipe, Matty, and Jesus Alou have worn the Escogido uniform, along with Bill White, Ray Dandridge, Willie McCovey, Frank Howard, Charlie Hough, Gaylord Perry, Tim Raines, Fred McGriff, Marquis Grissom, Willie Kirkland, and so many more.

Of special note is the Escogido all-star team link. When I logged on, the page was still under construction, but it promised to present "Escogido's All-Star Teams, made up of the best players that have been with the team in its 75-year history, according to baseball writers in the Dominican Republic."

The text on this site is available in English and Spanish.

Chinese Professional Baseball League

http://www.cpbl.com/tw/

This Web site comes only in Chinese. However, it is so visually appealing that it merits inclusion here.

Its home page features a mini-revolving baseball that transforms itself into a globe and a smiling cartoon face. The page is adorned with animated images of ducks with bobbing heads and smiling and waving ballplayers coming up to bat. The logos of the league teams are collectively colorful.

Also worth a quick look, for the same reason, is the Taiwan Major League Web site (*http://www.naluwan.com.tw/*).

TruNorth Baseball

http://www.bccc.com/TruNorth/tnbhome.html

This Web site spotlights "Canadian connections in baseball's major and minor leagues." It includes nicely done features, mostly written by John Lott, on Canadian-born ballplayers and those playing for Canadian teams. Most are minor leaguers. On my visit, there were pieces on Rich Butler, Vernon Wells, Todd Betts, Roy Halladay, Diegomar Markwell, Bob Henley, Mike Thurman, Milton Bradley, and, most prominently, Greg Morrison, a triple crown-winner (.448 average, 23 homers, 88 RBI) for the Medicine Hat Blue Jays in the short-season Pioneer League.

Baseball's past was covered in pieces on Bill "The Spaceman" Lee and a 1983 Skydome exhibition game between the Syracuse Chiefs and Tidewater Tides, the Toronto Blue Jays' and New York Mets' AAA farm teams. There also was a heartfelt piece on Kelly Gruber's attempted comeback after four years away from the game.

Baseball In Literature and the Arts

Plenty of Web sites focus on the manner in which baseball has been depicted in poetry, song, and fiction. Some consist of lists: indexes of baseball mysteries, melodies, and movies. Others are cyberspace art galleries that display paintings, lithographs, or photos. Some are wildly creative in and of themselves; the Cosmic Baseball Association, for example, qualifies as one of the sharpest baseball-oriented pages on the Internet. Still more feature reminiscences or wax nostalgic about long-ago summer nights spent on idyllic fields of dreams. And a few even attempt to cast the harsh light of reality on such recollections.

This chapter presents an assortment of some of the most engaging, unusual, or all-inclusive arts and literature-oriented baseball Web sites.

Baseball Book Survey

http://members.aol.com/aspira/books.html

The core of this Web site, maintained by Greg Spira, is a survey in which he charts "a selection of the best books which cover various angles of baseball itself from an analytic perspective. I have tried to come (up) with books that cover (an) extremely wide variety of baseball topics, including general histories, specific histories, biographies and autobiographies of both historical and more recent personalities, economics, labor-management struggles, scouting, defense, statistical analysis, the minor leagues, Japanese baseball, the Negro leagues, broadcasting, etc."

If you want an authoritative guide to baseball literature, this Web site is as good a place as any to start.

Another worthwhile site is The Essential Baseball Library (*http://www.kypris.com/Baseball/bb-essential.html*). It features a subjective list of the top 50 non-statistics-oriented tomes, compiled at the request of SABR by Lawrence Ritter, author of *The Glory of Their Times.*

The Total Baseball Online Discount Bookstore

http://www.totalbaseball.com/

This page is a link on the Total Baseball Web site. It enables you to order baseball-related books online from the Amazon.com online bookstore Web site (*http://www.amazon.com*). Amazon is among the best sites of its kind and is worth checking out for information on any and all reading matter.

However, this page is cited here because it includes a generally solid cumulative list of baseball books in print. They come under the following headings: "Statistics"; "General History"; "Team Histories"; "Fiction/Humor/Drama/Verse"; "Biography—Players"; "Biography—Managers"; "Biography—Collective"; "Biography—Executives";

"Anthologies, Anecdotes & Reminiscences"; "Umpires and Umpiring"; "World Series and All-Star Games"; "The Minors"; "Negro Leagues"; "Instructionals"; "Ball Park"; "Pictorials"; and "Miscellaneous."

Another fine baseball book-related page is Virtual Athlete (*http://www.webgrafxx.com/virtualathlete/books/baseball1.html*), which consists of a comprehensive A-to-Z list of baseball books (which also may be ordered through Amazon).

Casey at the Bat

http://rowlf.cc.wwu.edu:8080/~stephan/webstuff/poetry/Thayer-CaseyattheBat.html

This Web page consists of nothing more than the most famous baseball poem of all time, in all its glory: Ernest Lawrence Thayer's "Casey at the Bat."

The URL *http://www.historybuff.com/library/refcasey.html* is a good place to find out the story behind the poem.

Jeff Suntala's Web Site

http://w3.gwis.com/~sun/

A visit to this Web site is like a mini-trip to an art gallery. It is brightly designed and loaded with drawings created by artist Jeff Suntala. They include portraits of "classic baseball superstars," Negro leaguers, Cleveland-related art (Suntala is an Indians fan), and humorous illustrations.

The "self-portrait" with the bobbing head is a clever touch.

The Art of Baseball: Dwight Baird

http://www.iconn.ca/zone451/issue06/art/ar06bair.html

This Web page features more than two dozen pieces by artist Dwight Baird. Most are baseball-related, and are anything but traditionally posed; instead, they focus on torsos of players, hands meeting dirt as runners slide into bases, and fielders whose faces are obscured by their gloves.

Sights and Sounds of Baseball

http://www.oldbaseball.com/gallery/art.htm

Here is another cyberspace art gallery. This one consists of images of nineteenth- and twentieth-century baseball cards (which I have long maintained are individual pieces of art in and of themselves, which are as worthy of hanging on walls as storing in shoe boxes or card-collector albums). Each image serves as a link; click on it, and it will be enlarged and identified.

Additionally, with the proper software, you can download such "sounds" of the game as John Fogerty singing "Centerfield," Lou Gehrig's farewell speech, and Russ Hodges's call of Bobby Thomson's shot-heard-'round-the-world.

Sights and Sounds of Baseball is a link on the Online Baseball Cards Web site (*http://www.oldbaseball.com/*), which is dedicated "to the innocence of our youth when collecting was a hobby" and is worth perusing if you are interested in vintage baseball cards.

My Baseball Art...

http://home.sprynet.com/spry/igabbard/sportcol.htm

Not all art collectors collect for investment purposes. Some actually enjoy looking at their purchases.

This Web page mostly consists of reproductions of several lithographs (whose subjects are Ken Griffey, Jr., Reggie Jackson, and Nolan Ryan) owned by its anonymous host, who declares, "I don't know if the things I collect have any monetary value nor do I really care. I collect things solely for enjoyment, so if you have a burning need to know what these things are worth I guess you'll just have to ask someone else."

California KidsArt: Baseball Art

http://www.kidsart.com/kacal.html

This Web page features the photograph of a smiling, baseball-loving kid named Jacob, holding the three-dimensional baseball picture he designed.

The process by which Jacob created the piece is explained. It is not all that difficult, and the materials he used can be found in most any home. By using them and following the instructions, pint-sized baseball fans will be able to creatively express their affection for the game.

A Bibliography of Baseball Music Titles

http://www2.ari.net/home/odenwald/ballb/intro.html

"Take Me Out to the Ballgame," "Willie, Mickey & 'The Duke' (Talkin' Baseball)," and the individual numbers from *Damn Yankees!* are not the only baseball ditties penned over the last century-and-a-half. This bibliography, compiled by Susan Clermont, music specialist at the Library of Congress, contains more than 400 baseball-related musical works and songs. They are offered in alphabetical order and chronological order, and by miscellaneous titles and funny titles.

Among the oldest entries are "The Baseball Polka" (1858); "Home Run Quick Step" (1861); "The Base Ball Fever" (1867); "The Base Ball Quadrille" (1867); "The Bat and Ball Song" (1867); "Hurrah for Our National Game" (1868); "Home Run Gallop" (1869); and the ironically named "Red Stockings Schottisch" (1869), which was not penned by Marge Schott.

Some of the more amusing titles: "If You Can't Make a Hit in a Ball-game, You Can't Make a Hit With Me"

(1912); "Jake! Jake! The Yiddisher Ball-Player" (1913); "The Feds Are Here to Stay" (1914, which one can assume was no chart-topper); the patriotic "Batter Up Uncle Sam Is at the Plate" (1918); "I Can't Get to First Base with You" (1935); "There's Gold in Them There Phils" (1938); "Dem Flatbush Bums" (1949); and the quite shocking "Gay Ballplayers Play" (1954).

Diamond Cuts: A Compilation of Baseball Songs and Poetry

http://www.crosstownarts.com/CrosstownArts/client_music/diamond/diamon2.html

This Web page is a link on a site maintained by CrosstownArts, which describes itself as "a group effort by people active in the Washington, D.C. area music scene. Our intent is to bring together many independent musicians, performers, artists, writers (and) film makers that live in our area and the nonprofit arts organizations that labor to help these artists succeed."

CrosstownArts has put together this collection of baseball songs and poetry, which is available for purchase. All the numbers and their histories are briefly described. Some of the performers/musicians/readers—Bruce Springsteen, Buck O'Neil, Bob Costas, Bob Dylan—are household names. Others—the list begins with Kathy Kallick, Bill Kirchen, Yvonne Hood, and Sam Bush—are not. A few—Big Bill Broonzy and Jerry Jeff Walker—are legends and cult performers.

Proceeds from sales will go to various Washington D.C. and baseball-related charitable organizations.

Baseball Down by the Station

http://www2.netdoor.com/~crogers/

What this Web site lacks in graphics is counterbalanced by its content. Its home page features various lyrical answers to the question "What is baseball?" They are quotes by fans and from fiction, by baseball writers, ballplayers, and bat boys.

Links include everything from the Abbott and Costello classic, "Who's on First?" to Gina Hodges's poem, "America's Baseball"; Greg Bell's nostalgic ode to Mickey Mantle; and a piece on Robert Adair ("the only person ever to hold the title 'Physicist of the National League'") and his explanation of why a curve ball curves.

The Pedestalization of Baseball by Americans

http://www.middlebury.edu/~ac400b/costner.html.

This Web page consists of an essay, written by Luke Spencer, which opens with a quote from David Mamet's screenplay for *The Untouchables*, in which the character of Al Capone reflects on his enthusiasm for baseball.

Next comes the following: "Since the close of the Civil War, baseball has ascended to the somewhat lofty position of 'America's favourite pastime.' By 'pedestalization,' we mean the deliberately enforced elevation of an object to the point of obsession, where more often than not, the object takes the form of a screen-memory, which represents the 'idea' of something rather than the object principal."

Spencer goes on to illustrate how a false American mythology is depicted in such baseball films as *The Natural* and *Field of Dreams*. It ends with the declaration that "the move towards capitalist democracy proved to corrupt the ideals behind baseball, and the 1919 Black Sox scandal is the best signifier of this: Chicago as the epitome of the new urban America polluting the purest symbol of American individuality. Subsequent popular culture has attempted to overlook this, and imbibe the past with purity."

All this does make for provocative reading in that it explores how on-screen images and ideas, and the manner in which they are presented, impact on viewers.

Troy Soos Home Page

http://members.aol.com/troysoos/index.html

This Web site is promotional in nature; its purpose is to drum up books sales. Still, if you love baseball and enjoy reading mysteries, you should know about Troy Soos. He is the author of the Mickey Rawlins historical baseball mysteries, the titles of which are *Murder at Fenway Park*, *Murder at Ebbets Field*, *Murder at Wrigley Field*, *Hunting a Detroit Tiger*, and the latest, *The Cincinnati Red Stalkings.* Additionally, Soos has published one nonfiction book: *Before the Curse*, a history of early New England baseball.

Soos is adept at combining a love and understanding of baseball with entertaining fiction writing, and his site serves to introduce the uninitiated to his work. Mystery addicts will appreciate his links to mystery bookstores and other related sites.

Sport Literate

http://www.avalon.net/~librarian/sportlit/spring.html

Sport Literate is a magazine that offers what it describes as "honest reflections on life's leisurely diversions." One such distraction is baseball and, although this Web site exists to solicit subscriptions, it also features excerpts from issues.

When I visited the page, one on-line issue was devoted to "Spring Hits & Summer Runs." The downloadable pieces included reminiscences (Robert N. Georgalas's "In the Cards: Colden Ave. The Bronx. June 1961"); poetry (Robert L. Harrison's "Baseball: A Short History"); and several other goodies.

However, you will have to subscribe to read Philip Fountain's "Baseball and the Grateful Dead: Confessions of a Seamhead."

The Baseball Poems

http://www.pacificnews.org/marko/baseball.html

On this site, you will find a quartet of poems by Mark O'Brien, the titles of which reflect on a baseball fan's yearly cycle: "Magic Number"; "The End of Summer"; "In December, the Fan Looks Forward to Spring"; and "February Blues."

O'Brien's work also can be found at **A Collection of Baseball Poems** (*http://www.mansfield.ohio-state edu/mans/faculty/mallen/students/pclass/bball/bball.htm*), which also includes pieces by Grantland Rice, Robert Francis, and Richard Hugo.

The Double-Breasted Fedoras

http://www.concentric.net/~Kellyl/feds/

Who—or, more appropriately, what—are the Double-Breasted Fedoras? For openers, they are the creation of Rick Wilber and Randy Miller, professional writers and die-hard baseball fans. They describe the Fedoras (or "Feds," for short), as a "virtual reality baseball team comprised of a group of science fiction/fantasy/horror writers, editors, agents, and fans from all around the country."

This site is included in this chapter rather than in the Fun and Games or Humor chapters because the Fedoras publish their own online literary review. It can be downloaded from the site, or found at *http://thuntek.net/mandala/feds/flr.htm.*

Here is the first sentence in the opening paragraph of the short story "A Pennant from the Gremlin," written by James Brunet: "I got to the lab early that morning so I could allow myself an afternoon of playing hookey at the Ballpark."

The second paragraph begins, "So there I was, doing an experiment, trying to keep my measurements as accurate as possible."

Laboratories? Experiments? Ballparks? Would this fiction end up a combination of Frankenstein and Frank Chance or the Wolf Man and Willie Mays?

To find out, you will have to download *The Fedora Literary Review*.

The Artist Within

http://members.aol.com/artistwi/index.html

Lou Gehrig is as well-known for having a disease named after him as for his consecutive-games-played streak and other on-field heroics. That malady is Amyotrophic Lateral Sclerosis (ALS), otherwise known as Lou Gehrig's Disease.

This Web site features a collection of computer-generated greeting cards created by artist Bill Hemsing, who is afflicted with the disease. The cards are offered for sale, with profits going to fund ALS-related research.

"It's the only way I have to fight back," notes Hemsing. "I can't fight with my body, but maybe I can fight with my art."

KTG's Fine Sports Artwork

http://www.kt2.com/

On this Web site, you can view more than 300 individual pieces of art (which are available for purchase) covering a number of sports. The relevant home page links are "Baseball" and "Stadiums/Arenas." The "Baseball" link features autographed and unautographed portraits of mostly contemporary stars; the art on view at the "Stadiums/Arenas" link just begins with Jackie Robinson at bat in Ebbets Field, Kenny Rogers tossing the first-ever pitch at the Ballpark in Arlington, and Cal Ripken going long in Camden Yards.

Even if you are not buying, a visit to this site is the equivalent of time spent perusing the pictures in a museum's sports art exhibit.

Ballpark Classics, Inc.

http://www.osborn-eng.com/ballpark.html

In recent years, yellowed maps, blueprints, contracts, and renderings have come to be considered art. This Web site includes reproductions of original memorabilia relating to college and professional stadiums. All were fashioned by Osborn Engineering, which designed and redesigned ballyards between 1909 and 1970.

Click on the stadium name—among the choices are "Braves Field," "Comiskey Park," "Fenway Park," "Navin Field/Tiger Stadium," the "Polo Grounds," and "Yankee Stadium"—and you will view thumbnails of architectural renderings and construction photos.

Limited edition copies are available for purchase.

Matty

http://pages.prodigy.net/big6/

From this Web page, you can book your very own stage show: "Matty: An Evening with Christy Mathewson," a one-man production written by and starring Eddie Frierson.

The play enjoyed an off-Broadway New York run a while back, and there are excerpted reviews and comments—all raves, of course—from the *New York Post*, *New York Times*, *National Public Radio*, *USA Today*, Bob Costas, and Keith Olbermann. Frierson has taken the show on the road, where it has played in venues from the National Baseball Hall of Fame to Valencia (California) High School.

The site also features information on the Mathewson Foundation, a "not-for-profit educational organization established to support research, provide education...develop media and promote events which will encourage young people to identify their own unique combinations of talents and to nurture the important character traits exemplified in the life of Christy Mathewson."

Angela Fremont

http://users.infohouse.com/fremontappel/gloves.htm

You've heard of individuals sitting for artists and having their portraits painted.

Angela Fremont, a Miami-born artist who resides in New York City, paints commissioned oil portraits. However, they are not of people. They are, instead, of baseball gloves!

Fremont's creations would make ideal gifts for the "person who has everything." Truly everything.

Her Web site includes several examples of her work—including "Harold's Glove, Open" and "Harold's Glove, Closed." So even though the page exists to solicit customers, it qualifies as a mini-cyberspace art gallery.

Cosmic Baseball Association

http://www.clark.net/pub/cosmic/cba1.html

Although the Cosmic Baseball Association is a fantasy league, the home page explains that it is "not one that attempts to reproduce or simulate the past. Our focus on the game of baseball is more poetic than athletic. Beginning with the notion that the game of baseball is really a metaphor for the life of the mind, CBA expresses itself with the desire for and love of individual and collective creation. We hope the Cosmic Baseball Association will be experienced as an art exhibit or as an educational resource. It could also be enjoyed as just a fantasy game of the imagination played for fun and for pleasure and for laughs. Seriously."

Twenty-seven teams comprise the Cosmic Baseball Association. All are unusual. Among them are the Alphatown Ionians (a team of philosophers and scientists); Dharma Beats (Beat Generation personalities); Vestal Virgins (a women's team); Eden Bohemians (writers); Heartland Capitalists (entrepreneurs and economists); Vienna Songbirds (classical composers); Bolex Poetics (avant-garde filmmakers); Pranktown Busriders (Merry Pranksters); Telecity Superbas (television personalities); Psychedelia Woodstockings (1960s personalities); Delta Dragons (musicians); Bhutan Vanguards (artists); Barnum Stormers (circus personalities); Khe Sanh Commanders (marine commanders in Vietnam); and Plumbago Bay Graphites (graphic designers, illustrators, typographers).

The players on some teams are not even human: Vermeer paintings (who play for the Paintland Vermeers); movies about the planet Mars (Martian Kinotypes); tarot cards (Riderland Tarotians); Frank Zappa albums (Franklinton Zappas); tropical hurricanes (Tropicland Hurricanes).

If you are of a certain mind-set, this site is fun to explore.

18 Baseball Humor

Some baseball-oriented Web pages that attempt to tickle your funny bone are as predictable as a George Steinbrenner temper tantrum. The sites listed in this chapter feature Chris Berman nicknames and David Letterman top-ten lists, Abbott and Costello's "Who's on First?" and Yogi Berra's "Yogi-isms."

A number are funny in and of themselves: the site devoted to SLUBA (the Sixto Lezcano Ultimate Baseball Association), a Seattle, Washington–based fantasy league. Some find humor in the futility of such teams as the Chicago Cubs and Boston Red Sox, who haven't been world champs since around the time that doughboys were soldiers and not cuddly cartoon characters in Pillsbury sales pitches. Others squeeze laughs out of the dubious accomplishments of major leaguers who *aren't* named Ruth, Musial, or Griffey, Jr. Still more feature your standard one-liners, mini-stories, and question-and-answer style jokes whose punch lines involve gloves and grounders rather than Henny Youngman's wife.

Bits of baseball drollery can be found on any number of Web pages. For example, this is from Total Baseball Daily: "On Sunday, the *New York Post* devoted an entire page—plus most of (the) front page of their news (not sports) section—to chronicling grammatical errors on plaques in Yankee Stadium's Monument Park.

"The *Post* was actually surprised to find poor sentence construction and grammar in Yogi Berra and Casey Stengel's plaques."

The Baseball Gallery

http://www.orst.edu/~protherj/bbl/

Two links on this well-put-together Web site qualify it for this chapter. The first is "Injuries During the Streak," culled from an article by the Knight-Ridder Tribune News Service, which lists the funny and strange mishaps that forced other ballplayers to miss games while Cal Ripken was on his way to breaking Lou Gehrig's consecutive-games-played streak. For starters: "Kevin Mitchell strained a muscle while vomiting"; "Pitcher Steve Foster injured his shoulder knocking over milk bottles during a segment with Jay Leno on 'The Tonight Show'"; "Florida's Randy Veres hurt his hand pounding on a hotel room wall trying to get the people in the next room to quiet down"; "Rickey Henderson missed several games because of frost-bite. In August"; and "In what must be considered the quintessential modern athlete injury, Tony Gwynn missed a couple of games after he smashed his thumb in the door of his luxury car. While going to the bank."

The second is "Quotes from Yogi/Stengel," which is lengthy and self-explanatory. "The Wisdom of Casey Stengel" begins with, "I broke in with four hits and the writers promptly declared they had seen the new Ty Cobb. It took me only a few days to correct that impression." "Yogi-isms" opens with, "If you can't imitate him, don't copy him."

At this site, you also will find some nice, crisp photos of ballplayers from Walter Johnson to Josh Gibson to Barry Bonds.

Berman's Baseball Nicknames

http://www.op.net:80/~lmk/baseball/berman.htm

gopher://wiretap.spies.com/00/Library/Media/Games/berman.nik

http://web.mit.edu/patton/www/humor/berman
and
http://www.eden.rutgers.edu/~mrrosa/baseball/berman.txt

"Berman" is, of course, ESPN sports personality Chris Berman, who has become fabled for concocting middle names that are verbal spin-offs of ballplayers' given monikers.

Hundreds of names are listed from Shawn "Little" Abner, Rick "see ya later" Aguilera, Roberto "Remember The" Alomar, Jesus/Felipe/Matty/Moises "Skip to my" Alou, and Brady "Bunch" Anderson all the way through John "stick it in your" Urrea, Andy "Dick" Van Slyke, Frank "Play the" Viola (who is also known as Frank "Hundred one strings" Viola), Ozzie "Like a" Virgil, Butch "Oil and" Wynegar, and Rich "Not" Yett.

In between are Ruben "High" Sierra, Ty "Corn on the" Cobb, Don "Down the" Gullet, Willie "Lost in the" Mays, and Dwight Gooden "Plenty."

How to Read *Having Fun with Baseball Nicknames*

http://www.sowashco.com/baseball/read.html

Chris Berman is not the lone wit to have fun with baseball nicknames. Although this Web site exists to promote its title book, there are plenty of entertaining examples of how *real* ballplayer nicknames, or those unlike the Berman kind, can be linked by subjects.

You name the topic, and there will be baseball-related AKAs: Travel (Leroy "Satchel" Paige, "Shoeless" Joe Jackson, Roger "The Rocket" Clemens, Harry "Suitcase" Simpson); Religion (Elwin "Preacher" Roe, Warren "Deacon" Newson, Frank "Sweet Music" Viola, Gil "Miracle Worker" Hodges); Las Vegas ("Black Jack" McDowell, John "Bid" McPhee, Clarence "Ace" Parker, "Neon" Deon Sanders); Food (Charles "Chili" Davis, Harold "Pie" Traynor, Arnold "Bake" McBride, John "The Candy Man" Candelaria); Forest Animals (Bill "Moose" Skowron, Don "Tiger" Hoak, James "Hippo" Vaughn, Ryne "Ryno" Sandberg"); and Weather (Vernal "Nippy" Jones, Johnny "Dusty" Baker, "Stormin"' Gorman Thomas, George "Storm" Davis).

Late Show Top 10 Lists

http://207.66.144.5/lateshow/ttlist.html

The "Late Show" is, of course, short for "The Late Show with David Letterman," where goofy top ten lists (brought to you from the home office in wherever) have been comic staples for years.

Type **baseball** on the home page search engine, and you will be taken to lists of top ten "Punchlines to Dirty Baseball Jokes," "Ways to Create More Interest in Baseball," "Signs You're Not Watching a Real Baseball Team," "Rejected Slogans for Major League Baseball," "Signs It's Spring in New York," "Proposed New Baseball Rules," and "Least Popular Attractions at the Baseball Hall of Fame."

You also can enter baseball-related names. "Ripken" yielded the top ten "Horrifying Things About Cal Ripken." "Steinbrenner" brought up the top ten "Least Popular Snacks Sold At the World Series."

Who's on First?

http://www.cs.nps.navy.mil/people/support/akin/Funny/Whos_On_First.html
also
http://math.whitman.edu/sun/whos_on_first.html

http://www.math.okstate.edu/~msepans/humor/WhosOn.html

http://www.alienbill.com/funny/whos.on.first.html

http://www.ece.uc.edu/~pbaraona/stories/abbott_costello.txt

http://www.shu.edu/~mondarvi/whoson.html

Who's on first. What's on second. I Don't Know's on third.

The next best thing to seeing or hearing Bud Abbott and Lou Costello perform their classic baseball routine is to read it on the Internet. One should not be surprised to find "Who's on First?" on so many Web sites; it is the most celebrated of all baseball vaudeville comedy numbers. It was derived from several burlesque routines, and is screened each day at the Baseball Hall of Fame.

"Who's on First?" is presented on-screen in the 1945 Abbott and Costello comedy *The Naughty Nineties.* Shorter renderings can be seen on the duo's 1950s television show, and they even performed it with Joe DiMaggio on TV's "Colgate Comedy Hour." And of course, it was paid homage in the Dustin Hoffman-Tom Cruise feature, *Rain Man*, in which Raymond Babbitt, the autistic savant played by Hoffman, recites the routine whenever he feels threatened and obsesses over "trying to find out...what's the guy's name on first base."

SLUBA

http://www.eskimo.com/~oolon/sluba

The concept behind the formation of a number of fantasy/roto leagues occasionally is quite funny—some intentionally and, I am sure, some not.

Upon perusing scores of fantasy/roto Web sites, one stands out for its originality and sheer audacity. It is the Sixto Lezcano Ultimate Baseball Association (or SLUBA—not to be confused with "Shotgun" Shuba), a Seattle–based fantasy league "named after legendary outfielder Sixto Lezcano, who played mostly for Milwaukee." Sixto, needless to say, is far from a legend. But he did have a respectable major league career, lasting 12 years in the bigs while compiling a .271 lifetime average and bashing 148 homers.

According to the Web site home page, SLUBA owners "have included a member of the Seattle Mariner front office, a major players agent, a member of the Seattle Mariner broadcast team, W.P. Kinsella who wrote the great book *Shoeless Joe* and a bunch of regular guys who usually won because they knew more about baseball than these 'experts.'" The home page includes a photo of Sixto himself posing with SLUBA bosses Bob Rosenzweig ("of the powerhouse Skillets"), Jack Fleming ("of the formidable Flemengos"), and Sam Martin ("of the expansion Suns").

SLUBA even has an official Championship Traveling Trophy: a baseball autographed by the one and only Sixto!

Ya gotta love it!

Hairface's Major League Baseball Wall O'Shame

http://www.inetnow.net/~ferenczy/thon.html

The "Wall O'Shame," a link on The Dickie Thon Fan Club Web site, is an ode to "players who gave their 110% to achieve mediocrity, but could never quite get there."

Members include Kelly Mann ("released after failing to live up to his .208 rookie campaign"); Onix Concepcion ("groomed as the successor to U.L. Washington" as Kansas City Royals' shortstop); Wayne Krenchicki ("a lifetime .188 hitter vs. lefties w/0 extra bases"); Brad Komminsk ("the Braves' biggest disappointment of the '80s"); Oswaldo

Peraza ("catcher turned pitcher because he couldn't hit...found out he couldn't throw a strike either"); Tony Perezchica (a career minor leaguer who "has toiled in the trenches so long he's been a minor league double play partner of both Matt Williams and Derek Jeter"); Shawn Abner ("what list of baseball disasters would be complete without Lil Abner"); Sammy Khalifa ("since Rafael Belliard reached the majors he has been a defensive replacement for many shortstops, but sadly enough he tended to be the offensive replacement for Sammy"); Alexis Infante ("the versatile .109 hitter could play anywhere but hit nowhere"); and Jimmy Kremers (a third-string catcher who "would have been the worst hitter in the past 20 years, if not for Infante").

Others to make the Wall: Buddy Biancalana; Bobby Meacham; Argenis Salazar; Orlando Mercado; Juan Espino; Domingo Ramos; Tom Lawless; Billy Jo Robidoux; Beau Allred; Mike Loynd; Steve Jeltz; Houston Jiminez; Steve Fireovid; Hensley "Bam Bam" Meulens; and Luis "Funky Cool" Medina.

Let us not forget Billy Bean ("#4 pick of Detroit in '86, .226"), Billy Beane ("#1 pick of NY Mets in '80, .219"), and Billy Bene (pronounced Buh-nay and the "#1 pick of LA in '88. Drafted because of fastball, never reached majors because of everything else").

Griffey in '96

http://www2.netdoor.com/~grant/griffey.html#Running

The 1996 presidential election may be history, but this Web site happily remains on the Internet. At the top of its home page is a reproduction of a "Griffey '96" campaign button along with a photo of Junior belting a dinger in front of a large American flag.

On the site, you will learn why Griffey is tough on crime, a leader, honest, and ever-ready "to take on the issues that concern us all."

There even is an endorsement from James Carville, the noted political strategist: "People don't want someone coming out of left field and they sure don't want someone too far right. Griffey's in the center, perfectly positioned."

Another 50-homer season, and this site surely will be updated to "Griffey in 2000."

Famous Yogi Berra Quotes

http://www.yogiberraclassic.org/quotes.htm

What would a chapter on baseball humor be without a mention of Yogi Berra? Indeed, what would the game of baseball be without this colorful and beloved legend, who is the type of personality you can cherish even if you despise the New York Yankees.

The top of this Web site's home page features a color illustration of Yogi with cocked bat in hand, next to a black-and-white still of him just after he has swung at a pitch. Scroll down, and you will find not only such celebrated Yogi-isms as "It ain't over till its over" and "This is like deja vu all over again" but "I couldn't tell if the streaker was a man or woman because it had a bag over its head."

Here is Yogi, after seeing a Steve McQueen movie: "He must have made that before he died."

Another related page: "Yogi-isms" From Berra's Montclair State Commencement Speech (*http://cgi.nando.net /newsroom/ap/bbo/1996/mlb/mlb/feat/archive/051696/mlb24396.html*).

For yet more Yogi quotes, along with humorous ones from an array of baseball wits, check out *http://members.aol.com/bbsvhome/quotes.htm*, which is a link on the Web site maintained by the Bavarian Baseball and Softball Federation!

Casey Stengel's 1958 Congressional Testimony Wavs

http://www.earthstation1.simplenet.com/stengel.html

Despite its visually stunning home page, you do not so much see as hear this Web site. With the proper software (which you can download from the site), you will be able to listen to four minutes'-worth of The Old Professor's legendary, hilariously rambling appearance before Congress—spoken in pure Stengelese. In it, he "explains" why a bill should be passed that would allow Major League Baseball to remain exempt from antitrust laws.

A complete text version of Casey's testimony can be found as a link on the Fastball Web site (*http//www.fastball.com/foulpole/casey/casey1.html*).

Baseball Humor

http://www.eden.rutgers.edu/~mrrosa/baseball/bbquotes.txt

This page is a collection of baseball buffoonery compiled by "Mark." Included are "Jay Johnstone's Twenty Best Answers to Every Question Ever Asked by Sportswriters," "Don Carman's 37 Responses to Reporters," "Johnstone's Three Dumbest Answers I've Ever Heard From Athletes," "Top 25 Classic (Jerry) Colemanisms," and individual quips. Among the latter: "They shouldn't throw at me—I'm the father of five or six kids" (Tito Fuentes, upon being brushed back); "I don't know, I never smoked Astroturf" (Tug McGraw, on being asked whether he preferred grass or Astroturf); and "Either you give me what I demand, or I take what you're offering" (Joe Torre, while negotiating a contract).

Baseball Jokes

http://www.cpba.org/sean/jokes.htm

"MLB is deciding whether or not to reinstate Pete Rose in the 98 season. When asked about it, Rose said, 'I hope they do, cause I've got $50 riding on it.'"

"What's the difference between Mel Rojas and UPS? UPS knows how to throw a strike."

"Well, at least the Cubs are trying. They installed a new pitching machine the other day. Unfortunately it beat them 4-1."

These and other similar gems can be found on this entertaining Web page.

A more cornball-style humor dominates Baseball Jokes (*http://www.laughnet.net/archive/jokes/baseball.htm*). For example, "Why is it so windy at Candlestick Park?"

"Because of all the Giant fans."

"What do you get when you cross a tree with a baseball player?"

"Babe Root"

Among the baseball "quotes": "I watch a lot of baseball on the radio." (Gerald Ford, 1978); "I won't play for a penny less than $1,500." (Honus Wagner, upon turning down a contract offer for $2,000).

Religion as Baseball

http://www.cs.ccsu.ctstateu.edu/~pelletie/newhumor/religion-baseball.html

This briefest of Web pages, culled from an "unknown Internet source," humorously links religion and baseball.

Several examples: Calvinists believe the game is fixed; Quakers won't swing; Amish walk a lot; Pagans sacrifice; Televangelists get caught stealing; Evangelicals make effective pitches; Atheists refuse to have an Umpire; and The Pope claims never to have committed an error.

The Hot Corner

http://www.thehotcorner.com/

This web-zine is in this chapter because, in addition to offering "news, commentary (and) original research," it also features "plenty of humor."

When I logged on, there was a list of "top ten new locations for the New York Yankees"—and you can bet your 1959 Topps Mickey Mantle baseball card that none are in the Bronx. Upon Wade Boggs's being sent in to pitch in a game, there was a "top ten best future stunts for Wade Boggs." My favorite citation: "Ride Steinbrenner's horse in Kentucky Derby."

Mystic Sports Journal

http://www.sirius.com/~regent/MSJ/Mystic.html

If your funny bone is tickled by the declarations at the top of the journal's home page—"Invisible cows control my destiny" (from John Wetteland) and "I've never been to heaven or been to hell, but if this isn't hell, it's got to be a suburb" (Kirby Puckett)—you more than likely will be entertained by this web-zine.

It is crammed with quirky observations ("Mal Fichman, manager of the Johnston Steal of the Frontier Baseball League, set fire to his undershirt in a fit of superstitious anger in front of his team"); lists (a "Top Ten Great Things About Major League Baseball," the first of which is, "If you want to get a player injured, just roll a tarp up his leg"); and predictions (such as a *Mystic Sports Journal* "Excloosive," headlined "Dodgers to Leave L.A. for Brooklyn").

Odie the Wonder Dummy

http://www.inetnow.net/~ferenczy/odie1.html

This Web site merits a spot here if only for the title of the poem that appears on its home page: "Remember the Alomar."

Page 2 of the site is "Honest Odie's Used Closer Lot," in which relief pitchers are compared to used cars.

Page 3 consists of one-liners, puns, and other nonsense.

Page 4 contains a "conversation" between Felipe Alou and Cito Gaston.

Only on the Internet!

Answering Machine Messages

http://www.clari.net/rhf/jokes/91q1/ansmg.html

In some ways, men and women will remain eternally different.

During the baseball season, Bob Dashman once put a message on his answering machine that was an authentic-sounding re-creation of the radio commentary of the final game of a campaign. In this fiction, the Cubs and Mets are battling for the pennant. They are playing, and the team that wins the game goes on to the playoffs. It is the ninth inning, with two outs. The Cubs trail by a run, but have a runner—Shawon Dunston—leading off third. BOB comes up to bat against Dwight Gooden. The hurler fires a hard one to the plate. BOB swings and belts a long drive deep to rightfield. Darryl Strawberry "RACES OVER AND MAKES A LEAPING CATCH AT THE WALL AND BOB IS OUT!!!! Yes, Bob is out, but he'll be happy to return your call as soon as possible."

Dashman reports that the response to his message, which lasted 60 seconds, "was interesting. Men loved it, and passed my phone number around so that their buddies could call in and hear it.

"Women, in general, didn't understand it, and left messages complaining that it was too long, too loud, or didn't make any sense."

How 'bout them cubs?

http://comedy.clari.net/rhf/jokes/88q1/7433.19.html

Speaking of the Chicago Cubs, this Web page is a list of all that has happened in the world since the team won its last World Series—way back in 1908.

The final entry sums it all up: "Hundreds of boys were born, raised, played inept baseball for the Cubs, retired and died of old age."

If you are a die-hard Cubs fan, however, you will not be amused.

The content on the preceding two pages originally appeared in the *rec.humor.funny* newsgroup. More can be found by typing in **baseball** or specific baseball-related terms on the search engine located at *http://www.clari.net/rhf/search.html.*

Jeff Northrup's Depressing Red Sox Page

http://www.tiac.net/users/northrup/baseball.html

Northrup—any relation to Jim?—feels it is his "duty to continue to depress those of you whose Hose are Carmine and whose hearts are sore from the burden of 79 years without the attainment of Baseball Nirvana. Come on in, grab a box of tissues, and read on."

As any baseball fan knows, the Bosox sold Babe Ruth to the New York Yankees in what may be the most infamous one-sided transaction in the game's history. For this reason, as Northrup so aptly declares, "Contrary to historical belief, the Depression began in 1918" for Red Sox fans.

However, if you click on the "Worst Trades Ever" icon, you will find a list of other Bosox blunders, accompanied by Northrup's caustic commentary.

Other site highlights: the "Yess, Genulmens, Speling Kounts" note in which Northrup offers his thoughts on what should be the proper pronunciation of Jimy Williams and his views on the Bosox bullpen, as assembled by "the lovely Dan Duquette."

Those who are not Red Sox devotees will find this Web site witty and imaginative.

Those of you who are will find it dispiriting, just as Northrup promises.

Joe DiMaggio's Lame Home Page

http://www.eden.com/~joed/

Bet you didn't know that Joe DiMaggio maintains his very own Web site.

This is it. Only trouble is, *this* Joe D. is not *the* Joe D.

Before you can ask, he offers his "answers to the usual questions":

"Yes, it's my real name."

"No, no relation that I know of."

"No, my parents weren't baseball fans."

"Yes, I get comments about it all the time."

"No, I don't play baseball."

"Marilyn's dead."

"I am a coffee achiever."

If the "lame" photo included on the home page is insufficient proof that *this* Joe D. is not *the* Joe D., he even posts a reproduction of his driver's license!

The Internet is crammed with endless Web pages offering Yankee Clipper memorabilia for sale ("Joe DiMaggio: Great 8x10 color photo of this all-time legend: $90"; "Joe DiMaggio signed 8x10 sepia print, action shot: $195"; "Joe DiMaggio Autographed Ball: $275"; "Joe DiMaggio: 12x15 Autographed Baseball Statistical Plaque: $275").

How much do you suppose this DiMaggio's autograph is worth? Perhaps he could sell them online. They *would*, after all, be authentic Joe DiMaggio signatures!

Defaced Baseball Cards

http://www.hightimes.com:80/~hightimes/ht/sl/art/cards/

Despite the fact that this Web page is a link on the *High Times* magazine site, you will not need to be stoned to be amused by its content. It consists of examples of defaced cards from the collection of Paul Kuhrman, who since 1979 has been sponsoring baseball card defacing parties.

Most of the marred cards are commons and have been included in art exhibits. But a number of valuable ones, including a Rickey Henderson rookie card, have been defaced—and devalued.

Would Kuhrman mark up a *really* expensive card? It is noted that he "dreams of getting the opportunity to deface a Honus Wagner tobacco card (which has sold at auction for hundreds of thousands of dollars), or a Mickey Mantle rookie card (also worth way too much money for its own good)."

Among the cards reproduced on the site: a Topps Brad Arnsberg with a diaper across the ballplayer's face; a Donruss Vince Coleman in which a stick of dynamite replaces a bat; a Donruss Billy Hatcher featuring a dinosaur and a chicken; a Topps Mets Leaders featuring Gary Carter and Darryl Strawberry along with a pair of GIs walking arm-in-arm; a Donruss Rance Mulliniks with a turban replacing his baseball cap and featuring a sacrificial lamb; an indescribably goofy Bowman Ellis Burks; and a Topps Tony Armas featuring, appropriately enough, gigantic arms.

Why Softball Is Better Than Sex

http://www.safari.net/~sky/freedom/softball.htm

The humor on this Web page is clever and never rated anything less than PG-13 or R. Among the entries:

> In softball, the other team pays attention throughout, even if they're done scoring.
>
> If you don't score in a softball game, the other team doesn't ask you if you've had that problem often.
>
> You don't mind if your parents come to watch you play softball.
>
> Rest assured that the other team will not invite you to the ballet.
>
> No matter how drunk the other team is they never throw up in your bed.

A Guide to the Bases

http://web.mit.edu/patton/www/humor/Bases

For years, the expression "getting to first base" meant, well, getting to first base with a romantic partner. It usually connoted kissing, and hitting a home run "was ALWAYS sex, although it was rarely reached in the times when you had to refer to it in terms of bases."

This Web page includes a contemporary (and very R-rated) variation on the above. Among the entries: "Error" (condom breaks during sex); "Banned For Life For Gambling" (sex without condom); "Pine Tar" (KY jelly); and "Rain Delay" (parents/roommate return home unexpectedly).

The Inside Pitch

http://pegasus.rutgers.edu/~tarose/

This web-zine features brief articles and analysis, and its focus is not baseball humor. But on my visit, there was a bit of caustic wit on its home page in the form of a survey in which participants were asked to vote for "the most idiotic owner in all of sports."

You could choose between any one of five candidates—each named Jerry Reinsdorf.

19

Fun and Games

Although plenty of baseball-related computer games and trivia competitions exist as links on Web sites, an astounding number of individual pages are devoted solely to contests. Some are interactive diversions that you can play directly off the site either for free or for a fee. Many more are sponsored by computer simulation leagues that use Diamond Mind, Tony LaRussa, Strat-O-Matic, or other software.

Some of the most helpful game-related sites are those that feature reviews of software written by players who have purchased the product and those that offer how-to-play hints and strategies. Unfortunately, among game-oriented Web sites, these come fairly infrequently. Finding a solid and intelligently written game review page is almost like finding a Web site that is giving away free baseball cards.

CyberSkipper

http://www.cyberskipper.com/

This free interactive Web game (which supports itself via advertising) describes itself as "a baseball forecasting game for fans of every major league team and every major league player."

For openers, click on the CyberSkipper logo on the home page. You will learn that there is a different game for every team and that CyberSkipper involves predicting player performance.

Before signing up, you can play several simulated "spring training games" to get a feel of what CyberSkipper is all about.

Home Run Challenge

http://www.ipass.net/~homerderby/homerunchallenge/

The rules of this free fantasy game—which is played during the baseball season and features "a special affinity for home runs"—are explained on its home page.

I liked the clever line at the bottom of the page: "This page has had more hits than Tony Gwynn."

The Games People Play...

http://www.mindsync.com/swatson/

Here is a self-described "newsletter for serious sports gamers!" Although it is a subscription publication, sample articles are available online.

When I visited the site, many free files also could be accessed from the "TGPP Download Page." They included "the 1946 International League season for 'Baseball for Windows,' created from scratch by Chuck Partington" (see the following entry) and "the 1950 Pacific Coast League season for 'Diamond Mind Baseball' (Version 7.0), created from scratch by Stephen Davis," with quite a few in between.

Chuck's Baseball Replays

http://pw2.netcom.com/~ctpart/chuck.html

On his Web page, Chuck Partington posts the results of his replays of major league and Pacific Coast League seasons using APBA and Diamond Mind simulation games. Among them: the 1947 and 1949 ML seasons, and the 1949 PCL campaign.

In 1947, the Brooklyn Dodgers won the National League pennant with a 94-60 record, and the New York Yankees emerged victorious in the American League at 97-57. The Bronx Bombers went on to beat Brooklyn's Bums in a seven-game World Series. You could look all this up in your handy baseball encyclopedia.

Although Chuck's final standings for that season had the Yankees and Dodgers copping pennants, his Bums won 111 games and no longer needed to wait 'til next year as they took the World Series four games-to-one.

What a way to rewrite history!

The Official World Series Baseball and Information System Game

http://users.deltanet.com/~tdb/wsbb.htm

Although you must order this simulation game—which you can do after downloading a demo version—it is cited here because of its special quality: It is a "baseball game for sight-impaired owners of IBM computers and clones."

The game was created by Harry Hollingsworth, who describes himself as a "retired economist and statistician and ultimate baseball fan." Particularly notable is the "History of WSBB" link, in which Hollingsworth writes about his lifelong love of baseball games and how he came to develop this particular one in the early 1980s, "when I retired on disability with bad eyes."

GameSpot

http://www.gamespot.com/

Interested in purchasing a baseball computer game but don't know where to begin? This Web site offers basic data on and critiques of a wide assortment of sports and other games.

Click on the "sports" icon, found on the right of the home page, and you will be taken to a game list. When I logged on, the baseball-related games included "Aaron vs. Ruth," "Baseball Mogul," "Baseball Pro '96," "Baseball Pro '98," "Frank Thomas Big Hurt Baseball," "Grand Slam," "Hardball," "Tony LaRussa Baseball 3," "Tony LaRussa Baseball 4," "Triple Play 97," and "Triple Play 98." For each game, you'll find reviews, player comments (which are solicited), previews, demos, hints, and more.

The Cheap Seats (*http://webcube.volstate.net/~marv/*) also features evaluations of baseball-related games, offering numerical ratings in various areas (playability, realism, statistics, options, and graphics) and an "Overall" assessment.

StratWeb

http://www.enter.net/~adamw/strat.html

This Web site, maintained by Adam Wodon, is described as "a hub for the latest in news, history and information about the Strat-O-Matic World. This site has the blessing, but, as of yet, not the official endorsement of Strat-O-Matic."

Perhaps this is because Wodon does not go about hyping Strat-O-Matic as the greatest game since the evolution of baseball. Although he does offer new product information, he reports on bugs and oversights found in the already-marketed product. And he actively solicits opinions, playing tips, and strategy comments from game players who happen to come upon his site. The only requirement for posting is that it is "well-written, and informative or entertaining."

An especially interesting link is the "Nameless Player Info," in which Wodon notes that, because of its contract with the Major League Baseball Players Association, Strat-O-Matic was "unable to put names on the cards or in the appropriate spots on the roster disk for players not in the MLBPA last year. I have, on my own and independently, done the research to determine which players these are supposed to be." Then Wodon presents the list.

If you are at all interested in Strat-O-Matic, this Web site is a must-read.

Strat Research Associates

http://www.dnaco.net/~velten/

This Web site is designed for the more serious Strat-O-Matic player. It is maintained by Vince Velten and devoted "to the quantitative study of Strat-O-Matic baseball."

The essays found here are titled "Manager Tactical Impact," "Stealing: A Runs Created Analysis," and "Team Strength Estimate." Additionally, Strat Research Associates has developed LINEUP, a spreadsheet that addresses "perhaps the central question in SOM player selection—when to trade-off glove for stick or 'stack' against a backwards/forwards pitcher."

You will not be able to make it through this Web site without straining your brain. But it just may add to your knowledge and enjoyment of Strat-O-Matic.

Diamond Mind/PTP Leagues

http://wsrv.clas.virginia.edu/~mij6t/otherlg.html

This handy, link-loaded Web site is an excellent starting point for anyone interested in the who, what, and how of Diamond Mind, a popular computer baseball simulation game designed by Tom Tippett and previously known as Pursue the Pennant.

From the home page, you can link to various Web pages that will tell you the ins and outs of the game or clue you in on leagues looking for managers and players seeking leagues.

Links are provided to a number of Diamond Mind leagues. Among the latter, my favorite is The Cold Stove League, a 14-team outfit.

APBA Online

http://broadcast.simplenet.com/apbaonline/

Anything—and I do mean anything—you ever could want to know about the APBA computer simulation baseball game can be found on this Web site, which is "the home for APBA Baseball Players; hosted by APBA Players."

It is, indeed, a model Web site of its type. You'll find information on national APBA tournaments and conventions, ratings of game upgrades, game strategies, an online message center, and much more. Most helpfully, a search engine allows you to look for documents on this very busy site.

APBA Sports Simulation Central

http://home.maine.rr.com/sports/

This Web site is maintained by Ron (any relation to Carlos?) Bernier, who notes, "My emphasis...is on APBA products...I have played many others, but have grown to like APBA products the best."

Bernier includes an impressive array of APBA-related material, from news to software updates to leagues.

APBA Central

http://pw1.netcom.com/~mcclureb/apba.html

If after perusing APBA Online and APBA Sports Simulation Central, you *still* are hankering for APBA-related information, you probably will find it here. Although the home page is just a bit too self-congratulatory ("Would you believe over 7,500 hits have been registered since APBA Central's inception just a few short months ago?"), this Web site is loaded with a potpourri of material.

Twentieth Century Baseball Association

http://www.geocities.com/Colosseum/3211/

The Twentieth Century Baseball Association, or TCBA, has been in existence since 1975. It includes three baseball leagues: TCBA Yesterday, which replays past baseball seasons and heads back in time; and TCBA Today and TCBA/NL, which deal in the present. All utilize the APBA game.

Managers have hailed from across the United States, Canada, and Europe; they even have come from Saudi Arabia and on board a U.S. Navy ship cruising the Pacific.

The TCBA is highly organized—there even is a league constitution. Franchises "are not awarded lightly....Criteria for accepting new managers include baseball (and APBA game) knowledge and the reliability to complete a home schedule on time." However, there is a ten percent annual turn-over rate among managers. Also worth a look: the material in the self-explanatory "How We Started The TCBA in 1975" link.

Dave Vandal's Tony LaRussa Baseball Simulation

http://members.aol.com/popout/index.htm

All you need to know about this Web page is that it is "devoted to players of the Tony LaRussa 2 and 3 baseball simulation. If you would like your name added to the waiting list for a future league, you can e-mail me."

If you click on the icon under the blinking "In Progress League," you will come to a page that resembles one on a well-designed super-site or official team site. It includes news items, head shots, and game-action photos of real major leaguers and links to scores, schedules, statistics, and such. The only difference is that these big leaguers play for the Bedford Downeaters and Framingham Muskrats rather than the Boston Red Sox and Florida Marlins, and the page is spotlighting happenings in the AOL Tony LaRussa 3/96 League.

Nick Keren's Ultimate Utilities

http://ourworld.compuserve.com/homepages/NickKeren/

From this Web site, you can download additional software for Tony LaRussa games. Keren designed them himself as shareware add-ons. "My goal was to enhance this fine baseball simulation to make it more enjoyable, for both myself as well as others," Keren observes.

On the "About This Site" page, it is noted that, for those who have registered or purchased the utilities, the site "provides an environment where you can get the most recent updates to your release of the utilities free, find out what Nick might be coming out with next, and get answers to questions you may have about the utilities. To registered individuals, the site becomes a 'support central' of sorts. For those who have not tried the Ultimate Utilities, this site provides an environment where you can download evaluation versions to test drive, you can browse through feedback from others who are using the utilities, or get further information on how to register/purchase them."

Also on the site: everything from how-to information regarding the game to a list of LaRussa baseball leagues on the Internet.

Baseball Quiz

http://huizen.dds.nl/~etb/e-knotty.htm

Think you are an expert on baseball rules? Your knowledge of ballyard regulations will be tested on this Web site, which is maintained by Erick T. Barkhuis.

The questions Barkhuis posts are not trivia-related, but involve baseball policy and strategy. There may be a game situation. Then a specific play occurs, and you are given a multiple choice of answers regarding the correct umpire ruling or solution. You also can download previous quizzes and their answers.

Those who make correct choices have their names posted on the site. Barkhuis ranks frequent participants by "times-at-bat" and "number of hits" and lists champion players in a Baseball Quiz Hall of Fame.

OBFLB

http://virtual.union.edu/obflb/

OBFLB stands for Original Bitnet Fantasy Baseball League, a 24-team organization "run completely through electronic mail and completely free of charge since we were founded in 1989"—which makes it a graybeard among ongoing online games.

Home page links include a league history and season-by-season data, league information files, and "other league stuff." If upon exploring the site you think you might like to play, you can have your name added to a waiting list to become an assistant owner. When one of the established owners departs, a new one is selected from the assistant owners pool.

Note that the site currently has "a long waiting list, and there is little hope that someone being added to the list now would even become an assistant this season." But this Web site does serve another purpose; it offers an illustration of an e-mail league that has successfully operated for a long period of time, and the information on it can be used as a model for establishing a league of your own.

Another related Web site is Internet Baseball League (*http://www.ibl.org/*), "an electronic play-by-mail league which uses a modified version of the 'Pursue the Pennant' board game known as 'The IBL Game.'"

National On-Line Baseball League

http://www.mich.com/%7Eserra11/

The National On-Line Baseball League is yet another free Internet baseball competition. To play, all you need is any version of Sierra's Front Page Sports Baseball. The home page emphasizes that "this is a FREE league, you don't have to pay a dime. This is just a group of people who love baseball, and enjoy 'owning' their own teams."

On this Web site, you will find an explanation of how the game works, the basics of ownership, and stats from the initial seasons.

Interested players are advised that "the NOBL is running at near capacity, with almost every team having an owner...e-mail us and see if a team has popped open."

Baseball for Sale

On the Internet, you can find hundreds—no, make that thousands—of Web sites that exist solely to sell you baseball cards, autographs, caps, T-shirts, jerseys, press pins, paperweights, yearbooks, programs, magazines, posters, balls, bats, bat weight donuts, batting cages, batting machines, pitching machines, gloves, batting gloves, glove lacing kits, wrist bands, uniforms, shoes, sunglasses, warm-up pullovers, instructional books, and videos. Many even offer baseball memorabilia for bidding via auction. You can find practically anything for sale—with the exception of a minority share of your favorite major league team.

Some of the memorabilia-oriented sites are elaborately designed using nifty graphics, reproductions of baseball cards, and so forth. (After perusing scores of these sites, my one discovery was that more feature images of Ken Griffey, Jr., than any other ballplayer past or present.) Others dispense with visuals—except for the VISA and MasterCard logos, which may be used to complete your purchase.

Some sites are generically named. In the baseball card category, there are All Star Sports Cards; Ballpark Sports Cards & Collectibles; Card Connection; Classic Cards; and Vintage Baseball Cards. Some tell you the name of the dealer: Al Young's Baseball Cards; Collectibles and Memorabilia; Alan Sunderman's Baseball Cards; Bob's Baseball Cards; Bill's Baseball Cards; Bill Henderson's Baseball Cards; Curt's Cards; Vern Gorman's Baseball Trading Cards; Amy's Sports Card Auctions; Peggy's Baseball Cards; and Sheryl's Card Shop.

Some try to be clever: Baseball Card "Kid" or Chas-Ra-Tazz Baseball Cards. Others attempt to evoke nostalgia: Baseball Card Time Machine; The Bicycle Spoke Sportscards; Diamond Dreams; and Street Corner Sports. Still more sound corporate and official: AGG Sportscards & Collectibles, and Mid-Atlantic Sports Cards, Inc. Still more simply claim to be amazing: Amazing Baseball Card Auction, and Amazing Yankee Bob's Sports Cards and Memorabilia.

The equipment-oriented sites range from Accubat (a practice aid which, it is claimed, allows you to "hit grounders, fly balls and line drives with the accuracy of a professional") and ASMI Sports (makers of "the natural baseball/softball system") to SportsFrame, Inc., (which, according to the company CEO and president, offers "the most innovative, portable batting/pitching net on the market").

For logical reasons, the word "baseball" often is found at the beginning of the Web sites' names.

At Baseball Direct, you can order historic World Series tapes.

At Baseball Express, you can purchase equipment.

At Baseball Fantasy Broadcasts, you can be the hero of a "simulated 'radio' broadcast on cassette tape, scripted especially to your baseball fantasy."

At Baseball Imuggination, you can order special digital baseball cards featuring your own photo and statistics.

At Baseball Songs—Required Records, you can purchase cassettes of baseball music written and performed by Barry Feldman.

This chapter spotlights selected baseball-for-sale Web sites. Some are of special interest, whereas others are really out of the ordinary or offer more than just items for sale.

However, a citation here (or, for that matter, a mention in the preceding introduction) should in no way be construed as an endorsement of a product or service.

Beckett Online

http://www.beckett.com/

The Beckett sports card/memorabilia price guides are the bibles of the hobby. Its Web site offers links to the "Beckett Hobby Insider," a weekly newsletter offering industry news; previews of Beckett publications (including *Beckett Baseball Card Monthly*); "Hobby Happenings" (offering everything from results of major sports card auctions to data on baseball card company products); even a Beckett-sponsored newsgroup.

If you register with the company's Web site—at last look, enrollment was free—you will have access to a convention calendar and further hobby information. You also can subscribe to one or more of the site's interactive price guides, which include the same data found in Beckett's monthly publications.

Tuff Stuff

http://www.tuffstuffonline.com/

Tuff Stuff is a sports/non-sports card price guide and hobby magazine, and its Web site is loaded with useful information

When I logged on, there were articles ("Would a new home-run record propel Maris' memorabilia?" and "Collecting Publications," about amassing old sports magazines); lists of newly released card sets; a survey of the "hottest selling cards"; reviews of new sets; an address list of card companies; results of recent auctions and information on upcoming ones; even an interactive Kenner sports figurine price guide and a buy-sell-trade bulletin board.

A handy search engine allows you to look up names found throughout the site. However, a password is required to access the Tuff Stuff price guide.

Comparison shoppers might want to check out the "Price Guides" link found on the World Wide Collectors Digest Web site (*http://www.wwcd.com/*) and Sports Collectors Universe (*http://card-universe.com/prices/*), which offers its own theories on card grading along with prices for dozens of sets from 1909 to the present.

Another site featuring helpful bits of hobby information is Baseball Card News (*www.baseball-cards.com*). Here you will find brief articles ("Ted Williams' son says 'Watch out for fake autographs" or "Problems with Signature Rookies Autographs Redemptions").

At the top of the home page is a quote from Pete Rose: "I'm no different from anybody else with two arms, two legs and forty-two hundred hits."

The Topps Company

http://www.topps.com/

Admittedly, baseball card company Web sites exist to advertise their products. Yet a few do extend beyond self-promotion and offer more than just "What's New and Hot" and "Cool Things to Buy" links.

This site features an informative "Topps History" link, which explains how the company was founded in 1938 by four brothers, Abraham, Ira, Philip, and Joseph Shorin. Originally, Topps just marketed chewing gum. During World War II, it sported a slogan that mirrored the nation's defense-mindedness: "Don't Talk Chum, Chew Topps Gum." Baseball cards did not become a part of the Topps product line until 1951.

Other card company sites do have their pluses. The home page for Donruss (*http://www.donruss.com/*) is dominated by an imaginatively conceived image: the inside of a closet, with animated shoe boxes of cards opening and closing amid the shirts on hangers and athletic equipment. But beyond this, there is little more on the site than lists of the company's product and a skimpy timeline covering its history. Fleer Skybox International (*http://www.fleerskybox.com/*), meanwhile, is ruled by boring, self-serving declarations ("dealers swarm to Flair Showcase Baseball Legacy Collection Masterpiece Tracker"; "1997 Fleer Ultra MLB Series 2 & Fleer MLB Series 2 Sold Out"; or "Baseball's Superstars Come to Life on 1997 Metal Universe Cards").

The essence of the manner in which card collecting has changed from a child's pastime to a big-bucks business where greed rules is captured on the Web site of Pinnacle Trading Cards (*http://www.pinnacle-brands.com/*). When I logged on, the first words I saw were "BOUNTY $35,000," relating to a company promotion. ("Collect four Authentic Press Plates from the same card and win $35,000.")

Other baseball card manufacturers Web sites:

Pacific Trading Cards:
http://www.pacific-trading-cards.com/

Signature Rookies:
http://www.wwcd.com.whatsnew/sigrook/sigrook.html

Upper Deck:
http://www.upperdeck.com/

Internet's Baseball Card Auction

http://www.baseball-cards.com/market/

If you have baseball cards to sell or are looking to purchase them, this Web site is a simple and handy way to do so. A search engine allows you to explore the site's entire database for the cards in stock. Type in the year and player's last name, select the team, and click on "Begin Search," and up pops a list of available items and prices. After searching for a couple of dozen arbitrary names, I determined that the database is stronger on current and recent players and cards and weaker on older ones.

Small fees are charged for listing cards in the database or taking out ads. The search is free.

www.baseball-cards.com

http://www.baseball-cards.com/news

This handy Web page, a link on the Internet's Baseball Card Auction site, earns its own special mention for its content. It features the latest information on card set releases and news and notes. Of special interest: the warnings regarding cards or autographs that may be stolen or in any way unauthentic and the reportage of beefs collectors have had with card companies.

www.baseball-cards.com is the equivalent of a mini-baseball card web-zine. If you are interested in this hobby, this site makes for essential reading.

Hasbro Toy Group's Starting Lineup Page

http://www2.startinglineup.com/startinglineup/slu.htm

This Web site is maintained by the company that markets the popular Kenner Starting Lineup (SLU) sports figures. The site will be helpful for collectors who want information on new products, want to download year-by-year lists of every Starting Lineup figure the company has produced, want a schedule of Starting Lineup conventions held across the country, or simply are curious about the manner in which the figures came to be marketed.

Near the top of the home page is a solicitation for a "Starting Lineup Collector Registration." It is explained that "we'd like to know more about you and be able to let you know about special events or product announcements....we'd appreciate it if you would take a moment to fill in the registration so that there can be a real 'two-way' communication between us." However, the questionnaire (which asks for correspondents' ages, the number of figures they own, and the publications they read) seems to be strictly for market research purposes.

Dave's Starting Lineup Cyberspace Oasis

http://oeonline.com/~slu2/

This busy and colorful Web site spotlights SLU sports figures, which are aptly described as the "Unique Sport Collectible 'Toy.'"

It contains plenty of news and information via such links as "SLU Tabloid Hobby News," "Future SLU Issues," "Trade/Shipping Tips," "Grading," and even "Dave's (not Letterman) Top Ten Lists" (which, of course, relate to the hobby).

Additional links will take you to everything from the Tuff Stuff Web site (see entry earlier in the chapter) from which you can download the latest sports figure price guide to the Hasbro Toy Group's Starting Lineup Page (also see entry earlier in the chapter) to the Web sites of various chain stores that sell SLU figures.

If after perusing this site you still are hankering for Starting Lineup information, check out Gordon's SLU Stop (*http://home.cwnet.com/sluhunt/*).

World Hardball League

http://www.whl.com/welcome.htm

This Web site introduces you to one of the more unusual fantasy-oriented associations: the World Hardball League, described as a "global baseball league featuring teams that represent cities and countries from all corners of the world. The World Hardball League teams are packed with larger than life players who are capable of tremendous heroics both on and off the field! They pound it out on the pages of World Hardball League comic books."

Furthermore, "WHL players play in the league for their love of the game and they never go on strike! Truly, a fantasy world of baseball!"

World Hardball League teams include the Tijuana Tornados, Cairo Desert Dogs, Tel Aviv Crocs, Singapore Stingers, Bombay B's, Mombasa Cheetahs, Kobe Vultures, Perth Great Whites, and Yukon Ice Cats.

The comic books, which are published by Titus Press, are available for purchase. And it is noted that they do not only offer escapist entertainment. "The players and stories are designed to be a positive influence on young people by showing that the team philosophy of winning baseball can be utilized for achieving real life success."

About At Bat

http://yes.net/jAmBoneComics/AboutAtBat.fun

At Bat is described on this Web page as "a fun-filled 'interactive comic book' about a young boy called Joey who knew everything there was to know about baseball—except how to play. It is the story of how Rudy, his big sister and star of the local baseball team, and her fellow teammates who come from different racial backgrounds, teach Joey the fundamentals of baseball while learning about life."

The comic includes animated talking characters; children can click on the dialogue bubbles, which allows the characters to say the dialogue as it is read. Players also can choose to follow the story, play various games on the "Interactive Television," and look for "Hidden Discoverables."

Examples of the comic book's "screen-shots," along with information on ordering At Bat, can be found on-site.

The Nolan Ryan Foundation

http://www.lonestar1.com/nryan/

Some ballplayers even have their own Web sites from which they offer autographed paraphernalia for sale. From this page, you can order Nolan Ryan baseballs, bats, jerseys, pennants, posters, books, photographs, envelopes, and caps. Dozens of items are available, and personal ones also can be sent in for autographing. Flats cost $25; signed baseballs are $35; bats, gloves, or jerseys are $40. If you would like a stat added (for example, "324 wins"), it will cost an extra $10. If you would like a message or additional words (for example, "Best Wishes" or "Happy Birthday"), the price also goes up $10.

However, all proceeds go to the Nolan Ryan Foundation, a nonprofit organization that supports the Nolan Ryan Center for Continuing Education at Alvin (Texas) Community College. The center is a combination Ryan museum and continuing education program/resource center.

Ted Williams Family Enterprises, Ltd.

http://www.hitter.com/

Stan Musial is listed in the membership directory of the Society for American Baseball Research. Under "Expertise," other SABR members might cite the Northern League or Wrigley Field or Jackie Robinson. Stan the Man simply lists "Hitting a baseball"—and who is to argue!

Similarly, this Web site's URL is as appropriate as any on the Internet. So is the initial image on its home page: a black-and-white photo of Teddy Baseball way back when he was barely old enough to shave along with the appellation "the greatest hitter who ever lived."

For after all, of the several dozen Hall of Famers present at the 1997 Cooperstown induction ceremony, Williams was the *lone* one to earn a standing ovation!

This site pays homage to Williams and offers memorabilia and autographs for sale. (The prices, by the way, are positively stratospheric.) But it also includes some fascinating material, from Ted Williams trivia (offered in the form of pop quizzes) to an actual photo taken on February 17, 1953, of Williams crash-landing his F9F Panther after being shot down over enemy territory on a bombing mission during the Korean war.

The Official Site of Babe Ruth

http://www.baberuth.com/

This Web site is copyrighted by the Babe Ruth Family and Babe Ruth Baseball League and "officially licensed" by CMG Worldwide, a business and marketing agency. On it, you will find an exhaustive list of Sultan of Swat merchandise, from figurines to tankards, talking plaques to serigraphs.

Happily, you'll also find links to Ruth's career highlights, quotes by and about the Babe, a Bambino Photo Gallery, and a "Did You Know..." page.

Upon perusing this site, you will learn that, on January 28, 1993, "a beautiful chestnut colt was born with bloodlines pointing him to the winner's circle. With championship stature waiting in his future, what better name for him than Babe Ruth?"

The name of the link that will lead you to this information is "Babe Ruth: The Horse."

The Official Web Site of Yogi Berra

http://www.imall.com/stores/yogiberra/)

This Web site (presented by LTD Enterprises, a "Berra Family Corp.") may offer for sale "the complete line of Authorized Yogi Berra Memorabilia and Photographs along with the new Signature Sportswear line of clothing." But it is enjoyable to browse for its vintage photos of the Yankee Hall of Famer (including a shot of Yogi, garbed in a U.S. Navy uniform and pictured with his father and brother in St. Louis in 1944, and one of him and a pair of fellow GIs taken "somewhere in Italy" in 1945).

The site is a work-in-progress. And browsers with knowledge of the exact number of vintage Berra baseball cards are encouraged to send an e-mail.

Other official ballplayer Web pages include New York Yankee Legend Don 'Bad Boy' Larsen Memorabilia (*http://rand.nidlink.com/~bhbi/yankee/index.html*), from which you can purchase signed photos, display plaques, caps, baseball card collages, baseballs, and books. And you will learn that "Don Larsen is available for personal appearance bookings for autograph sessions, conventions, trade shows and special events." Upon logging onto the Gaylord Perry Memorabilia Store, (*http://www.gaylordperry.com/estore.htm*), you will learn that "you can *now* order *authentic* memorabilia direct from Gaylord Perry Enterprises *online!* Authenticity *guaranteed by Gaylord!*"—and VISA and MasterCard accepted.

Not all ballplayers hawking merchandise are old-timers or Hall of Famers-in-waiting. Right below the "biography" link on the home page of the Official Tom Candiotti Web Site (*http://www.tomcandiotti.com/*) are the flashing bright red words, "Online Gift Shop Now Available!" Here, you can purchase autographed Candiotti game jerseys, baseballs, and photos; official Candiotti Web site T-shirts (available in child and adult sizes) and baseball hats; and even a Tom Candiotti photo key chain. On the "Gift Shop" link is a photo of Candiotti clutching a baseball in one hand and a supermarket cart in the other!

There never will be a plaque in Cooperstown commemorating Candiotti's career. Nor did he ever pitch a perfect game in the World Series. He is at best a journeyman hurler with a below .500 lifetime record.

Yet he expects you to fill your cyberspace shopping cart with Candiotti merchandise, cover your chest with a Candiotti T-shirt, and attach your car and house keys to a Candiotti key chain.

And you wondered why professional athletes are viewed as greedy egomaniacs!

Send $3, it will come

http://www.roanoke.com/Marquee/collector/moonlight.html

One of the primary characters in W.P. Kinsella's *Shoeless Joe* and the movie *Field of Dreams* is Moonlight Graham, an elderly doctor who, decades earlier, barely sipped a cup of coffee with the New York Giants. There of course was a real Moonlight Graham, and he became a physician who practiced in Chisholm, Minnesota, for nearly a half-century.

Doc Graham has been honored in a set of four baseball cards, priced at $3 each; one is reproduced at the top of this Web page. The cards are described as "a great collectible—one that relates to sports, medicine, literature and even Hollywood—that helps out a terrific cause." That cause is the Doc Graham Memorial Scholarship Fund, which awards monies to deserving Chisholm High School graduating seniors.

Be sure to click on the "Moonlight Graham" icon near the bottom of the page. Here, you will find more information on the fund and on Graham.

Legendary Ladies of Baseball

http://members.aol.com/legendlady/index.html

Although you will find a brief history of the All-American Girls Professional Baseball League and player biographies here, this is not a historical Web site. Rather, its purpose is announced at the top of the home page, right by the illustration of the "legendary lady" swinging a bat: to sell AAGPBL autographed memorabilia.

Offered for sale are signed baseball cards, photos, baseballs, bats, jerseys, pennants, posters, sketches, and "There's No Crying in Baseball" T-shirts and sweatshirts.

Jack Aker Baseball

http://www.jackakerbaseball.com/

Aker, who pitched in the major leagues between 1964 and 1974 (all in relief, compiling a 47—45 record with 123 saves and a 3.28 ERA), describes himself as "the only former major league player and coach providing baseball instruction and baseball camps to amateur players year round as a full-time job."

On his Web site, you will find information on the various products and services Aker offers. And you can evensend him a video of yourself practicing or playing ball. For a nominal fee, Aker will "critique your play and show you how to improve your game in a one-of-a-kind video made specifically for you."

Dominating the home page is a photo of Aker meeting President Clinton at a White House reception after being honored with a Giant Steps Award, presented by the Center for the Study of Sport in Society for his "outstanding and dedicated work teaching student-athletes."

Personal Pitcher

http://www2.connectnet.com/~spc/

Do you know a Little Leaguer who desperately needs to develop bat speed and hand-eye coordination? Or, for that matter, do you spend hours (not to mention many dollars) belting baseballs at batting ranges? If so, this product—a backyard portable, battery-powered pitching machine—might be worth an investment.

It is advertised as being "safe enough for a supervised 8 year old, but challenging for the college player who needs to react to 85 mph speeds."

On the home page's "History" link, you will learn that the machine was developed in the late 1980s by the father of 14-year-old Chris Richard, who was desperate to make his high school's junior varsity team and felt he needed an inexpensive and accessible way of getting in extra swings.

Richard, a centerfielder, grew up to be drafted by the St. Louis Cardinals. At last report, he is toiling in the team's minor league system.

Russian International Baseball

http://www.public.iastate.edu/~airedale/rib.html

Legions of baseball fans demonstrate their loyalty to the New York Yankees or Chicago Cubs or Colorado Rockies by sporting team caps, T-shirts, or jerseys. Others favor minor league, Negro League, or AAGPBL gear. On this Web site, you can purchase the hats and T-shirts of "teams that participate in the great sport of baseball in Russia."

The page may exist primarily to sell merchandise, but it also features data on baseball in Russia and such nines as the St. Petersburg Lions, Moscow Red Devils, the Moscow State University squad, the Russian National Team, and the Russian Army Team.

Revenues from all sales help supply these squads and three Russian Junior National Teams with hats. Additionally, a predetermined percentage of all monies goes to each team.

Ballpark Vacations

http://www.clark.net/pub/rothman/ballpark.htm

Elsewhere in this book, you will find above-average Web sites devoted to individual trips to ballyards around the country. Bruce Adams and Margaret Engel did those fans one better: They published a book on their experiences. It is a Fodor's travel guide, titled *Ballpark Vacations: Great Family Trips to Minor League and Classic Major League Baseball Parks Across America*.

This bright Web site includes the book's table of contents, an explanation on how Adams's and Engel's love of baseball is "a genetic thing," and links to articles and interviews on the book from nationwide publications.

Oh, yes, *Ballpark Vacations* is available at your local bookstore.

Ball Park Baseball Tours

http://www.roadtrips.ca/baseball.html

Would you relish a vacation visiting ballyards but do not want to be bothered with making hotel reservations or planning itineraries? If so, you might want to pay a visit to this Web site, which promises that, on its tours, you will "stay in wonderful hotels, sit in great seats and we'll take care of everything, so you can just relax! All you have to do is to be there."

The site even includes photos of happy customers enjoying the game—and each other's company.

The Charlie Rose Baseball & Softball Specialists

http://www.crose.com/

This visually pleasing Web site grabs the attention, beginning with a mini-figure of a player swinging a bat at the top of its home page. Primarily, this is a commercial site that hypes itself as "the nation's only baseball and softball specialty store. We've got all the gear for men, women and kids, from the tee-baller to the big leaguer. You'll find a wide variety of the best gear in any of 10 stores, our catalog, and throughout this web site."

Upon perusing its links, however, it becomes clear that Charlie Rose does offer an astonishing range of products. Although you can have a catalog sent to you, this Web site actually serves as an online product inventory.

Furthermore, from the "Hot Tips" page—the link to it is "Tips"—you can e-mail questions regarding baseball and softball to "professional ballplayers, professional coaches, pro and college scouts, high school coaches, baseball company representatives and the professional Charlie Rose staff."

I decided to test the waters by sending in a question—What are your feelings on the DH?—directed "to professional ballplayers." I never did get a response.

Online Sports Catalog

http://www.onlinesports.com/pages/top,sprt,base.html

Online Sports describes itself as "an interactive, online directory, catalog and showplace for sports and recreational products, services and businesses."

Thousands of for-sale sports items are listed throughout the site. On my visit to the "Shop By Sport: Baseball" page more than 2,000 separate objects were listed from accessories and autographed items through trading cards, videos, and watches. The autographed items included limited edition art, baseballs, photos, bats, caps, magazine covers, and jerseys signed by everyone from Joe DiMaggio to Joe Morgan, Luke Appling to Len Dykstra. The videos mostly were instructionals but also included the likes of *Amazing Sports Bloopers.* And there was an impressive array of merchandise in between.

In many cases, you can view an image of the actual article on your computer screen before ordering. Additionally, a handy search engine allows you to look up specific names or items.

21 Rotisserie/Fantasy Baseball/Player Projections

Rotisserie/fantasy baseball leagues are for fans who want to play at drafting and managing winning teams (whose "performances" are based on major leaguers' actual on-field statistics). A staggering number of Web sites focus on roto/fantasy baseball, stat services, and the like, devoted to serving this fervent audience, which can't seem to get enough forecasting and number-crunching. A query for "fantasy baseball" on the HotBot, AltaVista, Excite, and Infoseek search engines yielded, respectively, 4,981, "about 2,000," 5,450, and 2,365 documents.

Many of these sites are strictly commercial in nature and exist to sell their product. They are crammed with ad hype, telling you that they are the absolute best at what they do.

They promise top quality and endless entertainment: "Welcome to the best baseball pool on the Net!"; "the most exciting Fantasy Baseball contest on the Web!"; "the ultimate in Fantasy League enjoyment."

They guarantee hours of fun for low prices: "Special: 5 teams for only $99"; "All of the above can be yours for just $25"; "1997 Orphan Teams Available Now! Prices Slashed!"

They mimic slick-talking carnival hucksters and traveling salesmen desperate to pawn off sets of encyclopedias as they promise riches: "Our Customers have received over $100,000 in Prizes"; "Step up to play for $12,000 in cash and merchandise"; "CASH PRIZES—WIN UP TO $500" and you even can "make money recruiting friends."

Stat services, meanwhile, offer "the simplest and quickest way to maintain your league's stats"; "a fast and fun way to compare player performance"; or "custom Rotisserie and Fantasy League reports *updated daily* on the WWW."

Some lay on the hype, while the actual price of the service is not immediately apparent. Within the Web site, the price is practically an asterisk, to be found only after wasting minutes of your life perusing the site, downloading its various pages, and exposing yourself to the hard-sell.

Upon spending hours surfing the fantasy/roto/stat service Web sites, a fundamental question emerges: How do you find a truly entertaining and reliable fantasy/roto league or stat service on the Internet?

For openers, a disturbingly high percentage of Web sites listed on search engines are dead. One can imagine the number of individuals who were sucked in by the hype and sent in checks to the managers of these Web pages, only to find them out of business in the instant it takes for Mark McGwire to reach the upper deck.

One URL (which was a link on another Web site) even advertised itself as a "Fantasy Baseball League that uses real major league players." Wow! Does that mean that you can join this league and actually draft Andruw Jones or Albert Belle? Or if you sign up, will your favorite Cleveland Indian or Colorado Rockie come knocking at your door to sit by your side and offer tips on how to win? Alas, upon attempting to link up with the site, I was informed that the file could not be found.

Regarding the formation of leagues, one sure-fire way not to be ripped off is to organize your own confederation with a bunch of friends or coworkers. Another is to play a game sponsored by a reputable source: *The Sporting News* Fantasy Baseball Challenge (***http://www.cdmnet.com/fsi/baseball/***), for example, or CBS SportsLine Fantasy Baseball (***http://ww2.sportsline.com/u/fantasy/baseball/index.html***), or ESPN SportsZone Fantasy Baseball (***http://games-espnet.sportszone.com/cgi/flb/request.dll?FRONTPAGE***).

This is not to say that all small, independent leagues are fly-by-night. Far from it. I am sure that plenty of privately (as opposed to corporately) operated leagues are A-1 quality. However, to join each, play each, and then rate them is fodder for an entirely different book.

Additionally, many fantasy leagues—from the Abner Doubleday Memorial League and All-Ohio Fantasy Baseball League to the Virtual Baseball League and The 'We Can't Get Dates' Rotisserie Baseball League (whose motto is "We have no lives!!")—have their own Web sites on which they offer current standings, league rules, and constitutions. However, these sites will be of interest only to those owning league teams.

Many of these sites do, by their very nature, exude a pure joy and love of baseball and are worth noting. For example, there is the cleverly named Moonlight Graham Fantasy Baseball League, whose divisions are named for Ring Lardner, Harry Caray, and (of course) W.P. Kinsella. Team names in the Berks Montgomery Chester Rotisserie Baseball Association include the Salem Warlocks, Wichita Shockers, Springfield Isotopes, Dallas Eliuks, and Albuquerque Dogs. Three of the teams in the Shoeless Joe Jackson Fantasy Baseball League are Kramer's Komets, Abner's Army, and Dave's Dugout; they are *not* named for Chick Gandil, Eddie Cicotte, or Buck Weaver.

On the subject of data and analysis: If you are willing to pay for such material, there are established and reputable sites. One is Baseball HQ (*http://baseballhq.com/*), sponsored by Ron Shandler's *Baseball Forecaster*. There are some freebie teasers here, but you must subscribe to download most of the goodies.

On perusing player projection-oriented Web sites, I came to realize that plenty of free material is available on the Internet. Some are on sources cited elsewhere in this book. An excellent starting point is the Web site maintained by *USA Today Baseball Weekly* (*http://www.usatoday.com/bbwfront.htm*), which offers John Hunt's lively and authoritative fantasy/roto coverage. You also can download *Baseball Weekly* fantasy/roto pieces from the past year. If figures and facts from last February are outdated, you might be able to find helpful information by linking to the more recent issues. (Hunt also has his own Web site, which is cited below).

Baseball Weekly is not the lone "super-site" to offer stats, strategies, and other fantasy/roto news. Another exceptional one is the fantasy baseball link on the Web site maintained by *The Sporting News* (*http://www.sportingnews.com/*). Here you will find John Benson's Scouting Fantasy Baseball report along with links to lists, tips, and analysis.

You also will find fantasy links at ESPN SportsZone (*http://www.sportszone.com/*) and CBS SportsLine (*http://sportsline.com/*), among others. You can download *USA Today* columnist Rod Beaton's Rotisserie Roundup column (*http:www.usatoday.com/sports/baseball/colrod.htm*); Jeff Sagarin's computer ratings of major league batters and pitchers (*http://www.usatoday.com:80/sports/sagarin.htm*); and *USA Today* FanTrack (*http://www.usatoday.com:80/leadpage/fantrack/fantrack.htm*), a statistics viewer that provides free of charge "instant access to the most up-to-date information on Major League Baseball from the Elias Sports Bureau."

Two basic types of Web sites are listed in this chapter. The first type is not necessarily roto/fantasy league oriented but more theoretical in nature. These sites deal with numbers and projections from mathematical angles. Although these sites are of special interest to students of baseball statistics, roto-geeks should find them engrossing. The second type of site is intended more for typical roto/fantasy players. All are similar in that they primarily deal with statistics and player projections.

Many of the sites analyze the abilities of up-and-comers—minor league .300 hitters or strike-out kings on the verge of making it in the majors. Will they stick in the bigs this year, or are they a season or two away? They may have compiled estimable records at Louisville or Syracuse or Phoenix, but will those numbers be duplicated in The Show—and are these players worth a gamble on roto league draft day? Other sources of information on young ballplayers can be found in the "Minor and Independent Leagues" chapter of this book. One outstanding Web site in this area is Prospects, Projects and Suspects (*http://www.dmlco.com/pps/*).

Finally, before considering the opinions or numbers offered on any site, be sure to note when they were last updated. After all, an opinion on drafting Robin Ventura for your 1997 team was rendered obsolete by the fact that the Chicago White Sox third baseman was injured in spring training and did not return to the majors until well past midseason.

Baseball Engineering

http://www.best.com/~kwoolner/bbeng/

This Web page, maintained by Keith Woolner (moderator of the *rec.sport.baseball.analysis* newsgroup), offers "discussions of baseball engineering and modelling, with an explicit focus on making better strategic and tactical decisions for a baseball team. Over time, you'll find info here related to statistics, performance, strategy and economic issues pertaining to baseball, primarily analyzed from a mathematical or engineering point of view."

There are stats, evaluation systems, and essays galore at Baseball Engineering. One of many fascinating inclusions: a review and analysis, written by Woolner, of a 1954 *Life* magazine article by Branch Rickey "which anticipates the conclusions of the next 40 years of sabermetrics." For those not in the know, *sabermetrics* (as defined in "The Sabermetrics Manifesto," included on this site) is the "attempt to answer objective questions about baseball, such as 'which player on the Red Sox contributed the most to the team's offense?' or 'How many home runs will Ken Griffey hit next year?' It cannot deal with the subjective judgments which are also important to the game, such as 'Who is your favorite player?' or 'That was a great game.'"

Woolner also is interested in receiving e-mail on statistical questions and issues, or historical rankings not contained on the site.

Pay Vs. Performance in Major League Baseball

http://www.pcc.com/~chip/95diff.html

The title tells all on this Web page maintained by Chip Hart, who has "concocted a subjective, but reasonably accurate, methodology for comparing player salaries to their actual performance." It will make good reading for those interested in Hart's subject matter; however, fantasy/roto players also might be able to utilize Hart's analysis.

Statistical Studies of Baseball

http://pacer1.usca.sc.edu/~jfj/baseball.html

This intriguing Web site, maintained by mathematician/college professor John F. Jarvis, explores statistics from the point of view of "numerical analysis"—and is fashioned for serious students of baseball data.

High Boskage House

http://highboskage.com/MAINPAGE.HTM

High Boskage House describes itself as having "a twenty-plus year track record in the field of baseball statistical analysis; for most of that time, it has been providing consulting services to major-league clubs."

At this impressive, exhaustive Web site, which you can spend hours perusing, you will find what are described as "baseball performance measures": daily data focusing on overall team performance, individual performance by team, individual batter performance, batter performance by position(s) played, individual pitcher performance, and top-ten and bottom-ten lists.

There also are complex explanations of the theories behind the manner in which the statistical analysis is derived.

Fantasy Baseball Central

http://www.dcache.net/~gkscalf/index.html

Fantasy Baseball Central describes itself as being "dedicated to providing a site in which owners can access information quickly by providing links to the latest information." It is indeed a one-stop Web site and is must-viewing for fantasy/roto enthusiasts.

The site is crammed with invaluable links, beginning with "Fantasy Players Dollar Values," "Current Depth Charts," "MLB Rosters," "Player Evaluations," "MLB Prospects," "Player Tip Lists," and "Position Eligibility." And you can download data and analysis culled from, among other sources, *Baseball America*, *Baseball Weekly*, *The Sporting News*, CBS SportsLine, and the Web sites of individual fantasy/roto experts.

The number of links and sublinks found on this Web site is mind-boggling.

John Hunt's Fantasy Beat

http://www.fantasybeat.com/

Many fantasy/roto journalists have their own Web sites. Hunt, who writes on the subject for *Baseball Weekly*, maintains this one. On it, you will find helpful fantasy/roto feature pieces, evaluations, tip sheets, answers to readers' questions, and oodles of stats.

In the middle of the pack is Alex Patton's Web Site (*http://www.alexpatton.com/*), which exists primarily to sell products. However, if you explore the site, you will find useful bits of data and analysis—and Alex Patton (who has written for ESPN SportsZone and published several books, his first being *Patton's Price Guide for Fantasy Baseball* in 1989) is one of the most respected names in roto/fantasy/stat analysis.

At the other end of the quality scale is John Benson on Baseball (*http://www,johnbenson.com/*). After you get beyond the staggering amount of unabashed Benson hype (in which he is described as "the original master, the most published author and the expert most often cited in the national media"), this Web site features "free samples" of Benson's fantasy baseball analysis. However, be forewarned: the purpose of the site is not to offer you information but to sell you products.

For Benson's commentary, your best bet is to download the appropriate pages from *The Sporting News* Web site (see the URL listed in this chapter's introduction).

John Mosey's Fantasy Baseball

http://www.mosey.com/

This comprehensive Web site offers links to fantasy baseball articles, current fantasy values, fantasy classifieds, newsgroups, and the like. The player evaluations are especially thorough.

Fantasy Sports Headquarters

http://www.fantasysportshq.com/baseball/theshow.htm

This Web site is an outgrowth of *Fantasy Baseball Weekly*, advertised as "the only television show dedicated to the Fantasy Baseball general manager." The hosts are Paul White, editor-in-chief of *Baseball Weekly*, and Norm Hitzges, the Texas Rangers' telecaster.

After you get beyond the site's hype and self-promotion, you will find informed and intelligent chatter, sleeper picks, and analysis.

Prior to the season, and for a fee, you also can register to play the site's Fantasy Baseball game.

RotoNews

http://www.futures.net.roto/

and

http://www.rotonews.com/

This is yet another top-flight Web site offering oodles of roto/fantasy information and analysis, including links to a "Player Status Database," "Draft Day $ Values," and various other features.

Furthermore, you can sign up for a free "Injury Update," which you will receive by e-mail twice a week.

Baseball Weekly's John Hunt has labeled RotoNews "the best fantasy information site on the Web." He just may be right.

Scott Arnold's Fantasy Baseball Player Rankings

http://members.aol.com:80/scotarnold/homepage.htm

This site includes "fantasy baseball rankings for each major league player...TOTALLY FREE!" The rankings are calculated, Arnold continues, "by comparing each player's performance in various statistical categories to the league as a whole. The rankings are done using a mathematical calculation. During the season, these rankings will be updated at least on a weekly basis. They reflect year-to-date performance for the current season. They are not projections...."

Baseball Prospectus

http://www.baseballprospectus.com/

This Web site features fact and opinion-filled sample entries from *Baseball Prospectus*, an annual publication featuring player analysis, performance projections, and so forth, as well as a "Newsletter" and various "Special Features" (which just plain fans as well as fantasy players might enjoy).

When I logged on, some of the available articles were "Picking It: Deivi Cruz tops American League SS," by Gary Huckabay; "Dusty Luck: The 1997 San Francisco Giants Explained," by Steven Rubio; and "Rotisserie Turns: September Call-ups Worth Knowing About," by Keith Law.

On another occasion, pieces included James Kushner's "Can the White Sox Catch the Indians? A Probabilistic View"; Chris Kahrl's "Transaction Analysis" (in which he offered projections on how trades and minor league recalls and DL activations will impact on teams); Gary Huckabay's "Cause and Effect" (a column on the manner in which sports media analysts offer opinions and "grasp at straws" without knowing all the facts); and "The Week in Quotes," an entertaining compilation by Steven Carter.

Player Projections

http://www.playerprojections.com/

This Web site is chock-full of news, stats, and so forth. Of particular interest are the "Strategic Essays" regarding the ins and outs of fantasy/roto ball. Their subjects are wide-ranging: "September Stats" and "Winter League Myths";

"Computers in the Draft"; "Phantom Inflation"; and "Draft Day Tips."

You also will find information on the League of Alternative Baseball Reality (LABR), a fantasy league whose members include fantasy baseball columnists. Log on here, and you will find out who they are, what transactions they have made, and an analysis of these deals.

Sean Forman's Baseball Info

http://soli.inav.net?~sforman/Baseball.html

The high point of this no-frills but nonetheless solid Web site is Forman's ratings of young talent, listed team-by-team. On one of his home page links, he offers a detailed explanation of how he comes to these evaluations.

Fantasy Baseball Advisor

http://webfronts.com/fantasy/advisor.htm

Here is yet another Web site featuring links to stats, schedules, and injury reports. One handy feature, found on the link "Cheat Sheets," lists rankings of each player in several formats.

Express Stats

http://www.express-stats.com/

This company's stats come at a price. However, from its home page, you can search, at no cost, several months' worth of columns written by rotisserie expert Steve Lombardi.

Lead Dog Stats

http://www.leaddogstats.com/

This "absolutely FREE always" Web site provides sophisticated statistical information. To access it, you will have to download software.

I especially like Lead Dog Stats' mission statement, which opens with the following: "Information on the Internet should always be free to the end user. There is nothing wrong with commercial uses of the Internet, but users have already paid their way to our door, and should not be asked to pay an entrance fee as well."

rotoball.com

http://www.rotoball.com/

More roto-related links can be found on this Web site (which is "created for Fantasy Sports players by Fantasy Sports players"), including a stat center, cybercolumns, "mlb notes," and a roto-related chat line.

One of the site's best features is "rotomatch," which allows those seeking to join or complete leagues to post messages.

Roto-Whip

http://www.ctwired.com/rotowhip

This Web site features links to player projections, offered by team, position, and in alphabetical order. The Roto-Whip FAQ link explains how its valuations are attained and that the page is "intended to be an alternate viewpoint of information."

A to Z Fantasy Central

http://www.usbusiness.com:80/webworld/fantasy/index.htm

On this Web page, you will find fantasy baseball articles "written by fantasy baseball fanatics just like you." On my visit, the titles included "Drafting with a Purpose," "Sleepers and Weepers," and "Tribe has 3 Hot Players but where are they going?"

There also is a fantasy sports chat room (which you only can use if your browser is Java-enabled) and lots of links—along with solicitations for stat services.

Ted Nye's Top 500 Players

http://www.interlog.com/~tednye/html/top500.html

This totally subjective list of baseball's best may be of use to roto/fantasy players and is interesting to scrutinize just for fun. The two key points Nye makes about his list are that "players are ranked according to their current ability to help win baseball games" and "this is not the result of a numerical study—just an opinion of a knowledgeable baseball fan and sabermetrician."

When I logged on, Nye's top ten players were Barry Bonds (ranked first), Mike Piazza, Ken Griffey, Jr., Frank Thomas, Greg Maddux, Roberto Alomar. Alex Rodriguez. Albert Belle. Barry Larkin. and Chuck Knoblauch.

What is most noticeable (and, to many, controversial) about Nye's list is its lack of focus on pitching. After Maddux, his next hurler is John Smoltz, in 31st place.

Baseball Mogul

http://www.imonkey.com/

Although the main purpose of this Web site is to sell you the title game (described as "an addictive baseball franchise simulator"), it is listed for its helpful Fantasy League Resource Page.

One of its most useful features is a list of bids for American and National League hitters and pitchers and an explanation of how they were calculated. This section "describes the basic assumptions about your fantasy league that were made in calculating the bids, and the statistics and formula used. It also discusses the importance of league size, the relative value of stat categories, and defense (yes, defense) in making your fantasy bids."

Plus, those designing Web pages also can download free baseball art!

The Masters of Baseball Daily

http://www.masterball.com/

This Web site describes itself as "your daily source for fantasy sports analysis." It features chatty (and often funny and deliciously opinionated) columns by Jason Grey, Chris Adams, Todd Zola, Paul "Baseball" Jones, David Macias, Joe Caruso, and Scott Souza.

A handy archives index allows you to download previously posted pieces.

CREATiVESPORTS

http://www.creativesports.com/

CREATiVESPORTS is a self-described "fantasy sports resource" that features "all kinds of writing, writing, writing...." Some of it is by Lawr Michaels and is found on his chatty Fantasy Baseball Hotpage, an advisory/resource offering opinions on which players are hot and which are not.

Ryan's Fantasy Baseball Page

http://homepages.together.net/~rphillip//baseball/

This Web site offers opinions on roto/fantasy major and minor league drafts and game strategies. Its maintainer describes himself as "entering my seventh season of fantasy baseball and I now consider myself a student of the game rather than a casual observer."

When I perused this site, I found essays on "The Draft/Auction," "The Minor League Draft," "Playing Dirty," (a piece on "really lousy things that some people I know have done" while managing fantasy league teams), and "The Importance of Naming (your team, that is)."

Ryan does not solicit ads and will not run them on his Web page. "I don't want any hint of commercialism to TAINT MY MESSAGE," he says.

Larry's Baseball Resources

http://www.op.net/~lmk/baseball/index.htm

Larry does the talking at the top of his home page: "The purpose of this page is to gather the best FREE resources for the Rotisserie team owner to find up-to-the-minute information on MLB players." He goes on to explain that the site is "really nothing more than the bookmarks I use to check in daily on news concerning my Roto teams and Baseball in general."

The site consists of these bookmarks along with brief descriptions of what the roto player can find at the individual site.

What works for Larry just may work for you.

22

Chat Rooms/Mailing Lists/Message Boards

Countless Web sites feature links to their own chat lines. Some focus on baseball in general; others center on specific subjects from fantasy and roto to memorabilia to specific teams. On occasion, those connected to the baseball supersites schedule chats with baseball celebrities. It would be impossible to list them all; a few notable ones are cited in this chapter.

However, some sites exist for the sole purpose of offering an opportunity for Web surfers to sound off on baseball-related topics. A number of these lines are moderated; in general, these sites will feature the most stimulating and intelligent conversation. Others are not moderated—and, unfortunately, on these lines, anything goes.

Chat lines can be divided into two categories: those in which the repartee is lively, perceptive, and about baseball, and those in which the participants seem to be clones of Beavis and Butt-head. On the latter sites, the level of conversation is that of a foul-mouthed 15-year-old boy who is only interested in flirting with any girl who happens to be online.

For example, Omni-Chat (*http://www.4-lane.com*) offers chat groups relating to a smorgasbord of subjects from religion to politics to music. One group is called "Sportschat!," which features such links as "BackpackChat!," "HoopsChat!," "SnowSkiChat!," "OlympicsChat!," and "BaseballChat!." I logged onto "BaseballChat!" on several occasions, and the level of discourse was inane. Typical is a comment from "Braves Fan": "Who thinks Canadians can play baseball?" And here is one from "mikey": "Mariners are a hell of alot (sic) better than them Braves." Plenty of observations were loaded with expletives-deleted.

Similarly, on the several occasions I logged onto Dugout Chatter (*http://www.fastball.com/echat/login.html*), the conversation was at the same level found on Omni-Chat.

Omni-Chat and Dugout Chatter serve as proof that the Internet truly is a democratic (not to mention uncensored) medium.

ESPN SportsZone Chatter

http://espnet.sportszone.com/editors/talk/chatter.html

This busy chat line will allow you to converse with players from all sports and ESPN SportsCenter personalities. Among those scheduled when I perused its Web page were ex-major leaguer Bill North (the chat guest on "MLB Memory Lane") and Jose Cruz, Jr. Previous guests included Sparky Anderson, Eric Davis, Ben Grieve, Todd Helton, Tim Foli, Reggie Jackson, Paul Konerko, Buck Showalter, Bobby Valentine, Tug McGraw, Travis Lee, Monte Irvin, and Jim "Mudcat" Grant.

Regular programs include "Monday Night Trivia," "The Answer Man," and "The Farm Report." Plus, there is a pregame chat show (hosted by Jon Miller, Joe Morgan,

Major League Baseball (MLB@BAT) Fan Forum

http://www.majorleaguebaseball.com/fanforum.sml

MLB@BAT's Fan Forum (a link found on the Major League Baseball Web site) allows fans to chat with ballplayers past and present, baseball broadcasters, and the like.

Additionally, through this feature, fans can chat with each other about the major and minor leagues, the Negro Leagues, and fantasy baseball. A chat line even is available for youngsters, offering "a forum for kids to talk about baseball."

The "About the Fan Forum" link describes the page as a place "where diehard baseball enthusiasts as well as newer fans discuss topics, express opinions and share insights with people from every corner of the world. Before you join the discussion, we'd like to remind you that there are certain guidelines and rules of etiquette that you should follow in order to get the most out of your online experience...."

Total Baseball Chat

http://206.40.77.230/chat/chatTB.html

This chat group (which is a link on the Total Baseball Web site) offers lively conversation. The occasional idiotic declaration is nullified by the general intelligence of those participating in the chat.

Sporting News Chat

http://www.sportingnews.com/chat/

Here, you will find chat rooms for various sports, including baseball, and "auditoriums" where users can query celebrity guests and sports experts.

To get on board, you first must register. It also is helpful to check the "Chat Schedule" to find out who will be appearing when and where.

Infield Chatter

http://www.fanlink.com/CONTENTS/IFCHAT/INDEX.HTML

This Web page is connected to *Baseball America*/Fanlink. You will find several current listed topics, which might range from a pro-and-con discussion of interleague play to opinions about minor league ballparks. However, the dialogue focus generally is on the minor leagues.

There even is a "FanLink 'Singles' Sports Bar," described as a place where "a single minor league baseball fan (i.e. unmarried and looking for a 'significant other')" can come to "meet other single fans looking for love."

And there are rules: no "cussin', fussin', fightin' or foolin'."

Dugout Chatter

http://www.fastball.com/chat/

Dugout Chatter is a link on the Fastball Web site's home page. To participate, you must be a registered user; however, guests are welcome to participate.

When I visited, current topics included a general baseball discussion, realignment, trade talk, who will make the playoffs, remembering Mantle, and the best and worst of baseball.

Nando Chat

http://www.nando.net/xwebchat/chat.html

This Web page, sponsored by Nando Net, includes chat lines for all sports. Clicking on the "General" link will lead you to the "Nando 12 Commandments," an in-your-face list that might serve as ground rules for any chat line. Included are: "Ignore assholes"; "No swearing in vain (but feel free to swear, if it's justified)"; "Don't pretend to be 21 if you're 13"; "Don't use all caps, it's very annoying... Don't post big text messages that go on forever about whatever you might be talking about today because tomorrow it won't matter anymore anyways so who cares!"; and "Contribute! Don't just say 'anybody wanna chat?' or what'zup?'"

Because this is an unmonitored chat room, participants are further advised to "respect your fellow chatters, be polite, avoid abusive language or being offensive to others."

WBS Open Forum

http://wbs.net/

WBS is short for WebChat Broadcasting System. On its home page are subject icons. Upon clicking the "Sports" icon, you will arrive at a page that features a scrollbar. When you scroll down to "Major League Baseball," click on "Go," and you will access the site's Major League Baseball page.

You can click on a "Visitors" icon and view the chat room. Or, you can fill out a registration form, which will allow you to join in the conversation.

On this site, you will find a handy link to "Chat Lingo," on which you will learn that *AFAIK* is short for As Far As I Know, *CSG* means Chuckle Snicker Grin, and *YBS* means You'll Be Sorry.

The Dugout Chat Room

http://www.baseball-links.com/wwwchat30/

This unmoderated chat room is a link on the John Skilton Baseball Links Web site. Like most responsible chat rooms, it is suggested that participants conduct themselves appropriately. Before entering, you are requested to read, and consent to, the following message: "While we welcome you to stay and chat as long as you like, please remember that there are often minors in this room. Making rude, obscene, racist, suggestive or otherwise offensive remarks is NOT acceptable. We are sorry to even have to mention this, but we remind you that you and your computer may be banned from this server for improper conduct."

However, to participate in The Dugout Chat, your browser must be Java-enabled.

The Baseball Soapbox

http://www.baseball-links.com/wwwboard

The Baseball Soapbox, yet another Skilton link, is a message board that "has been created so that baseball fans can discuss all aspects of the game without the flames and spams associated with the newsgroups."

When I logged on, the subjects were all-encompassing: "Your Favorite Baseball Books"; "Baseball caps"; "Looking for jobs in baseball"; "Pete Rose"; "Aluminum bats are ruining the game"; "Little League Baseball a Joke!"; and "Baseball's Re-Alignment." Not surprisingly, these last three had quite a few responses.

SportSite Sports Talk

http://www.sportsite.com/chat/Baseball/group.html

The home page of the "baseball" section of this easy-to-use chat line features links to the various discussions already in progress along with the number of articles already posted. On my visit, they covered a range of topics: "Surprising Mets"; "Old baseball memorabilia"; "breaking in a new glove"; "My encounter with Cecil Fielder"; and "Girls Fastpitch." The number of articles in each ranged from 1 to 53; the liveliest discussions were found on those with the most postings.

Click on each, and you can read the articles as well as enter the discussion. Or, you can start a thread of your own.

Rotisserie Chat

http://www.alexpatton.com:80/Q&A_frm.htm

Of all the roto/fantasy-oriented chat lines, this quick and easy-to-use one is as good as any. It is sponsored by roto expert Alex Patton and features lively commentary on an exhaustive range of subjects.

You can post a new article, start a new thread, or search the articles for a word or pattern. Every article has links that enable you to reply to it and navigate the article list.

Forum: The Negro Leagues Conference

http://www.the-coop.com/cgi-bin/netforum/negroleagues/a/1

This is a "discussion forum" designed for "fans of Negro Leagues baseball and students of the national game." On it, you might find data relating to recent Negro Leagues research, Negro League art and artifacts, specific ballplayers and teams, requests for information—or you can start your own discussion thread.

Around the Horn—Baseball Mailing Lists

http://www.mcs.net/~crawford/bblistservs.html

This handy, frequently updated Web site maintained by Brian Crawford, describes itself as "the most complete compilation of baseball mailing lists on the Internet." Here you will find e-mail addresses of major league baseball-related discussion groups to which you must subscribe to participate. Included are the addresses that will put you in touch with the list owner and enable you to subscribe, and the address that members use to communicate with each other.

You also will find a thorough inventory of e-mail addresses for major and minor league teams, e-mail baseball publications, and "other" baseball mailing lists—an intriguing one is BEISBOL-L, featuring discussion and information, in Spanish, about Venezuela baseball, the Caribbean, and the major leagues.

All the addresses are listed as links, so all you need do is click on any one you want to use.

23 Newsgroups

Most of the top baseball-oriented Usenet newsgroups begin with the prefixes "*rec.sport.baseball*" or "*alt.sports.baseball.*"

Others do exist, though. Take, for example, *clari.sports.baseball*; *clari.sports.baseball.games*; *clari.sports.baseball.major*; *clari.sports.baseball.major.al.games*;*clari.sports.baseball.major.al.stats*; *clari.sports.baseball.major.nl.games*; *clari.sports.baseball.major.nl.stats*; and *clari.sports.baseball.minor*. All are supposed to be moderated and are cited on many Web sites offering links to baseball newsgroups. I attempted to log onto the *clari* groups on several occasions, over several months, from the Yahoo! search engine and the links on the *clari* home page (*http://global.gvi.net/clarinet/sports.html*).

Each time, no one was home.

Other alleged baseball newsgroups did have postings. I found two upon logging onto *us.sport.baseball*, which supposedly is a general baseball discussion area. One was pornographic. The other was an offer to sell a baseball-related CD. The newsgroup *us.sport.baseball.college* allegedly focuses on American college baseball. On the day I logged on, there only were four postings. One was a solicitation to "earn upwards of $10,000 per week" on a "less than $30 investment." Another hawked pagers and cellular phone cases with NFL or college logos. The third posed a question: "Does anybody use this newsgroup?" The fourth offered an answer: "I've subscribed for about a year now and not much happenz (sic)."

When I checked out *pdaxs.sports.baseball*, I found five postings. Four were non-baseball-related and were designed to separate me from my money. The last was a solicitation for a new simulation baseball league. Upon logging onto *nctu.club.baseball*, I found just one posting. On it, I was told that I was "about to witness, first hand, the most unique and revolutionary money making program ever offered to the general public!!"

But all I wanted was a baseball newsgroup.

Major League Team Newsgroups

There is a newsgroup for every major league ballclub. On them, you will find get-rich-quick and memorabilia-for-sale postings. These groups all are unmoderated, and general baseball postings offer opinions on everything from greedy players to idiotic owners to the pros and cons of realignment and the designated hitter. Most prominent, however, is the repartee on any and all aspects of the individual team. Often, those participating in the group are die-hard team loyalists, and so the discussions can be quite fiery (and occasionally R-rated).

Undoubtedly, in 1998, 1999, and beyond, there will be fresh controversies galore involving players, managers, and owners; ungraceful falls by teams predicted to run away with pennants; and mad rushes into first place by teams expected to wallow in the second division. You can be sure that they will be hotly debated by the die-hard subscribers of their teams' newsgroups.

This chapter lists, based on the perusal of thousands of postings, the major league newsgroups with the liveliest gab.

alt.sports.baseball.atlanta-braves

The Braves are the most successful baseball team of the 1990s, even if they do not have a bunch of World Series victories to show for it. For this reason, many postings on this newsgroup are protests—about Turner Field, Andruw Jones, manager Bobby Cox, the Braves' bullpen, even the team's announcers.

This sense of frustration—which reflects on the American attitude that all that matters is being Number One—is epitomized in the following comment about Cox: "Ted will run this jerk out of town if he doesn't win it all."

alt.sports.baseball.balt-orioles

The names "Alomar," "Bordick," "Mussina," and "(Davey) Johnson" regularly appear here. But one should not be surprised that the name most frequently posted is "Ripken": "Ripken Autographed Items"; "Ripken and the Streak: Time to Be Unselfish"; "(Thomas) Boswell on Cal"; "Ripken, His Bad Back, and Motivation"; "Ripken Getting Lazy!" (which ends with, "He is still my hero").

alt.sports.baseball.bos-redsox

It is a bad sign for a ballclub when the name of its general manager pops up just as often as that of its all-star first baseman or Rookie-of-the-Year shortstop. Such is the case here, where there are plenty of postings on Dan Duquette, the Bosox's controversial general manager.

On several visits to this group, I came away with a sense of frustration among its participants that, season after season, the Yankees usually win more games than the Red Sox.

alt.sports.baseball.chicago-cubs

This newsgroup mirrors its Boston Red Sox counterpart in that there is a sense of futility expressed by participant after participant. The Cubs have not made it to the World Series since, roughly, the Millard Fillmore administration, and the postings are, for the most part, of the "who should be the new manager"/"what should the Cubs do?"/"hang in there, it's got to get better" variety.

alt.sports.baseball.chi-whitesox

The White Sox newsgroup is fun to peruse and promises to remain so for as long as Jerry Reinsdorf is the team's owner. As any baseball fan who has not been on Mars knows, Reinsdorf conceded the 1997 pennant during the season, when the Pale Hose were just three and a half games behind Cleveland, by trading away some of his best players.

At the time, some of the Reinsdorf-related postings were crammed with expletives. "Moron" and "idiot" were two of the kinder and gentler words found here.

alt.sports.baseball.cinci-reds

As one might expect, the dominant topic here is not Barry Larkin, Pokey Reese, Hal Morris, Ted Kluszewski, Dutch Dotterer, George Crowe, Ed Bailey, Bill McCool—or even Marge Shott. It is Mr. Pete Rose and the should-he-or-shouldn't-he debate regarding his reinstatement into the good graces of Major League Baseball and subsequent enshrinement in the Hall of Fame.

This most likely will remain so even after a decision is made regarding Rose's future relationship with baseball.

alt.sports.baseball.cleve-indians

Two threads running through this newsgroup offer contrasting opinions on Indians devotees. One: "Indians fans rudest & most obnoxious." The other: "Indians fans most loyal and enthusiastic." Suffice to say that, for every level-headed comment on an Indian, there were just as many of the "Albie Lopez Sucks," "Eric 'Ker' Plunk," "Grissom Stinks," and "Re: Manny (Ramirez) Bashing" variety. So perhaps Indians fans are, all at the same time, loyal/rude and enthusiastic/obnoxious.

Another observation: More often than not, whenever Albert Belle's name appears in a posting, he is sarcastically referred to as "Joey."

alt.sports.baseball.fla-marlins

After you get beyond the "sexy girls mud wrestling," "quit smoking—free trial," and "free Seiko watch! great deal!" postings, this newsgroup features commentary on what is wrong and right with the Marlins. Will they win or lose? Which of their players are the best at their positions? How do they stack up against the Braves, Dodgers, and Rockies?

alt.sports.baseball.houston-astros

Because he plays in Houston and not New York or Los Angeles, Jeff Bagwell is pretty much an underrated ballplayer. However, on this newsgroup, as one might expect, his virtues are constantly extolled. Other names that frequently appear are Larry Dierker, Billy Wagner, and Darryl Kile.

alt.sports.baseball.la-dodgers

In this relatively trash-free newsgroup, you will find postings related to Mike Piazza, Raul Mondesi, Brett Butler, and Hideo Nomo; scuttlebutt regarding proposed trades and top prospects; observations on the Dodgers/Giants rivalry; comparisons—mostly unfavorable—between Bill Russell and Tommy Lasorda; and comments on how there really are few true baseball fans in Los Angeles.

A typical comment: "Just got back from my upteenth (sic) game at Dodger Stadium. Once again I'm disgusted. Bases loaded, middle of a pennant drive, and...out come the beach balls, out comes 'the wave,' kids throwing paper airplanes by the dozens as their zombie-drunk parents gaze on. I asked over 50 people at random what the score was...and they didn't know.... It's really no wonder why L.A. is hated so much. They treat everything like a sority (sic) beach party. Vin Scully can't believe it either."

alt.sports.baseball.ny-mets

Both the Mets and Yankees newsgroups are jam-packed with postings. Here, you will find a potpourri of material.

Who should the Mets try to trade? Who should they pursue in trades, or in the free agent market? What must the Mets do to make it to the postseason? Who should be the next honoree in the Mets' Hall of Fame? What might the team do to improve the look of their jerseys?

Then there are the (Ralph) Kinerisms. Hall of Famer Ralph Kiner has been a Mets broadcaster since the team's inception, and he rivals Yogi Berra in his propensity for mouthing goofy comments. Two Kinerisms posted during my review of the group: "They sell 5000 standing room SEATS for every game"; and "Kiner didn't say 'Happy Mother's Day.' He said, 'It's Father's Day, so to all you fathers out there, Happy Birthday.'"

Another posting reflected on why Ralph Kiner is so beloved in New York: "The retirement of Ryne Sandberg will, unfortunately, deprive the world of dozens of future Kinerisms. Over the years, Ralph has identified him variously as Carl Sandberg, Ryne Sandbag, Carl Rheinberg, and Ryne Duren. And who could ever forget former Mets Gary Cooper and Darryl Throneberry?"

alt.sports.baseball.ny-yankees

Postings in this busy group range from the physical appearance of Joe Torre to a detailed analysis of why a specific player is slumping to comments on Hideki Irabu (whose name is spelled "Iraboo" and "I-rob-you").

There are questions: Who is the all-time best Yankee pitcher? How many times did George actually fire Billy? Which rivalry is greater: New York/Seattle or New York/Baltimore? Does Don Mattingly merit a place in the Hall of Fame?

And there are plenty of answers and opinions.

alt.sports.baseball.phila-phillies

The postings here (excluding those for "wild sex pics!" and "girl seeks man") mix the names of the past and present: Curt Schilling, Johnny Callison, Richie Ashburn, Rico Brogna, Scott Rolen, Steve Carlton, and, ultimately, the sentiment that "We Philadelphia fans gotta look for every little ray of sunshine we can get...."

alt.sports.baseball.pitt-pirates

The Pirates are a small-market team. They may trade any player after he establishes himself and commands a salary higher than $1.97.

So the names found on this newsgroup are not Bonds and Bonilla, Neagle and Leyland but Steve Cooke and Joe Randa—ballplayers whom even the most faithful fans might have trouble placing.

Here, Al Martin gets the kind of attention Cal Ripken or Ken Griffey receives in their teams' newsgroups.

alt.sports.baseball.sf-giants

This newsgroup is loaded with wear-your-emotions-on-your-sleeve postings. They feature everyone and everything from "Barrrry" (Bonds, of course) and "Roddd-neeeeeey" (Beck) to "ARRRRRRRRRRRGH!!!" (involving the quality of the team's infield) and "Wowwee—what a game" (regarding a contest described in one post as a "classic for Jint history").

Then there are such Giants-Dodgers rivalry comments as "Going into the ninth tied. They have Rudinsky and Osuna. We have Henry and Beck. Edge to the bad guys."

alt.sports.baseball.sea-mariners

If it can be said that many newsgroup subscribers like to gripe, then do not expect to find too many postings on Ken Griffey, Jr. Alex Rodriguez, and Randy Johnson here. What is there to *not* like about Junior, A-Rod, and the Big Unit?

On perusing the postings, I came away with the impression that Mariners broadcaster Ron Fairly is no Vin Scully or Harry Caray. Their general feeling can be summed up in the following pair: "Let's start the RID RON campaign and send Ron F. to Anaheim or some other hated team"; and "The best way to watch any Ms game on TV [unless it's on ESPN] is to turn the sound off on the TV, and turn the radio broadcast on. No Fairly on the radio."

I also liked another comment: "This newsgroup is second only to alt.support.depression."

alt.sports.baseball.stl-cardinals

The tone of this newsgroup can be summed up in three words: McGwire, McGwire, McGwire. This is unlikely to change, given the Big Mac's signing a long-term contract with the Cardinals.

Oh, yes, the names Eckersley, Fossas, Lankford, and Benes do pop up here occasionally.

alt.sports.baseball.tor-bluejays

Should the Jays have traded John Olerud? Will Alex Gonzalez ever rank alongside A-Rod, Jeter, and Garciaparra? Who should be the team's manager? What must the front office staff do to upgrade the team and fill the seats in the Skydome? Are any of the solutions down on the farm?

These are some of the questions addressed (but not necessarily answered) in this newsgroup.

Additional Major League Newsgroups

*alt.sports.baseball.*az-*diamondbacks*

alt.sports.baseball.calif-angels

alt.sports.baseball.col-rockies

alt.sports.baseball.detroit-tigers

alt.sports.baseball.kc-royals

alt.sports.baseball.mke-brewers

alt.sports.baseball.mn-twins

alt.sports.baseball.montreal-expos

alt.sports.baseball.oakland-as

alt.sports.baseball.sd-padres

alt.sports.baseball.texas-rangers

alt.sports.baseball.minor-leagues

In this newsgroup, you will find a cornucopia of minor league opinions and information: questions and comments on the Sioux City Explorers, Newburgh Night Hawks, and Daytona Beach Cubs; scuttlebutt that a certain hot prospect whose heavy spring training hitting won him a spot in the big leagues is about to be ingloriously sent back to the farm; or queries regarding why Ballplayer A has recently been out of the lineup or whether Ballplayer B has the right stuff to ever transcend his status as career minor leaguer.

beckett.hot-topic

This newsgroup, sponsored by Beckett Online (*http://www.beckett.com/*), features general observations on the sports card hobby (as opposed to want lists or "for sale" solicitations). Comments run along the lines of "if you had unlimited funds and unlimited access, what would your 'dream collection' of ten cards be?" and "why any dealer in their right mind would buy and sell new merchandise in this industry."

fj.rec.sport.baseball

Here is a newsgroup devoted to baseball in Japan. Not surprisingly, you will have to speak Japanese to be able to fully participate.

However, it is worth a quick perusal because some subjects under discussion are written in English. On the day I visited, one of the more popular ones was "Greenwell comes."

Those who speak Mandarin and are at all interested in Taiwanese professional baseball will want to check out the following newsgroups:

tw.bbs.sports.baseball

tw.bbs.sports.baseball.bears

tw.bbs.sports.baseball.dragons

tw.bbs.sports.baseball.eagles

tw.bbs.sports.baseball.elephants

tw.bbs.sports.btaseball.lions

rec.collecting.sport.baseball

If you are looking to buy or sell baseball cards and memorabilia and cannot wait until the weekend card show at the local mall, this is the newsgroup for you.

Items wanted or for sale might range from a 1967 Topps Bob Uecker card to a 1986 Fleer #647 Andres Gallaraga rookie card to 1996 Leaf Signature cards; assorted minor league cards to Panini stickers to *SPORT* and *Sports Illustrated* magazines from 1967 to the present.

Cards are offered for sale individually, in lots, and even via auction. And there are pleas: "Help i need to complete a 90 Leaf set," or "Help!!! NEEEEED Cal Ripken '97 Donruss DK (Diamond King)."

Similar newsgroups that may feature baseball memorabilia are: *alt.collecting.autographs* and *alt.autographs.transactions.*

And at *rec.collecting.cards.discuss*, there is a general discussion of all sports and non-sports cards. On my visit, there was sufficient emphasis on baseball from a query regarding the value of Mark McGwire Topps rookie cards to requests to purchase Derek Jeter cards.

rec.sport.baseball

The focus of this newsgroup is Major League Baseball. It covers a panorama of subjects: trivia questions; pro-and-con comments on teams, players, managers, and management; opinions on everything from placing ads behind home plate to the realignment issue to "rare and exciting plays."

Before logging on, you might want to check out the rec.sport.baseball FAQ (*http://www.rpi.edu/~jonesm2/bb_faq.html*). Here, you will find a handy index of baseball rules, a glossary of baseball terms, information on official scoring and baseball awards, and answers to such questions as who qualifies as a major league rookie, who is eligible for arbitration, what is a waiver claim, and what is the trading deadline.

rec.sport.baseball.analysis

In this moderated, technical-oriented newsgroup, you will find everything from statistics questions to the availability of past season game-by-game stats, formulas that could approximate a team's probability of victory to the possibility of "electronic replacement" of the home plate umpire.

rec.sport.baseball.college

If you are curious about, or avidly follow, college baseball, you will enjoy participating in this newsgroup. It is loaded with commentary on college teams and players, scores and stats, and opinions regarding the ease or difficulty of team schedules.

rec.sport.baseball.data

This newsgroup spotlights stat and record-related discussions. You will find scoring questions: "Batter hits a long single....He tries to stretch the single into a double, and is thrown out at second. How do you score this? I know he gets credit for a single, but how is he retired? I know he's not caught stealing. Do I simply score it as a single AND a put out at second [9-4]?"

There are trivia questions: "How many major league baseball players past and present have 5 syllables in their last name?"

There are stat questions: "Could anybody help me find COMPLETE 1996 stats for the International League (AAA)?"

There are technical questions: "Is there a site that will permit me to download month-by-month MLB data for past seasons?...(If) I want to find out what Ozzie Smith hit in April of 1991 or how many saves Lee Smith had in May of 1992, where can I go on the Net for the information?"

And there are plenty of answers.

rec.sport.baseball.fantasy

Here you will find lively and opinionated fantasy and rotisserie baseball discussions.

An extremely popular subject, one especially relevant to fantasy/roto league participants, is the status of injured ballplayers. A typical series of questions: "I have two Phillies hurlers on my staff [Mark Portugal and Mike Grace]. Both are on the DL. Any word about how they are progressing? What's the projection for their return? What are their ailments?"

There are queries and projections regarding the caliber of ballplayers: "With [Kenny] Lofton gone to the NL, who is the Most Valuable Roto Player in the American League? Considering position scarcity and the reduced amount of steals available, I would nominate Chuck Knoblauch... Who do you nominate as your 1-2-3 Most Valuable Roto Players in your respective leagues?"

On the other end of the quality scale, there are lists of "Roto ruiners": ballplayers who never should be picked for teams, or those whose lofty pre-Opening Day projections are not coming to fruition as the season progresses.

Opinions are sought regarding prospective trades: "I'm in an AL-only standard roto league. I poured money into starters this year so my staff is: Cone, Clemens, Fassero, Sele and Wasdin. My offense, however is power short...So I'm looking to deal a pitcher. And lo and behold, I found someone looking for a pitcher. He seems interested in trading Manny Ramirez and Marty Cordova for Clemens or Cone. Your opinions, please." This request came under the subject "Stop me before I trade again!"

There are comments regarding the positive or negative quality of commercial leagues, stat services, and roto/fantasy products. The responses from companies, regarding disapproving opinions of their product, make especially interesting reading. However, keep in mind that some of the more glowingly affirmative comments just might be submitted by the respective company.

Finally, there are pleas for sympathy: "Is there anybody else out there who owns Pat Rapp and was just forced to take a 2 2/3 inning, 10 ER hit on Tuesday night? Must I suffer my pain alone?"

rec.sport.softball

In this newsgroup, you will find information regarding softball and fast-pitch tournaments, solicitations for teams and players, information on softball/fast-pitch URLs, even comparisons between softball and baseball.

rec.sport.officiating

Although all sports are discussed here, baseball is well-represented. This site offers questions and answers regarding everything from plays and decisions by major league umpires to Little League, college, and softball officiating.

Among the topics discussed, in lengthy threads: balks; catchers' tossing their masks in the foul line; overrunning first base; umpires' camps; home plate collisions; softball scoring; differences in strike zones; and experiences when umpiring behind home plate for the first time.

Live Audio

With the right software, you can listen to sports-oriented radio talks shows and, better yet, live broadcasts of ballgames right from your computer. This may be meaningless if you are a Yankees or Mets fan and you live in upstate New York, where you can hear radio broadcasts or watch games on cable television with ease. But live audio will be a godsend if you favor these teams and live in Dubuque, Memphis, or Santa Fe.

As of this writing, the technology that allows the video broadcast of live games remains relatively primitive. But the technology is improving every day, and companies are making it available on the Internet.

Dozens of Web sites listed in this book feature live audio and video of major league, minor league, and college games, or historical audio and video. Usually, you will find a link and description on the home page along with information on the required plug-ins and software.

For those interested in further information on live audio/video, several individual sites are worth browsing.

AudioNet

http://www.audionet.com/

AudioNet describes itself as "the leader in Internet broadcasting. We deliver more live and on-demand broadcasts with more viewers and listeners than any other company in the world."

This Web site is a handy guide to the day's live sports and non-sports AudioNet broadcasts. When I visited, the site offered a link to a live baseball games schedule, which informed me that six major league and five minor league contests were being broadcast that day. Links were provided to live radio sports and talk shows, which led me to programming and schedule information. And I found information on "what you need to enjoy our programming."

A search engine allows you to see if and when your favorite team's games will be aired. And you can sign up for a free AudioNet e-mail newsletter.

RealNetwork: RealAudio/RealVideo

http://www.realaudio.com/

This Web site provides RealAudio/RealVideo programming information and software downloads. Some of the latter are free; others require a fee.

For a listing of all stations, Web sites, and businesses that provide RealAudio and RealVideo, click on "RealAudio Showcase/RealVideo Showcase" on the home page search engine and follow instructions. Many are baseball-related.

An explanation of what RealNetwork is and how it works can be found at *http://www.realnetwork.com/*.

SportsRadio

http://www.sportsradio.com

SportsRadio can be reached via the above URL or as a link from the AudioNet home page. Here, you will find schedules for broadcasts of sports radio shows, live sporting events, and year-round sports programming.

Links come under the headings "Today in Sports" (Which lists the day's sports programming) "Featured Sports Radio Station" (which spotlights one station's programming); "Sports Programs" (listing several radio shows originating from locales as far apart as Orlando, Memphis, and Phoenix); "Radio Stations" (listing two dozen sports radio stations); and "Interviews" (clicking on the "Archives" link will lead you to a list of sports interview shows).

The "Great Games" link is worth noting. Click on the "Great Games Archives" link, and you will be taken to lists of games available for replaying. On my visit, they included the first interleague game (Texas against San Francisco, June 12, 1997), the 1997 Single A Minor League All-Star Game, the 1997 Major League All-Star Game, and every game of the 1997 College World Series.

To state the obvious, the "What You Need To Enjoy Our Programming" section of the home page is essential reading.

SportsLine USA's Baseball Live!

http://ps1.sportsline.com/u/baseball/mlb/bblhome.htm

From this Web page, which is connected to CBS SportsLine, you can download major league baseball games as they happen, with the action played out in an animated ballyard. However, you must have Netscape or Microsoft Internet Explorer with Shockwave; the latter can be downloaded from the site.

Also available: play-by-plays for previous games, covering the entire baseball season to date.

Instant Sports

http://www.instantsports.com/

This Web site offers the same service as SportsLine USA's Baseball Live in that it produces "real-time, interactive sports reporting." The company's objective is to offer scores, statistics, and multimedia play-by-play coverage via state-of-the-art computer/telecommunications technology.

For a fee, you can download "up-to-the-minute play-by-play and statistics in text, and an animated Instant Ballpark so you can watch a game while it happens or in replay."

SportsFan Radio Network

http://www.sfan.com/radio/home/

Although you cannot find Pete Rose in the Hall of Fame, you at least can listen to him here. Via RealAudio, you can hear "The Pete Rose Show," his sports talk radio program, along with other telecasts. Times and schedules are posted on the site; shows can be heard 24 hours a day, seven days a week.

The site is sponsored by the SportsFan Radio Network, which describes itself as "a multi-media sports programming and production company with developing interests in television, on-line, print and wireless distribution channels."

WTKI

http://www.wtki.com/

This Huntsville, Alabama radio station broadcasts major and minor league games and other baseball-oriented programming. Its home page features an illustrated radio that seems to want to burst off the computer screen and shout "play me!" Click on it, and you can do exactly that, enabling you to listen to the station live. A link will inform you of its programming schedule. However, a Real Audio plug-in is required.

WGN-TV Audio Library

http://www.wgntv.com/news/audio.html

The audio that you can download from this Web page (which is a link on Chicago's WGN Web site) may not be live, but it is audio just the same.

Using various software, you can hear Harry Caray sing "Take Me Out to the Ball Game," or say "Ah, you can't beat fun at the old ballpark, friends," or shout "Holy Cow!," or welcome you to Wrigley Field.

If that isn't fun enough, you can download Ken "The Hawk" Harrelson, Caray's fellow WGN sportscaster, shouting his classic "Yes!" and making his home run call.

Don't ask why the other audio downloads on the page feature Barney Fife and Gomer Pyle.

25 Miscellaneous

Plenty of Web sites do not fit into any of this book's previous chapters. They comprise a potpourri: ballplayer home addresses and grave sites; baseball-related postage stamps; highly personalized views on any number of baseball-related subjects; prognostications on final statistics had there been no 1994 strike; quotes both famous and obscure from famous and obscure ballplayers, umpires, and baseball-lovers; and much more.

While putting together *Baseball on the Web*, I knew I was nearing the end of my research when I stumbled onto the most bizarre Web site, which shall remain nameless. Its very existence is proof positive that, if you search long and hard enough, you will find just about anything on the World Wide Web.

The site consists of nothing more than mostly candid, locker-room photos of major leaguers sans uniforms!

In plain English, that means buck naked.

As the home page was slowly downloading, I figured that I would not find anything that would qualify for publication in *Playgirl.*

Boy, was I wrong.

Autograph Seeker's Paradise

http://members.aol.com/vincent776/index.html

Many Web site maintainers offering lists of celebrity residences will make them available for a fee. This one, however, offers free of charge home addresses of hundreds of luminaries.

First, click on the "Sports Players Home Addresses" link on the home page. Then click on the "Baseball Players Home Addresses" link. (There also are links for basketball, football, and hockey). You then will download a list of hundreds of ballplayer addresses.

However, keep in mind that such sites easily become outdated. For one thing, individuals always are moving—and always are passing away. This site listed addresses for Curt Flood, Bob Grim, and Richie Ashburn, among others, even though these ballplayers already had died.

Additionally, some of the misspellings—Barry *Larking*, Bill *Console* (rather than Consolo), *Onestus* (as opposed to Orestes or Minnie) Minoso—almost qualify this site for the humor chapter.

Among the other Web sites that include some ballplayer addresses:

Simeone Co.
(http://www.geocities.com/Colosseum/Track/6451/);
Celebrity Addresses
(http://www.robots.ox.ac.uk:5000/~syss/address.html);
and Celebrity Address Emporium
(http://www.springrose.com/celebrity).

Insomnia and the Hole in the Universe Baseball Autograph Page

http://www.angelfire.com/pa/HOMEPAGEOF LIVE//

This Web site is maintained by 16-year-old Mike, a ballplayer signature collector who is happy to share his autograph-seeking experiences.

The two main links relate to current players and retired players/Hall of Famers. Mike not only lists addresses but reports on his successes and failures in obtaining autographs. He cites the length of time it took for the ballplayer to respond to his query and whether the player sends out personalized items or requests money.

The one quibble with Mike's page: it is loaded with misspellings.

Find A Grave

http://www.findagrave.com/index.html

This Web site features ballplayers whose addresses are a bit more permanent than those listed in the preceding URLs.

Ever wondered where your favorite old-timer is buried? Are you curious about what his grave looks like? If you answer in the affirmative, you will want to peruse this site. It is maintained by Jim Tipton, who has a most unusual avocation: "I collect dirt from the graves of noteworthy people."

Searches can be made by name, location, and claim to fame. The "Sports Figures" link in the last category yields a number of ballplayers, beginning with Grover Cleveland Alexander, Cool Papa Bell, and Three Finger Brown; heading through Lou Gehrig, Gil Hodges, Connie Mack, and Mickey Mantle; and ending with Honus Wagner, Moses "Fleetwood" Walker, and Cy Young.

Gravesite stills are online only for some of the players. Area maps are provided for those interested in making a pilgrimage to a specific site.

Bigleaguers.com

http://www.bigleaguers.com/

This site labels itself as "the players' choice on the Web." And it describes itself as "the only place on the Internet where you can find personal web sites for every player in the Major League Baseball Players Association. The players update their own sites; between games, on the road, or whenever. You'll hear it straight from them, in their own words."

Although you won't find lengthy discourses here—which renders the preceding declaration a misrepresentation—the site is worthwhile if you want to quickly download basic information on major leaguers. This is accomplished via a search engine, which you can use to reach the players' home pages. All are generic in nature in that they have the same format and design. They include a statement: "Hi, thanks for checking out my site. Click through my pages and come back again.... See you soon," along with "Vital Information," "Stats," "Schedule," "Contact Me," and "Virtual Card" links.

Other home page links will take you to baseball surveys, trivia contests, and interviews with foreign-born major leaguers.

Baseball Inc.

http://www.cpba.org/sean/main.html

This potpourri Web site, maintained by Sean Ohlenkamp, has a beautifully designed home page: white and gray on black, with images of an outfielder leaping to make a catch and the Bambino and the Iron Horse shoulder-to-shoulder in a dugout.

The "Pictures" link will take you to loads of stills, which you can download. Almost two dozen of Ken Griffey, Jr., alone are available. (As you explore this site, you will get the idea that Junior is Ohlenkamp's favorite player.) From the "Sounds" page, you can listen to (with the proper software) everything from Russ Hodges screaming "the Giants win the pennant," to Keith Olbermann saying "It's deep and I don't think it's playable," to baseball-related music. The "Jokes" link is loaded with one-liners. The "Quotes" link cites everyone from Preacher Roe to Shirley Povich to Ogden Nash to "Unknown."

Baseball

http://www.well.com/user/ruz/baseball.html

This Web site consists of one baseball fan's thoughts on the game he loves. That fan is Christian Ruzich and, as he notes, "This page is my way of celebrating our national pastime."

On my visit to the site, Ruzich had posted his feelings on major league realignment, an extensive team-by-team list of retired numbers, his take on the major league playoff system, and an analysis of the "ex-Cub factor."

What, you may ask, is the "ex-Cubs factor"? Simply put, it is the concept that the more former Chicago Cubs found on a pennant-winning team, the less of a chance that team has to win the World Series.

Baseball—The National Pastime (The Slop Shop)

http://www.geocities.com/Colosseum/3969/#top

Here is another highly personalized Web site, maintained by Terry Sloope. Although the site emphasizes links to other sites as much as it does original material, Sloope does offer his views (under the heading "Slop Talk") on a multiplicity of subjects.

On my visit, Sloope opined about realignment and who is most deserving of Hall of Fame enshrinement. Previous postings can be downloaded on the "Slop Talk Archives" ink. They range from how Paul Sorrento is one of the most undervalued major leaguers to "Much Ado About Marge..."

Internet Baseball Awards

http://www.baseballprospectus.com/awards

These prizes, which originally were called the rec.sport.baseball (or rsb) awards, have been handed out since 1990. The one exception was the 1994 strike year.

The winners are determined via votes, solicited at season's end, from online baseball fans. The categories are MVP, Cy Young, and Rookie of the Year for both leagues. The rules are simple and straightforward, and there even are lists of qualifying players to help you in your selections.

As you vote, you even can imagine that you are an actual member of the Baseball Writers' Association of America!

Carter for Commissioner Homepage

http://www.olemiss.edu/~egcah/carter.htm

Who will be the next baseball commissioner? Pete Rose? Newt Gingrich? George Costanza?

This Web site will remain noteworthy even in the event that a new commissioner is named because it eloquently reflects fan frustration with the game. "Baseball is in trouble," it begins. "The real problem is no leadership from the 'office of the commissioner,' no one with the fortitude to compel the players and the owners to act in the best interests of baseball....What we need is a steady, unbiased hand at the helm: a seasoned negotiator, a proven administrator, a man of unquestioned integrity, and a lifelong fan of the game." That man is former President Jimmy Carter.

For after all, if Carter has "mediated disputes between world powers" and "monitored free elections in 3rd world countries," he surely would be able to deal with the Albert Belles and Jerry Reinsdorfs.

Lex Alexander Should Be Commissioner of Major League Baseball

http://shellhost.nr.infi.net/~lex/commish.htm

Who says the new baseball commissioner has to be a former United States President or a high-profile personality? Lex Alexander is the self-described "benign despot" who feels he is the right man for the job.

The high points of his platform, as presented on his Web page:

- No interleague play. "If God intends the Mets and the Yankees to face off," Alexander notes, "he will let them both win pennants in the same year."
- No radical realignment "of the kind now being proposed."
- No artificial turf.
- No home run porches.
- No DH.
- "No player under contract to any major league team shall be permitted to receive any valuable consideration in exchange for autographs."
- "And Schott, Selig, Steinbrenner and Reinsdorf all are looking for honest work before sundown."

Inheriting Mickey's Mantle: Baseball on Strike

http://wwwdryer.www.media.mit.edu/godfrey/write/mantle.htm

This Web page is yet another baseball commissioner solicitation—but with a bitter twist. It consists of an essay, written in 1995, by someone who calls himself "Godfrey Daniels" (which is what a flustered W.C. Fields would utter in his movies whenever he wanted to say "goddamn").

As he offers his services as commissioner, an irate "Godfrey" declares, "I'd make Judge Landis look like Barney Fife. Landis banned a few players from baseball for life; I'd ban a lot of them. *And* the owners. In fact, I'd disband the major leagues altogether. Oh, we'd still have baseball. But it would be baseball with a small *b.* Local baseball. Real baseball."

What is the source of "Godfrey's" outrage? Like all red-blooded American youngsters, he once collected baseball cards. But unlike many Baby Boomers, his cards were not trashed by his mother during spring cleaning. "Godfrey" innocently sent Mickey Mantle about a dozen of his cards to sign—including a 1952 Topps, which now is valued so highly that it might have put three of his children through college.

"Godfrey" never did hear from Mantle. The cards never were returned.

"Mantle certainly doesn't need the money," Godfrey writes. "I just got laid off."

The captions under the photographs included on the site are clever and biting.And the postscript, written a year later when "Godfrey" learned that Mantle was dying, is extremely poignant.

The Boycott Major League Baseball Home Page

http://fresno.edu/~morris/nomlb.htm

This impassioned Web page is authored by one baseball lover who refuses to forgive and forget in the wake of the 1994 strike settlement.

He is as angry as Howard Beale, the televangelist from Paddy Chayevsky's *Network*, and on his page he proclaims that he is mad as hell and not going to take it anymore. Only the object of his wrath is Major League Baseball—*not* baseball as a sport but *Major League Baseball* and the "business of baseball" the avaricious owners and the overindulged players who callously dismiss the fan.

His alternative to the majors: attend collegiate and minor league games. Ticket prices are lower. It is easy to get good seats. The games are fun. The players are enthusiastic.

"It is obvious that a true baseball fan does not need MLB," adds this anonymous fan. "There are literally hundreds of places around the country where a fan can enjoy a game without supporting the greed...of MLB."

The material on one of the page's links is germane to the subject at hand. It is a provocative essay written by Louis Marienthal and titled "Major League Baseball Needs a Board of Directors."

Rob Mallicoat's Diary of a Comeback Kid

http://www.net-endeavors.com/diary

Back in 1992, Rob "Mallyman" Mallicoat, a Houston Astros pitching hopeful, had his very own Fleer Major League Baseball card (which appears at the top of this Web page). Three years later, the 1995 season began with replacement players rather than bona fide major leaguers in spring training camps. And Mallicoat, his visions of becoming the next Nolan Ryan faded, was in the Kansas City Royals' camp as a strikebreaker. Here is the diary he faithfully kept during this period, and it makes for fascinating reading.

Early in training camp, Mallicoat writes, "The game of baseball is something I have played for over 25 years of my short 30 year life.... I have lived, breathed and literally given up many things purely for the love of the game...never have I been running and sprint (sic) the last 100 yards thinking to myself...I can make 3 million dollars. I can only think of standing on a mound somewhere with a small white ball, waiting for the batter to get into the box.... This game was just that...a game...I have not forgotten the striking Major Leaguers...I was one for 2 years...but I had my dream shortened by numerous injuries at unfortunate times in my 10 year career...and have one more opportunity to pick up that baseball and stand on that mound.... I realize my fastball is 8 MPH slower and my slider is gone...but it is still a game...and it always will be."

The Phillies Fan Union

http://www.geocities.com/Colosseum/4957/indext.html

The Phillies Fan Union describes itself as "the official voice of the Phillies fan" and "an organization built on the premise that the fan is the most important part of the game." It also claims that its Web site is the most accessed on the Internet.

Although much of the site is Philadelphia-oriented, you do not have to live in Pennsylvania (or even be a Phillies fan) to enjoy many of its features. Among the links found on the Phillies Pfun page: a "Baseball Joke Page"; "Famous Baseball Quotes"; and a "Know The Philly Langwich," in which you will learn that Philadelphians do not so much talk as *tawk*.

When I visited, there was a special feature on one of the few bright spots of the Phils' 1997 season: Scott Rolen. It included an enormous photo of the phenom at bat (which took forever to download), along with a prognosis that he "could develop into not only a quality major league player, but one of the true stars of the game."

Another worthwhile Phillies-oriented site is The Broad & Pattison Weekly Review (*http://users.aol.com/jsweetman/phils/bnp70414.htm*), a well-done online newsletter that includes everything from news and notes to minor league reports to "This Week in Phillies History."

1996 World Champion New York Yankees

http://mars.superlink.net/fraz/tribute.htm

Most fan-maintained team sites are unimpressive. However, this beautifully designed Yankees homage is an exception and serves as a model for fan-hosted sites. Even if you are a Yankee-hater, this site can be savored for its sheer panache.

Of course, it is unabashed in its enthusiasm. Its focus is on the 1996 World Championship season, and Derek Jeter is described as a "Future Hall of Famer." But there is so much more here to be savored, including back page *New*

York Daily News Yankees-related headlines, a cleverly animated ticker tape parade photo, and a nod to Yankee tradition, as exemplified in the photo of Joe DiMaggio preparing to throw out a game-opening ball.

Kudos to Charlie Frazer, who maintains this site.

Mets Online

http://www.icu.com/mets/

This "Unofficial World Wide Web Site of the New York Mets" is stunningly designed and crammed with information on the Mets present and past. Links are available to an array of team-related data; articles from *New York Mets Inside Pitch*, the team's official fan magazine; "Mets Journal," a diary written by super-fan Jonathan Weissman; a guide to Shea Stadium; a "Rumor Mill," featuring the scoop on potential trades and roster upgrades; photo and sound archives; a year-by-year club history; a Mets trivia quiz; and a name the "Mystery Met" contest.

This all-around outstanding site is more fact-filled and fun-filled than quite a few official team sites.

The Miserable Cubs Fan Forum

http://www.geocities.com/Colosseum/Track/7004/

Although the name of this Web site, and some of the commentary found on it, might qualify it for listing in the humor chapter, it actually offers plenty of clear-headed commentary on "the woeful Cubs."

In this regard, it is the antithesis of an Official Major League Web site, and all the generic Joe/Steve/Fred's Oh-How-I-Love-The-Chicago-Cubs pages.

Among the links: "Issue of the Week" ("Is Ryno a Hall of Famer or Just Plain Over-Rated????"; "Is Sammy Worth All That Cash????"); "Cub News & Insights" (which "is not designed to keep you up to date with all the stats and stories, but to offer thoughts and insights into the issues and controversies surrounding the Cubs"); "Cubs Organization Praise & Criticism"; and the "Miserable Cubs Fan Survey."

ARMpit

http://net.indra.com/~skillz1/armpit/arm.html

This Web site relishes wallowing in obnoxiousness!

ARM stands for Anti-Rockies Movement, and a couple of questions are put forth on its home page: "Are you tired of listening to Rockheads babble about the brilliance of Dante Bichette? Are you appalled at seeing baseball played in a bandbox named after a watery beer? Break ranks with the lemmings and join ARM."

In fact, upon clicking on the site's "Bichette" link, a File Not Found notice came on my computer screen. One senses that this is part of a master scheme perpetrated by ARM.

Those who scrutinize ARMpit are invited to send in "rebuttals, fan mail and death threats."

Tony Gwynn's Official Web Site

http://web.sportsextra.com/magazine/gwynn/

Here is a rarity: a current major leaguer's "official" Web page whose main purpose is not to offer for sale bandaids, toothpaste, and cookies featuring the player's image. Tony greets you on the home page and declares that the site offers him "an opportunity to talk about the game of baseball from my own perspective, no holds barred, to let you know what I think about umpires, about travelling, about hitting against Greg Maddux."

With the proper software, you can listen to Tony as well as read what he has to say; you'll also find comments by Barry Bonds, Wally Joyner, Bruce Bochy, and others. But you do not need any additional doo-hickeys to send Tony an e-mail and read his replies, or play the Tony Gwynn trivia quiz, or download the images in the Tony Gwynn photo gallery.

7th Inning Stretch

http://www.geocities.com/Colosseum/1826/

This chatty, heartfelt Web site is maintained by Dan (aka "Dano"), a thirty-something lifelong baseball fan. This site is, according to Dan, "by, for, and about baseball fans. People who are more than the casual fan. The site is for those people who can tell you what teams played in the World Series for the past thirty years—and then quote the scores of each game! Okay, maybe not *that* fanatical, but if I said the Mendoza Line they'd know what I'm talking about." Dan laments that kids today "would rather pick up a basketball or football instead of the ol' baseball" and blames this development on the manner in which the sport has been promoted. On his site, he offers his own personal all-star picks from past and present, observations on different aspects of the game, and a selection of baseball quotes.

The Baseball Collection

http://home.sprynet.com/sprynet/hotoff/baseball.htm

This Web site consists of provocative, highly opinionated baseball-related essays, commentary, and declarations on a gallery of subjects. The headlines are sufficient to capture the essays' points-of-view: "An Argument Against Corporate Ownership"; "The Sad Case of Hideki Irabu"; "Umpires Out of Control"; "Another Reason Why Bud Selig Shouldn't Be Commissioner"; "Joe Jackson Belongs in the Baseball Hall of Fame"; and, finally, "Remove Charles Comiskey from the Baseball Hall of Fame."

Now there's a novel idea!

Diamond Times

http://www.friarpub.com/di/diamond.htm

This web-zine is a sweet ode to baseball in general—that is, any kind of baseball except for contemporary major league play.

It is noted on the home page that these are "trying times for the national pastime. It's been kidnapped by the suits.... The Major Leagues are gradually becoming less relevant to the game.... Do yourself a favor. Ignore the TV, bypass the Bigs. Take the trouble to get to a decent Minor League game once in a while. The seats are cheap, the beer's just as cold, the play's pretty good, and the parking's almost always free."

And so *Diamond Times* exists as "the place...for true baseball lore. That means everything *except* current MLB happenings."

On my visit, there were pieces on Australian baseball, a day in the life of a Little League manager, Mark "The Bird" Fidrych, Negro League hurler Hilton Smith, and the last World Series in which the Chicago Cubs appeared.

Regarding the latter, no, Andrew Jackson was not the United States president at the time.

MediaFinder

http://www.mediafinder.com/

Interested in landing your cyberspaceship for a while and actually reading a baseball publication printed on good old-fashioned paper? This handy Web site is an excellent resource for gathering basic information on magazines, newspapers, newsletters, journals, and the like that cover every conceivable subject.

A "baseball" query on the search engine found at the top of the home page resulted in 136 separate listings. Some—*Baseball America*, *Spitball*, *USA Today Baseball Weekly*, and various *Sporting News* publications—were familiar. Others—*Boston Baseball*, *Old Tyme Baseball News*, *Baseball Insight*, and *Big Bad Baseball Annual*—were not.

There even were baseball-related catalogs offering everything from baseball/softball supplies to baseball jerseys to baseball cards. Some entries have Web sites; others only have e-mail addresses. But in each case, you are given a brief description of editorial content plus subscription and contact information.

The Second Season

http://www.nando.net/baseball/strike/recreate/recreate.html

Had there been no baseball strike in 1994, which teams would have made the World Series? Who would have been batting and home-run champions? Would Tony Gwynn have hit .400? Would Matt Williams have belted 62 home runs?

We never will know the answers. But this clever Web page, which is a link on the Nando X Baseball Server, offers a projection—purely subjective, of course—on the direction of the season had there been no work stoppage. You will find game simulations, box scores, stats, and summaries. Exploring this page is one bittersweet way of pondering what might have been.

America's National Pastime: A Report on Participation in 1996

http://www.sportlink.com/teamsports/market/baseball/96baseballpartstudy/bb96_2.htm

How many Americans play baseball? How often do they play? Is baseball mostly a game for youth? Is it a boy's pastime, or are more girls participating? What percentage of blacks, whites, and Hispanics play? Is the popularity of baseball as a participation sport on the wane, or is it actually increasing?

All these queries and more are answered in this survey, conducted by SGMA Market and Media, which features simple explanations illustrated with charts and graphics.

I certainly cannot fault the survey conclusion, which is found on the home page: "In the final analysis, the future of baseball lies in its ability to attract and enchant the young participants who will carry this game in their hearts long after they stop playing."

Online NewsHour

http://www.pbs.org/newshour/

This PBS news-oriented program has aired numerous illuminating baseball-related pieces and discussions. The list begins with David Gergen, editor-at-large of *U.S. News and World Report*, questioning Roger Kahn about his "memories of summer" and baseball during the 1950s; Stephen Jay Gould bringing baseball into a dialogue about the "history of life"; and *NewsHour* essayist Roger Rosenblatt on the differences between baseball and basketball and the idea of bringing the Dodgers back to Brooklyn.

To find them, click on the home page "Search" icon and type in **baseball**. From there, you can download the transcripts.

Wrigleyville Web

http://ourworld.compuserve.com/homepages/David_McPherson/

Zillions of personal Web sites are dedicated to individual players or teams. This Web site pays homage to a neighborhood: the area on Chicago's North Side that surrounds Wrigley Field.

This is a smallish Web site but very down home: "Opening Day (of the 1997 season) was the best," reports David McPherson, who maintains the site. "I was able to stay through the first 5 1/2 innings in Wrigley, one on the roof (see his "Best Locations" link), and the final innings at Sports Corner. I had extra tickets so my friends and I went back in with the extra tickets to catch Harry sing."

The key links on the page are "Best Wrigleyville Bars," "Restaurants and Best Locations to Watch Cubs Game," "Getting Around Wrigleyville," and "A Day at the Park" (which includes excerpts from William Hartel's book about the history of Wrigley Field and other material).

Baseball on Stamps

http://www.www.edu/~stephan/webstuff/bbstamps/as.html

This fact-filled and nicely illustrated Web site, maintained by Ed Stephan, charts the manner in which baseball has been depicted on postage stamps.

On this site, you will learn that, to honor the opening of the baseball Hall of Fame in 1939, Postmaster General James A. Farley suggested the issuing of a baseball-related stamp. In a nationwide poll, stamp collectors overwhelmingly voted against the proposal. But they were overruled by President Franklin D. Roosevelt, and the stamp—with a three-cent value and featuring a purple-colored etching of boys playing sandlot ball—was issued.

Since then, Jackie Robinson, Babe Ruth, Lou Gehrig, and Roberto Clemente have been featured on stamps issued in the United States. Meanwhile, Don Mattingly, Robin Yount, Roger Clemens, and Kevin Mitchell have graced those issued by the Central African Republic, Guinea, and the Comoro Islands!

Women's Professional Fastpitch

http://www.diac.com/~wpf/

On this Web site, you will find out everything you ever could hope to know about Women's Professional Fastpitch, a league "created to provide elite fastpitch athletes with the opportunity to compete at the professional level."

The league was launched in June, 1997, with teams in Atlanta; Charlotte, North Carolina; Tampa, Florida; Orlando, Florida; Raleigh/Durham, North Carolina; and Hampton/Newport News, Virginia.

The site features a history of fastpitch, rosters and box scores, players of the week, and the promise of updates on league and team information.

Ladies League Baseball, Inc.

http://www.ladiesleaguebaseball.com/

This rah-rah Web site is a repeat of the Women's Professional Fastpitch page, only the pitchers, catchers, batters, and fielders play hardball. As such, the league is the first of its type since the All-American Girls Professional Baseball League folded in 1954.

The teams competing in the league's 30-game 1997 inaugural schedule were the San Jose Spitfires (winners of the first Ladies League Baseball World Series), Los Angeles Legends, Long Beach Aces, and Phoenix Peppers. Among the stars: former Colorado Silver Bullet Gina Satriano, a double-threat who hit .364 and led the league in pitching with a 1.21 ERA; Victoria Ruelas, the first American female to play in the Little League World Series, who hit .378 and topped the league with 30 RBIs; and P.J. Brun, who compiled a perfect 5—0 record, with a 1.98 ERA, and struck out 48 in 35 innings.

The King and His Court

http://member.aol.com/WndMillR/king.html

For decades, softball pitcher Eddie Feigner has been barnstorming across America with his blindfold and glove. He is best known not just for striking out his opponents but for having his eyes covered as he does so. Now in his early seventies, he still travels with a four-person team, the King and His Court, and plays 200 games a year.

Never heard of Feigner? That's because he pitches balls that are "soft" rather than "hard." So his fame has been limited even though *Sports Illustrated* has labeled him "the most underrated athlete of his time."

The purpose of this Web site is to solicit bookings for Feigner and company. But it also features an Associated Press piece that will tell you all you could ever want to know about Feigner and "his never-ending quest for respect."

Three gigantic photos of vintage Feigner in action are the home page highlights.

The Sandalady

http://www.sterba.com/cotati/sandalady/

Fran Fleet (aka The Sandalady) is a Cotati, California based baseball glove repairperson who will mend your mitt if you ship it to her.

What earns her Web page a spot here are the helpful hints she includes on "not just how to choose a glove" but on buying, breaking in, and caring for it.

As small Web sites go, its layout is way above the ordinary.

Take me out to the ballgame!

http://www.nwnews.com/wwissues/v20n09/school3.html

This unassuming little Web page describes a project initiated by parents at Woodmoor Elementary School in Bothell, Washington: a "baseball learning extravaganza," in which youngsters got to choose from a number of activities during a two-hour period. They could write baseball poetry, do math using baseball statistics, construct a mini-baseball stadium out of recycled materials, create personal baseball cards and a baseball collage, write a letter to the Seattle Mariners, play a baseball trivia game, attend a baseball skills clinic, and even cook and eat peanuts and cracker jacks!

Plus, the school's principal, Blake (any kin of Kirby?) Puckett, starred in a production of "Casey at the Bat."

Whoever said learning isn't fun?

Roy & Roxie Campanella Physical Therapy Scholarship Foundation

http://www.dennismc.com/baseball/dtw/dtwcampy.html-ssi

Campanella, the legendary Negro League and Brooklyn Dodgers catcher, was involved in a 1958 automobile accident that not only ended his baseball career but also left him paralyzed until his death 35 years later. This Web site offers information on the Campanella family foundation, which "awards academic scholarships to students who wish to pursue the health care field of physical therapy based on the student's ability to demonstrate a cultural sensitivity to the patient. These financial awards assist senior physical therapy students who successfully exhibit awareness of cultural and ethical considerations that contribute to optimum patient care and recovery."

Jackie Robinson Foundation

http://www.dodgers.com/jackfound.html

On this Web site, you will find information on the Jackie Robinson Foundation, a "public, not-for-profit national educational foundation" established by Robinson's widow, Rachel, in 1973. Its mission is "to assure that the legacy of Jackie Robinson's activism and commitment to social justice is carried forth in the personal, community and institutional lives of young people as they assume leadership roles throughout society."

Each year, the foundation supports approximately 130 Jackie Robinson Scholars, who each receive a $20,000 college scholarship.

Online Drive

http://www.baseball.org/baseball/Online-Drive/

Online Drive, published by Rich Donnelly and Adam Gordon, is a folksy Web-zine "written 'by fans, for fans.'" According to Donnelly and Gordon, "the idea behind the publication is to have a correspondent for each major league team who will contribute a monthly article, written from the fans' point of view. You will find *Online Drive* liberally laced with opinions, just like you'll get when you talk baseball with your friends."

Links are provided to several years' worth of back issues. Although the site's focus is on major league team reports, I also found features on broadcaster Lindsay Nelson, baseball clown Max Patkin, the "Japanese ballpark experience," the 1978 St. Petersburg Cardinals' season, and the Imperial Valley Brahmas of the Golden State Baseball League.

Quotes on America's Favorite Pastime

http://www10.geocities.com/Colosseum/Field/8435/quotes.html

This site offers a nice selection of baseball quotes culled from *Play Ball*, a "Quote-A-Page" book. They are at once funny, poetic, and true, and come from such diverse sources as Walter Johnson, Harry Reasoner, George Carlin, William Saroyan, Russell Baker, Humphrey Bogart, Charlie Finley, and Rod Kanehl.

The opening quote: "Baseball was, is, and always will be the best game in the world."—Babe Ruth.

The closing one: "The game is supposed to be fun. If you have a bad day, don't worry about it. You can't expect to get a hit every game."—Yogi Berra.

Quotations from the Dish

http://www.superaje.com/~brenmcla/u_quotes.htm

This Web page, one of many outstanding links on the Amateur Baseball Umpires site, consists of a choice assortment of quotes by and about umpires. It opens with what might be the most famous of all—Bill Klem's "I never missed one in my heart"—and goes on the cite Joe Brinkman, Nestor Chylak, Cal Drummond, Larry Goetz, Tom Gorman, Ron Luciano, Ed Runge, Beans Reardon, Jocko Conlon, and Bette Davis, Don Adams, and George Will.

Some are clever: Luciano's "Umpire's heaven is a place where he works third base every game. Home is where the heartache is"; and Will's "Umpires should be natural republicans...dead to human feelings."

Others are knowing: Drummond's "The worst thing that can happen to a man is to be born without guts and be an umpire"; and Runge's "(Umpiring is) the only occupation where a man has to be perfect his first day on the job, and then improve over the years." It is not clear whether Bette Davis's declaration relates specifically to umps, but it sure is applicable: "The person who makes it has to sweat. You've got to have the guts to be hated. That's the hardest part."

Baseball Quotations

http://www.intac.com/~butch/quotes.html

Here is yet another well-chosen selection of pithy baseball quotes. For openers, there is this from Herbert (father of

Hank) Aaron: "When Henry came up, I heard the fans yell, 'Hit that nigger! Hit that nigger!' Henry hit the ball up against the clock. The next time he came up, they said 'Walk him, walk him.'"

Jim Abbott declares, "I wanted to be like Nolan Ryan. I didn't want to be like Pete Gray."

Sandy Alomar observes, after being behind the plate when Mark McGwire launched a titanic home run: "If it hadn't hit the scoreboard, it could have gone all the way around the world and hit me in the back of my head."

Plenty of others follow including several from baseball movies, announcers' legendary calls, Lou Gehrig's farewell address, and even the testimonies on ballplayer monuments.

Other well-done baseball quote URLs:

Baseball As I See It
`(http://www.evansville.net/~yaz/bbstuff.htm);
Baseball Quotes
(http://students.cs.byu.edu/~dixon/bbquotes.html);
Famous Baseball Quotes
(http://205.180.58.12/~kewlkc/quotes.html);
Baseball Quotes
(http://www.cpba.org/sean/quotes.htm);
Advice From Baseball Managers
(http://www.success.org/legends/baseball_managers.html).

Best Quotes in Baseball

http://www.arches.uga.edu/~rytie/baseball.html

This short, ever-so-sweet Web site features astute baseball-related comments. No many quotes are here, but the ones selected are choice.

The first, spoken by Ernie Banks on the Cubs' winning their first division title in 1984: "Good things come to those who wait...and wait...and wait."

The last, attributed to Bill Veeck: "That's the harbinger of spring—not crocuses or swallows returning to Capistrano but the sound of a bat on a ball."

Baseball Links

Countless baseball Web sites, in addition to the information contained within them, offer links to other similarly themed URLs. Meanwhile, some pages consist almost entirely of baseball links. The best of them serve as embellishments to the information contained in this book.

The following selection of baseball link pages should help you in your search for baseball on the Web. However, this appendix contains just a sampling of link sites; hundreds are on the Internet. Their essence is captured at the top of Baseball Links (*http://pluto.njcc.com/~nieporen/links/bblinks.html*), a page maintained by David Nieporen. "I cannot begin to duplicate the work of some individuals who spend all their time just compiling lists such as this one," Nieporen explains. "Well, I actually can *begin* to duplicate it. I just can't finish duplicating it. But I'm going to start, just because it's fun."

Then there are Web rings, which are variations of links pages. Web rings are groupings of related Web sites that have been gathered together and "attached," one after the other. Several baseball-related Web rings can be found on the Internet. A typical one is the appropriately named MLB Web-Ring (*http://www.california.com/~rpcman/mlb.htm*).

The major problem with Web rings is that the sites on the ring appear in arbitrary order. Ballplayer homages, fans' team pages, baseball-cards-for-sale pages, and those whose contents cannot be discerned from their names (such as Home Field, Masterseal's Page, and Lords of the Diamond, which appear on the MLB Web-Ring) all are scrambled together. However, you can view the names of five entries at a time and download those you want to scrutinize.

Another quibble with this particular Web ring: Despite the home page claim that "only quality sites will be admitted to the ring index," I would in no way characterize all its pages as top calibre.

Though *Baseball on the Web* provides our selections of the best baseball Web sites, and you can access every site listed in this book at *http://www.mispress.com/baseball*, and this appendix lists a number of other top-notch compilations of Web links, there will come a time when you are ready to look for new baseball sites on your own. That's when you will need to use a Web search engine to sift through the innumerable baseball-related sites and find only the ones touching on the topic you want. Five search engines we recommend are:

Yahoo!
http://www.yahoo.com

Webcrawler
http://www.webcrawler.com

Alta Vista
http://altavista.digital.com

Metacrawler
http://www.metacrawler.com

nfoSeek
http://www.infoseek.com

Yahoo! is unique among these engines in that it is arranged by topic, sort of like a yellow pages. The other listed search engines will ask you for a word, set of words, or phrase, and will find only sites that contain that phrase. So if you have a clear picture of the subject area that you are researching, Yahoo! is your best bet. For more broad-based searches, try several of the other search engines listed here and decide which one works best for you.

What follows is a general list of baseball links. However, beware—one-too-many URLs on even the most up-to-date links sites are as dead as Eddie Gaedel's chances of gaining election to the Hall of Fame.

John Skilton's Baseball Links

http://www.baseball-links.com/

You practically could write a book about this unique Web site (which features an attractive pinstripe motif throughout its pages).

Baseball Links is its name, and baseball links galore can be found here. It features an all-inclusive list of subject headings, not just major and minor league teams but also "Amateur/Semi-Pro Baseball," "Ballparks," "Cards & Collectibles," "College Baseball," "Fantasy/Rotisserie Baseball," "High School Baseball," and "International Baseball." Other attractions are "The Dugout Chat Room," "The Baseball Soapbox" (a message board), and "The Baseball Links Bookstore" (which, like the publications on the Total Baseball site, is presented in conjunction with the Amazon Bookseller URL).

As the 1997 baseball season ended, more than 3,000 separate links were contained here! Needless to say, you can spend hours—let's amend that to days and weeks—exploring the nooks and crannies of this site.

John Skilton's Baseball Links tries to be as current as possible regarding old and new Web sites. Those who maintain URLs can e-mail submissions to have their sites listed or requests to change existing postings. Browsers are encouraged to report dead links and offer feedback.

However, this site is not flawless. For one thing, it offers *too much* material. And the site offers no URL evaluations. Mixed among the outstanding Web pages are the idiotic ones, the repetitive ones, and the just-plain boring ones.

The site can be viewed via three formats: Frames (which keeps the Baseball Links menu constantly on-screen); Graphics Enhanced (which is suggested for slower connections and those without Java support); and Mostly Text (recommended for older browsers).

The Baseball S.W.A.T.

http://www.theswat.com/probase/

If you find the Skilton Web site way too massive, check out this solid links-oriented site. Its subjects include box scores, schedules, standings, statistics, injury reports, rosters and transactions, previews and updates, and articles and publications.

Some links listed on this site are direct links to data on CBS SportsLine, CNN/SI, ESPN SportsZone, and other super-sites.

The topics covered will be of interest to everyone from roto/fantasy players to those who want to quickly link to a variety of Web pages on specific subjects.

America's Sports Headquarters

http://www.sport-hq.com/

Although the Skilton Web site focuses solely on baseball, this is one of many URLs which offers links to a wide range of athletic activities from Aerobics to Yo-Yo.

With regard to baseball, links are provided to major and minor league sites, college baseball sites, Negro League sites, amateur baseball sites, and women's baseball sites.

One of America's Sports Headquarters' best baseball-related features is a list of "Baseball Indices," which provides links to an impressive variety of other Web sites, with occasional brief commentary on what can be found there.

Baseball Think Factory

http://www.ici.net/customers/sportsim/

This Web site, maintained by Jim Furtado, is "dedicated to the thoughtful analysis of baseball, both real and imagined."

Essentially, Furtado has compiled a collection of links to a potpourri of Web pages. The "Essays" subject heading spotlights thoughtful pieces on general subjects, including "Of Dice and Men," a 1977 article by Thomas Boswell on the United Baseball League parlour game, and "Designing a Baseball Cover," by mathematician Richard Thompson. Under "Economics," you will find David Grabiner's "Frequently Asked Questions About the Strike" and Neil Weiner's "Major League Labor and Management." "Sabermetrics" features everything from Jim Albert's "An Introduction to Sabermetrics" to "Brock2 System Spreadsheet," Bob Collins's updates of Bill James's system for predicting a player's career.

Then there is the site's handiest feature: the "Newsstand" page, from which you can link directly to two dozen baseball columnists. (Furtado notes that "some columns may require [a] subscription fee from the originating website.")

Yahoo's Baseball Links

http://www.yahoo.com/Recreation/Sports/Baseball/index.html

At this Yahoo! search engine-affiliated URL, you will find a variety of links to baseball-related subjects (from "Amateur," "Chat," and "Coaching" to "Wiffleball," "Youth," and "Usenet"); a listing of the day's baseball-related chats, games, and programs; and a search engine from which you can seek additional baseball or non-baseball Web sites.

Links to the Best Baseball Info on the Web

http://members.aol.com/apsira

Despite the brazen claim in the heading at the top of this Web site, I was immediately won over by the first sentence in its second paragraph: "ESPNET is not the end all and be all."

The page, maintained by Greg Spira, offers one person's opinion on the very best baseball Web sites.

Tony's General Baseball Links

http://home.earthlink.net/~tblalock/linkdex.htm

As the title says, this Web site—with its bright and shiny baseballs adorning the left side of its pages—offers a potpourri of links. On the day I visited, there were 197 links to American League teams, 186 to National League teams, 6 to expansion teams, and 63 to other baseball-related sites.

Nerd World: Baseball

http://www.nerdworld.com/cgi-bin/page.cgi?cat=26

This useful page, found on a Web site maintained by Nerd World Media, allows you to hook into an eye-popping array of Web sites. However, baseball is just one of dozens of sports covered.

If you want to get right to the baseball URLs, scroll down to the bottom of the page. There you will find a search engine on which you can type in **Baseball**.

The left-hand side of the page presents a listing of general subjects from "Alternative Sports" to "Winter Sports." On the right is an A-to-W scroll, which literally begins with AAA (AAA Fantasy Sports) and ends with WWW (WWW Women's Sports Page by Amy Lewis).

The Dugout

http://www.best.com/~sbware/index.cgi

This fine links site, maintained by Scott Ware, includes extensive listings in the categories "Coaching," "College," "Fantasy Leagues," "List of Teams," "Little League,"

"Merchandise," "Minors," "Negro Leagues," "Players," "Tickets," and "Other."

Dan's Baseball Page

http://www.kypris.com/Baseball/index.html

Several subject links, from "Ballparks" to "Usenet Groups," are listed on this site, which is maintained by Dan Nichols. Some are crowded with Web site links, whereas others are not. For example, only six URLs are listed under "Minor League Teams."

The home page features three of Nichols's favorite baseball quotes by "Joe Jackson" in W.P. Kinsella's *Shoeless Joe*; A. Bartlett Giamatti in *The Green Fields of the Mind*; and Annie Savoy in Ron Shelton's *Bull Durham*.

One of the nicer aspects of this site is its design. Links are printed in pale blue over a field of bright green grass—real grass, I assume, and not artificial turf!

Baseball Yellow Pages

http://www.tdl.com/~chuckn/mlb.html

This Web site is maintained by "Chuck N." and is a basic links site with the following categories: "NL West"; "NL Central"; "NL East"; "AL West"; "AL Central"; "AL East"; "College Baseball Links"; Other Baseball Links"; and "Search the Web."

The "College Baseball Links" are especially thorough. However, calling this Web site a "Yellow Pages," with all that is implied by this label, is a vast overstatement.

And Chuck N. needs a remedial course in spelling: The team that plays in St. Louis is the "Cardinals," not the "Cardnils."

Slugger's Softball

http://www.sluggers-sports.com/

Any and everything you ever could hope to know about Internet softball Web sites can be found on this all-encompassing page. It consists of links to a variety of subjects, including men's, women's, Junior Olympics, collegiate, and international softball.

Among the individual pages found here are those maintained by softball stars Michelle Smith, Dot Richardson, and Lisa Fernandez; collegiate conferences; individual softball teams and tournaments; and coaches offering drills and tips.

If you are interested in any aspect of softball, Slugger's Softball is the Web site for you. However, if your hankering for cyberspace softball is still not met after scanning this URL, check out Stephen Willett's Fastpitch Softball Page (*http://members.tripod.com/~willett/softball.html*), which also is loaded with "Links for the Fastpitch Fanatic" and other goodies.

The WWW Virtual Library of Sports

http://www.justwright.com/sports/

The Virtual Library offers links related to several sports, including baseball. Regarding the latter, you will find a healthy list of subjects under the headings "Baseball Servers," "Baseball Leagues and Scores," "Baseball Organizations and Societies," "Baseball Teams (USA)," "Baseball Teams (World)," and "Baseball Misc."

Baseball Fanatic

http://www.geocities.com/Colosseum/8822/

This friendly little site—whose anonymous maintainer describes himself as "truly a BASEBALL FANATIC!"—offers many links, most of which extensively spotlight major league team-related sites.

You will also find a link to "The Baseball Fanatic Survey," which requests your favorite team, all-time team, stadium, players, manager, and specific game.

Dr. J's Baseball Page

http://lamar.colostate.edu/~drj/baseball.html

This self-described "compendium of Baseball Minutia"—which is *not* maintained by Julius Erving—features links to major and other professional league sites; baseball newsgroups; sites featuring up-to-the-minute baseball news, stats, and archives; and "Other Baseball Stuff."

Given its Web address, it is not surprising to also find a list of Colorado Rockies links.

SABR Members' Web Sites and Web Pages

http://www.wp.com/JOWO/SABR/memsites.htm

In general, the research-oriented members of the Society for American Baseball Research are meticulous scholars (as well as zealous baseball fans). Many maintain their own Web pages, whose URLs are listed and described here. Subjects cover "General Baseball," "Baseball History," "Individual Players," "Sabermetric (Statistical)," "Art," "Illustration and Photography," and "Team or League."

MegaSports Search

http://megasports.com/

This link site home page, which also includes a search engine, features connections to everything from auto racing to wrestling. In fact, the "o" in sports cleverly switches from illustrations of baseballs to footballs, golf balls, hockey pucks, and basketballs.

The "Baseball" icon will take you to a links menu of more than 20 baseball-related subjects. Related URLs also can be found under the headings "Cards, Collectibles and Memorabilia," "College Sports," "Softball," "Sports Merchandise," "Sports News and Headlines," "Stadiums and Venues," and "Stat Services."

Collector Link

http://www.collector-link.com/cards/

Still haven't found that one baseball card you are desperately seeking to complete a set? At this Web site, you will find a list of more than 2,000 URLs for "card magazines and price guides, card issuers, dealers and private collectors." More than 1,000 of these are baseball-related.

BMCRBA Collection of Links

http://members.aol.com/bmcrba/links.html

"Very soon it will be a Federal Law that all Web Sites must have a collection of cool links," it is written at the top of this site's home page.

The focus in this Web site is on rotisserie leagues, and you will find links to more than 100 "Non-Commercial Rotisserie-style Fantasy Baseball Leagues with pages on the Web."

Black Hole of Links

http://www.geocities.com/Colosseum/Track/9899/index.html

This Web site is maintained by Jay Rotz, sports editor of the *Harrisburg Patriot-News.* On its home page, you will find links to other sports. Its baseball page offers a nice assortment of connections to everything from major league URLs to the Mechanicsville, Pennsylvania, high school baseball team.

On the home page, Rotz promises that "these links are so clean you could eat off them...but you don't really want to."

Index

C

H

T

U

V

W

Y

Z